WITH LOVE STAN

A SOLDIER'S LETTERS
FROM VIETNAM TO
THE WORLD

Karen Ross Epp

Bloomington, IN   authorHOUSE™   Milton Keynes, UK

AuthorHouse™
1663 Liberty Drive, Suite 200
Bloomington, IN 47403
www.authorhouse.com
Phone: 1-800-839-8640

AuthorHouse™ UK Ltd.
500 Avebury Boulevard
Central Milton Keynes, MK9 2BE
www.authorhouse.co.uk
Phone: 08001974150

First published by AuthorHouse 1/9/2007

ISBN:1-4259-4037-4 (sc)

Library of Congress Control Number: 2006904931

Printed in the United States of America
Bloomington, Indiana

This book is printed on acid-free paper.

This book is lovingly dedicated to:

Sp4 Stanley Dennis Ross, a loving son, brother, friend, and brave soldier…May 13, 1949-October 20, 1969.

My parents, who gave me a sense of independence, family loyalty, appreciation for history, and to a mother who saves everything… including Stan's artifacts.

My brother, Phillip, who makes me laugh at our family's quirks and proud of our strengths; and who helped me locate Stan's friends and dig for the facts to complete this work.

My sister, Eileen, who has been a sounding board, a source of strength, and my inspiration for success.

Phil, my husband, who encouraged me to see this project through.

Kate and Justin, my children, and son-in-law Jason, who encouraged me and put up with my tears.
Daniel and Isabelle, my grandchildren, who will get to know a brave Uncle.

To the brave men of the 199th Infantry Brigade, 2/3 "The Old Guard," Jayson "J" Dale, Greg Breeckner, Tim (Obie) Oberst, Arrol Stewart, James McGinnis, Melvin Ploeger, Norm Sassner, Lewis "Snake" Ruth, Ronald Divoky, Tom Schiefer, Jim Faber, David Garshaw, Terry Wanner, Tad Kawahira, and Lee Lanning who fought beside my brother in Vietnam and gave me a better insight into who Stan really was.

Robert Rhodes, 101st Airborne Div.

Steve Klaus, Mike Kitch, Bill Lane, Don Crowl, and Bob Richards— childhood friends of Stan's and fellow Vietnam veterans, who provided me with stories of their friendship and love for my brother.

Denise Rhoades, who polished my work and gave me the tools to see this through.

Judy Entz, who first encouraged me to write Stan's story.

My fellow educator and friend, Beverley Buller, who was a phone call away when I needed her.

To Michael (Lee) Lanning, Tim O'Brien, Bernard Edelman, Donald Stephen, Ches Schneider, and Robert Gouge—all authors of their own experiences in Vietnam, who permitted me to quote them.

To all those brave men and women who keep us safe while we sleep and stand guard for freedom.

Table of Contents

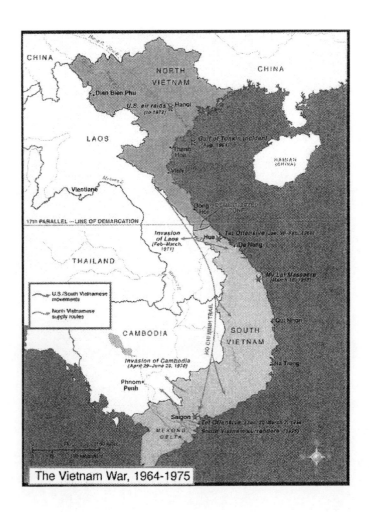

The Vietnam War, 1964-1975

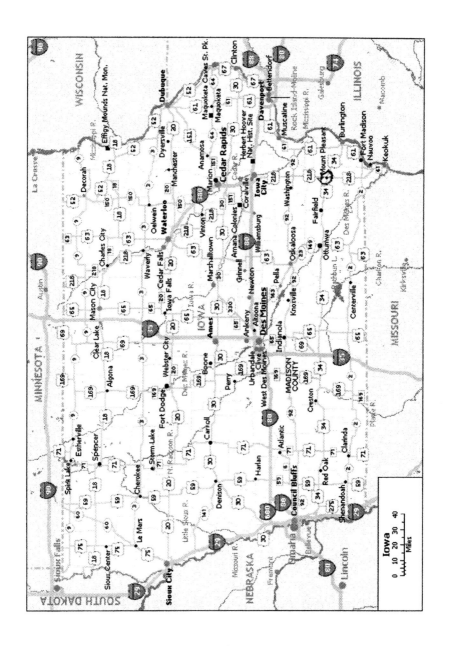

Map of Iowa

Author's Note

In 1969, the world was a very different place. We enjoyed modern conveniences that fifty years before were unheard of; most everyone had electricity, refrigeration, televisions, and transistor radios. The Beach Boys made Bermuda shorts and madras shirts a fashion statement. Men wore their hair longer than they had for decades. Women demanded liberation from traditional mores and their bras. We enjoyed sex without the fear of pregnancy, thanks to the pill, and more of us went on to college, striving for a better life than our parents had. There was, however, a growing seed of dissent within our country. The Vietnam Conflict was something I had heard about in my junior year of high school in U.S. History. It didn't concern me, I had never heard of Vietnam. I was much more frightened of the Russians and Khrushchev and the threat of nuclear war. We were constantly reminded that we could all be blown to bits by just the press of a button. Fall-out shelters were built faster than swing sets, in the backyards of America's suburbia.

Just two decades before we had been united in a World War that our parents felt was holy and just. We were now involved in a "military conflict" that had the nation and its youth divided. Nothing seemed clear cut; what our parents had struggled so hard to accomplish, my generation found repulsive and shallow. We had all the answers and any one who was thirty or older, just didn't get it! We would not go blindly into a battle thousands of miles away for a corrupt government who had imperialism as its goal. My generation chose to challenge the establishment at every turn, through dress, music, tradition, and political conscience. We did not honor the military as our parents had; anti-war demonstrations and burning draft cards were everyday occurrences. The Vietnam War defined my generation (baby boomers) and is still a reference point to which we often reflect. It was a tremulous, yet creative time. It was a time of experimentation and excess for which our children are marked. It was an exciting time, full of stimulus and adventure, and it was a time of lost innocence for thousands of young men who fought and died for the traditions our parents and forbearers held so dear. Two popular bumper stickers of the day said it all, "America, Love it or Leave It!" and "Make Love Not War!"

This work started out as a small weekend project. I had no idea what a ripple effect it would have on my life and that of others. Simply put, I wanted to preserve my brother's letters and other memorabilia by putting them into a more secure and permanent form.

My younger brother, Phill, had used Stan's letters for a history class while he was attending Iowa State University in the 80s, returning them to the green metal trunk where they would remain until I revisited them in the fall of 2004.

When I reopened the trunk that held Stan's belongings—viewing letters, and other artifacts deteriorating with age and neglect—I wasn't sure what I wanted to do with the pieces of Stan's life that lay before me. I knew I wanted to honor my brother's memory by sharing his experience through his letters and photographs. Putting the letters and artifacts into a printed binder would preserve them once and for all. It was to be a gift to my family and perhaps a few close friends of Stan's.

It wasn't my intention to write a book. My brother's life wasn't that much different from any other nineteen-year-old American that served in Vietnam. His death was recorded in the local paper newspaper and the Des Moines Register the fall of 1969. His death was like so many other young GIs in the 60s and early 70s, just another casualty of an unpopular war. It was, however, his story, life, and his sacrifice, that I felt should be remembered. Stan was a living, breathing person, a good boy and a bad boy, not just a casualty or grave marker in his hometown cemetery.

While doing research, I located and communicated with several of Stan's Army buddies and officers from Basic Training and Vietnam. I wasn't prepared for the emotional, yet healing effect it would have on me and the rest of my family. I wasn't sure what I wanted to find out about my brother, and his final days on this earth. I knew he had been killed in an ambush, along with private, Benny Jackson. I knew all the official details from reading the Army reports collected in that green trunk. I wanted to know what my brother had meant to his fellow grunts and officers. As I located these men, it was with trepidation that I dialed their phone numbers and typed in e-mail addresses; I wanted to know how Stan lived and died, but I wasn't prepared for the responses I would hear and read about. The conversations with these men were a combination of surprise, sadness, regret, humor and compassion. Every man had a story to tell. Though they made it home, they had suffered in their own way; each had dealt with the war, some better than others. Wounds are not always visible, as I would discover. I am forever grateful to these men for their encouragement, their service to this country, and their contribution to my brother's memory.

I have included reflections, and letters from Stan's friends and acquaintances: Jayson "J" Dale, Tim (Obie) Oberst, Robert Rhodes, Lewis "Snake" Ruth, Greg Breeckner, Arrol Stewart, Tadaaki Kawahar, Mike Kitch, Steve Klaus, David Garshaw, Jim Faber, Tom Schiefer, Michael (Lee) Lanning, Melvin Ploeger, James McGinnis, Terry Wanner, Ronald Divoky, Bill Lane, David Clines, and Bob Richards, because they give testimony to the brother, son, and man that Stan was. They all knew him, each in his own way. They reveal Stan's character from a friend's perspective, and a soldier's trust. Four of the friendships go back to elementary school. Many of the men corresponded with my parents after Stan's death, which meant a great deal to them. The loyalty and love these men had for each other has been, and is, unwavering and eternal. I learned much from them and gained comfort and understanding that made Stan's story worth telling, because it is ultimately their story.

Other contributions and quotes are from fellow Vietnam vets who had similar experiences and chose to write about them. It is important to note that Vietnam grunts came from different professions and experiences, like teacher, Ches Schneider, who was drafted, in spite of the fact that he would be too old in a matter of months. Ches was a SFC 4, Delta C. 2/16, 1st Infantry, (Big Red One). When Nixon pulled that unit out of Vietnam, he was assigned to Bravo C. 1/8, First Air Cav. Ches would hump the battle fields of Vietnam, just as my brother had done, and live to tell his students about it.

Robert Gouge, whose father Jack Gouge, served with the 199th in Vietnam, wrote a comprehensive book, These Are My Credentials, giving the history of the unit, the war, and the people of Vietnam.

Stan's love of photography gave me a treasure of images that represented his life in the military and his seven months in Vietnam. He took many still photos and several 8-mm movies of his tour in Vietnam, whenever the opportunity presented itself. The photos, many faded and torn, explained what Stan talked about through his correspondence; descriptions of how it felt to sleep in the rain, the absolute darkness of the jungle at night, rats crawling over his pallet as he tried to get a night's rest, and Army fatigues that hung rotting from his weary body, after being in the field for days and weeks at a time. Even in those conditions, he managed to smile for the camera, and wrap his arm around a buddy as they ate cookies from home or posed with his rifle.

His life as a soldier and warrior was not unique; other GIs in American history had fought the enemy and survived or perished in cornfields and pastures in our Southern states, forests in Europe, streets in France and the jungles in the South Pacific. But it was my brother's life and his experiences he shared with family and friends during those turbulent months in 1968 and 1969 that brings life to his journey.

This work is a collection, not only of what was written by Stan to me and my family, but also to friends and other relatives at home. He used words that we might find offensive today in our politically correct world. As the author, Tim O'Brien, writes in his book, <u>The Things They Carried</u>, *"A true war story is never moral. It does not instruct, nor encourage virtue, nor suggest models of proper human behavior, nor restrain men from doing the things men have always done. If a story seems moral, do not believe it. If at the end of a war story you feel uplifted, or if you feel that some small bit of rectitude has been salvaged from the larger waste, then you have been made the victim of a very old and terrible lie. There is no rectitude whatsoever. There is no virtue."* He goes on to say, *"You can't tell a true war story if it embarrasses you. If you don't care for obscenity, you don't care for the truth; if you don't care for the truth, watch how you vote. Send guys to war, they come home talking dirty."*

Stan tried to smooth over much of the danger he faced, but we read between the lines and knew how perilous each day and minute had become. His writing wasn't scholarly, it was straightforward and honest, permitting us to see, feel, and almost smell the humid air of Vietnam. He always closed by telling us, "not to worry," and how important we were to him.

Looking at the pictures and reading the letters through to the last one dated October 17, 1969, my brother's face and body went through a transformation, from a well- nourished young recruit to a lean, muscular man; his face grew gaunt and exhausted.

His letters are that of a young soldier describing, as best he could, his day-to-day routine in a way that would not alarm his family. He would hint at skirmishes but would not go into detail, as he knew we were hanging on every word.

Many of the days not spent in the field, enduring ambush, or fire fights, were filled with monotonous routines—a time to clean weapons or "get a letter off," as he would put it. He used crude language, vernacular that was typical of a soldier in war and battle. Stan spoke of things that sickened him, "better ways to kill the enemy," soldiers picking up the remains of the VC and putting body parts into garbage bags, laughing while they (soldiers) did it. Killing was never easy for him. The Vietnamese were still human beings, but in the heat of battle, survival was Stan's, and all other grunts, objective. That attitude would seem utterly savage to most Americans, not suitable material for discussion or conversation. But that was my brother's life for the seven months he was in the rice paddies and jungles of South Vietnam.

As Edelman describes in the beginning of Chapter 2 in his book, Dear America, *"They were called grunts, and most of them, however grudgingly, were proud of the name. They were the Infantrymen, the foot soldiers, of the war. They 'humped the boonies' in their own special nightmare, hacking their way."*

The terms and expressions that Stan used became defined for me after reading, The Only War We Had: A Platoon Leader's Journal of Vietnam, by Vietnam veteran and author Michael L. Lanning. Lanning, who was stationed at Blackhorse, as well as other fire base camps where Stan was, kept diaries of his twelve-month tour of duty. In his second book, Vietnam, 1969-1970: A Company Commander's Journal, Lanning recalls Stan's death as well as the other soldier killed with him that day, PFC Benny Jackson. Reading Stan's name in that entry was a pivotal moment for me as I began to realize how his life and death touched more than our family. I felt pride knowing that he was remembered as a good and brave soldier by one who led many young men into battle. Much of what Lanning recalls, correspond with my brother's letters. His book explained what Stan and other GIs meant when they asked, "How are things back in the world?" He describes the day-to-day life of foot soldiers, the unpleasant duties such as burning human waste in oil drums drenched with diesel fuel. Stan sent home a picture of himself doing just that, stirring something in a caldron with a long stick!

I had the opportunity to visit with Michael Lanning by phone and in person. His recollection of Stan was simply, *"Stan was a sweet guy and a good soldier, well liked and respected by his men. He was smart and deserved the promotion to Sp4. He took his job as a squad leader seriously and was dedicated to his men."* He (Lanning) had just returned from his own R&R in Hawaii, when he got the news of Stan's death. Today Lanning is an accomplished author of many books with the military as subject matter.

Stan's good friend, Jayson Dale, a member of his company (Charlie Company), has been a wonderful source of information. Jason returned home from the war in April, 1970. His recollections of the day-to-day contact he had with Stan helped me to grasp what he and my brother experienced. It enriched what Stan wrote about those seven months. It was Jayson who told me about Michael Lanning's books, and that my brother was mentioned in the second journal. Lanning's October 21 entry is his recollection of the day he returned from R&R. LT. Norm Sassner informs him of two deaths the day before. His first entry reads, *"Bad news— learned this morning C CO had 2 KIA—(Killed in Action) SGT Ross and PFC Jackson—Knew Ross well—Damn fine man."* He explains in detail, *"Death of a parent was important enough to allow a son to leave the war zone to pay last respects. But the fathers of Ross and Jackson would bury their sons, who would never reach twenty. I was beginning to understand a major difference between war and peace: in peace sons bury their fathers—in war fathers bury their sons.*

Sassner said he hated to be the one to tell me because he knew SGT Ross and I had been close. As a member of SGT Breeckner's squad in the third platoon, Ross had been one of the men who found me and my recon team back on August 7. I never had the chance to tell him thanks."

As I mentioned, I was so moved, I couldn't stop the tears as I read that entry. Lanning's book was published in 1988 and I had only learned of it weeks before. The layers to this project kept pealing away and there was no turning back.

Lee Lanning's books also define and explain the bigger picture of war and its effect on soldiers and their families. His chronological journals enlightened me on the contents of Stan's letters and what he went through. When I visited with Lee in person he told me that he always told his men, "If something happens to me, make sure my journals are secured and sent home."

Bernard Edelman's <u>Dear America,</u> a collection of Vietnam veterans' letters home, emphasized that this war and its casualties did not respect class, religion, ethnic backgrounds, or gender. When I recorded Stan's last letter home, I thought of the last chapter in Chapter 8 of Edelman's book, which is solely dedicated to "last letters," so many last letters, so many tears.

I don't think I had ever truly grieved or mourned for my brother until I started typing his letters. When he died, I was newly married, finishing up an undergraduate degree, and thousands of miles away from him and the war. I had other things to think about and my student friends weren't concerned about my loss; protesting and anti-war sentiments were the norm. I just didn't talk about it.

In 2004, I retired after a 30-year teaching career. As I sat at my desk each day and typed out the words for this work, Stan's ageless face looked back at me from a framed photo, taken 35 years ago. When I felt discouraged or unsure, that face gave me the courage to go on and fulfill the commitment I made to him. His spirit has moved me forward, pushing me to find answers and make those human connections that were dormant for so many years.

Stan always encouraged me when it came to furthering my education; he talked of doing the same one day. He, like many other young men of that era, answered the call to fulfill their military duty before they went on to careers, marriage, and parenthood. I know he would be proud of what I chose to do with my life.

I finally took the time to truly understand what my brother was all about and shed those tears that were locked up for so many years. My siblings, Eileen and Phillip, have encouraged me every step of the way and I love them for it.

The letters in this book are my brother's voice. I have tried to transcribe his language and thoughts as accurately as possible. I have intentionally not corrected some of Stan's unique ways of communicating, even when the wording or syntax was not perfectly correct; I wanted his voice to come through.

I located as many of Stan's friends as I could through records, the Internet, and word of mouth. If I have left anyone out, or misinterpreted any of the facts of the war, I apologize. I, as well as my family, would love to hear from you.

This is my story, as Stan's sister. It is the story of my family, his friends, and a story about that tumultuous time in our history, the 60s. It is the story of how one life affected others, like a pebble tossed in a stream, rippling through time and memories, never to be forgotten.

I hope that by sharing these letters and pictures readers will find some comfort in knowing that our loved ones and their lives, no matter how brief, impact our own. We should embrace and acknowledge that their lives influence and mold us in ways that we may never be able to fully comprehend.

Introduction

Growing up in rural Southeastern Iowa was idyllic, laid back, and uncomplicated. Winter days were cold, the nights were long, but the change in seasons provided us with many activities like ice skating, sledding, and snowball fights.

Summers were hot and sultry. Many hours were spent swimming in the farm pond or nearby river. We dug night crawlers for fishing, bicycled over dusty gravel roads to our friends' houses, and helped with the family chores. Life on the farm wasn't easy by any stretch of the imagination. There was always something for us to do. We rarely complained of being bored, because we knew what the solution would be.

All of us attended country schools and formed lifelong friendships with our school mates. Our lives centered around school, church, and farming. Potlucks and PTA meetings were a community affair. Mothers cooked their favorite dishes, fathers huddled together discussing farm prices or weather conditions.

We discovered that baking potatoes on top of the heating stove in the winter was a wonderful way to spice up our dull lunches. Keeping Edwin Egli's bull out of the school yard was a top priority. That was an experience I will never forget. We were play tag one minute, and the next we were eyeball to eyeball with a thousand-pound Angus.

Today's educators would have a hard time understanding how one person managed to instruct all eight grades, and keep her sanity, while making sure her pupils mastered the three R's. If our teacher felt like taking the day off, calling it a field day and packing picnic lunches while we swam in a farm pond, we did it. No permission slips were signed, no safety issues addressed, we just did it!

When we were old enough, we worked alongside the adults, baling hay, canning, or whatever the routine the day held in store. We were farm kids, and our dad worked the rich, black soil on the river bottom from dawn 'til dusk, praying for nature's kindness when the heavy rains came and the river flooded its banks. Stan was driving a tractor by the age of seven, cultivating corn, pulling hay wagons, working with livestock, whatever Dad asked him to do.

Stan learned a lot about responsibility because our parents expected it. He was taught how to hunt with a gun and dress game at an early age, tagging along with Dad through the thick timber and rolling Iowa hills. He became a pretty good marksman and respected the power and danger of a weapon. He would rather go fishing than go to class, as our dad found out from our high school principal, George Stanley. Mr. Stanley was an imposing man, who took his job seriously. He had a soft place in his heart for my brother. It seems that Stan and a friend had been fishing every day instead of attending school. When Dad heard this he met my brother at the screen door and said, "So you don't want to go to school? Then I guess you can pack your bags and get a job!" That was the end of playing hooky for my brother, as far as our parents knew. Mr. Stanley would become someone my brother came to respect. They stayed in touch with each other until he left for Vietnam.

Stan held many jobs in his short 20 years. He worked at the Fina gas station in town, drove a school bus, did carpentry with Lyons & Miller Construction, worked and drove for Ideal Ready-Mix, and of course helped Dad and neighbors with field work.

Our rural setting provided endless places to explore and hide, hills to climb, and streams to wade in. Stan enjoyed every minute of those childhood adventures. I'm sure he never dreamed that the cowboy and Indian games we played out as kids—dodging make-believe bullets and surviving play arrow wounds—would someday become real for him, a world away.

Stan and I were close in age and we had our share of brother-sister conflicts. Like all brothers, he enjoyed teasing me and my sister Eileen. Mom's "wait until your dad gets home!" along with some Italian she rattled off would put the fear of God in us until Dad stood larger than life, looking down on our remorseful souls. We'd point accusing fingers at each other, shirking the blame, knowing that all of us would get it in the end, literally!

Our baby brother or the "Little Man" came along when most couples think their family is complete. Phillip arrived in 1965. Leaving him and not seeing him grow, was one of the hardest things Stan endured. He loved being Phillip's older brother and asked about him in almost every letter. I know Stan would be proud of the man Phill has become.

2

Stan and Karen, holding baby brother, Phill.

Dad Ross in his Army uniform, 1945.

Mom Ross gets a taste of the rural life, feeding
chickens. It's a long way from LA!

Waterskiing—one of our summer activities. Karen on
skis. Stan's thinking, "Dunk her!" (Which he did.)

Stan's graduation picture, May, 1968.

My sister Eileen was 15 when Stan left for Vietnam. She was there the day the uniformed figure stepped on our front porch with the news that would change us all forever; Stan had been (KIA) "Killed In Action."

Our mother, Rose or Rosie, as most people knew her, (and still do) met our dad, Russell, at the Lockheed Aircraft plant in 1945, in Los Angeles, California. They married and moved back to the Midwest. I came along the following year.

Moving to an Iowa farm was quite an adjustment, but Mom was a real trooper and put even the natives to shame with her resolve to become a farm wife and mother.

5

Stan got much of his lust for life and out-going personality from Mom. His openness and affection for friends and family was something everyone loved about him. Dad was always the stoic one, the strong arm of reason: I know those traits served Stan well on the battlefields of Vietnam. He looked and acted rough and tough, yet underneath it all, he was tenderhearted and compassionate.

I've wondered many times what he would have made of his life, had he come home to us. Would the war have changed him, eaten away at who he was?

After his death I tried to picture his features, his smile, laugh, and walk. As time wore on, the familiarity of his face and character grew a little dimmer, but I hear traces of his voice when my younger brother Phill speaks. Sometimes it was too painful to think about him, I would pretend he was just away on a trip.

I believe he spoke to me this winter and ask to be remembered, not just for him, but for all those brave men and women whose fate was his. I realized it was time to revisit his memory, to share and to celebrate his life, not his death.

Stan's story is like so many others who have gone to war. That seems especially true now with the current war in Iraq. Sons and daughter still write home, and parents still worry and grieve. Knowing human nature and history, this will not be the last war our nation will face.

Mom and Dad's wedding picture, February 18, 1945.

Mom and Dad, 1945.

Stan with Queen, our Golden Retriever, circa 1959.

Mr. Stanley, our high school principal, and Stan while
on leave, spring 1969.

Stan posing by the school bus he drove. Eileen poking her head out of the window. Linda Burden, a friend and neighbor of Eileen's in the doorway, and Phillip behind our other Golden Retriever, Sandy.

Stan with his diploma, May, 1968.

Reflections
By
Phillip Ross

A man in a uniform came to the door one autumn morning. For a moment I thought it was Stanley. My brother had a uniform like that, with shiny buttons and colorful patches and a nifty hat that fascinated my young mind.

He wore that uniform the last time I saw him when he climbed aboard a huge United airliner in Des Moines. Moments later the big plane climbed into the sky shrinking away in front of a long trail of exhaust.

I thought for a brief moment my brother was back from the far away place he'd taken the plane to. My big brother, who drove a blue Chevelle SS that he once let me help wax-down in the front yard. Big brother who let me sit behind him in the big bus he drove part time for the school district as he parked it in the driveway. The big brother, of a few scattered, brief, but lasting memories, like driving up to Trenton for a bottle of pop at the filling station, sharing some spearmint Certs and teaching me to spit out my gum instead of swallowing it. Singing songs to me and putting my name in the lyrics. But it wasn't him. The man in the uniform was an Army Master Sergeant who had come to say words I'd always remember, along with his image in the front door: "Stanley was killed."

My mother began to scream. Soon Dad was at the back door, after running in from the barnyard, the feed buckets from the morning chores still in his hands. They swung from his grasp and hit the ground as he yelled, "What's the matter!"

I was four years old when my brother died in Vietnam, obviously too young to really mourn or understand much about the war that took him away. Only as I grew up, listening to stories about him, looking at pictures of him, and learning the history of the war that claimed him, did the grieving process begin for me. Through these pieces he left behind after his death, I finally got acquainted with a brother I barely got to know during his life. I learned and never forgot that every memory was precious.

The first time I looked at Stan's letters home from the war I was 22 and a journalism student at Iowa State University studying Vietnam in the best history course I ever had.

After I began reading the letters, I decided to type them into a collection for my parents. While doing this, I also looked at every photo he sent us and examined every piece of memorabilia we had. There were medals he earned, along with the letters of commendation, letters of condolence from friends and commanders, and even the personal effects sent home when he died. The special photo "yearbook" of his unit, the 199th Light Infantry Brigade, was sent to us. And our family even had a video cassette, a compilation made from 8-mm movies he filmed while in country.

Revisiting the war through Stan's letters was an experience I'll never forget. I had long been taught to honor him as a hero and patriot through the eyes of my parents. But not until I read his words scrawled on sweat-soaked pages smudged with red jungle mud, did I begin to understand. I read of his days in the rice paddies and the jungle around Saigon, enduring the daily hardships and dangers he and the other "grunts" faced. I also began to witness the strength of his character as he fought bravely alongside his buddies in the firefights and skirmishes he wrote about. My eyes swelled with tears of pride as I read how he not only gained the respect and friendship of his companions, he also distinguished himself among them, earning a field promotion and the charge of his own squad. I realized he did the best he could and his comrades and commanders appreciated him for it. He became my hero in those letters. He lives on in them. Phillip Ross

Stan, home on leave with Phillip, Christmas 1968.

Reflections
By
Eileen Ross Ensminger

October 22, 1969, I remember being upstairs and getting ready for school. I heard some commotion downstairs, sensing something wasn't right. When I came down, I could see into the bathroom. Dad was holding on to the legs of the vanity as if he couldn't breath or was going to be sick to his stomach. I then remember the soldier standing in the kitchen; I think he was Hispanic, a small guy. He stayed for a while discussing the upcoming events or notices that they (my parents) would receive in the mail and by phone. I remember I finished getting ready for school and felt I just had to get out of there, so I went on to school.

I don't recall the exact time, but I was in Biology class, staring out the window when the garage door of the funeral home across the street, lifted; and a hearse backed out. I started to cry, left the class, and drove home.

I don't remember the weather exactly, other than ever since that day, I always admire the beautiful fall leaves during or around the 20th to the 22nd of October. It still amazes me that back then in 1969, it took two whole days for the news of Stan's death to reach us…amazing! How long would it take today?

Mom made calls, and Dad made some too. I remember the noon hour brought the mailman, Mr. Hankins, a kind man, who was a member of our church. He delivered a letter from Stan, dated October 17th. Also that day a telegram arrived with more details of Stan's death. The next 24 or 36 hours we were informed as to where his body would be flown to, so we could claim his remains. The folks who owned the funeral home in Wayland, Iowa came down the next day to talk with Mom and Dad about the funeral arrangements; they were very supportive. I remember Vivian and Lyle, family friends and the funeral directors. They took over and that was a good thing.

Our dad's brother, Paul, and his sister, Geraldine, went with my sister, Karen, and I to Moline to pick Stan up. I watched as everyone departed from the planes, knowing nothing about the bottom cargo bay that held our precious brother. I remember watching the men who worked for the airline push the crate/box down a long plank. It seemed to hit the tarmac and it shook me and angered me at the same time. Even though I was the youngest person there, I asked the most questions, and took charge.

Al Towle, the soldier who escorted Stan's body, was very kind, and I remember asking him if we could see Stan. He answered, "Yes, he's presentable." You would have thought he had said he had "Risen." I knew so many guys were coming home in bags; our parents wanted so much for this not be the case. I felt we had been blessed! I called Mom and Dad and let them know that. They were ecstatic!

The next few days were filled with emotions, people coming and going. Mom and Dad were strong one minute and the next, weeping uncontrollably.

As a fifteen-year old I became very attached to Al in the days that followed. He became my hero. He seemed so important and I followed him around a lot. I recall him helping my dad with the decision to bring Stan home to the house, where I still live in today, before the funeral. This had been Stan's wish if something happened to him. It had been

13

a custom in our family to bring the deceased loved one home. Dad threatened to fly to Oakland to talk to anyone regarding his wishes. Al made many long distance calls, hanging up the receiver, and looking at Dad, shaking his head, and saying, "I'm sorry, Mr. Ross Stanley is the property of the U.S. Army and they are not going to alter the normal procedure here, Russell." Dad raised his voice, with respect for Al but yet letting him know, that he would do whatever it took to make good his promise to Stan and bring him to our home. In the end, Al put his job and career on the line to allow Dad his wish. My parents were very grateful. It helped to ease some of the pain they were feeling, knowing that their son would spend one more night in his childhood home. They would be able to sleep that night.

It was a dark and sad time in my life. I remember getting Stan's trunk home; and that trunk would stay in my parent's home for many years until we opened it in the fall of 2004 and remembered Stan.

Eileen Ross Ensminger, age sixteen.

Forward
By
Michael Lanning

During the summer of 2005, I received a telephone call from Karen Epp who asked if I had served in Vietnam with the 199th Light Infantry Brigade and if I was the author of several books about the war. When I acknowledged both, she said she was the sister of Stanley Ross. No further introduction was needed.

I indeed remembered Stan Ross. Although we had been in different platoons in Charlie Company, 2nd Battalion, 3rd Infantry, we had arrived in-country about the same time. On August 7, 1969, when I and a half dozen other soldiers were cut off from other friendly forces and were nearly out of ammunition in a desperate fight with a much larger force of North Vietnamese regulars, I was not surprised to see Ross among the few who risked their lives to come to our assistance. Less than three months later Ross fell mortally wounded in still another battle.

Since that first phone call I have had the privilege of meeting in person with Karen and her younger brother Phill at her home in rural Kansas. The visit had its sad moments, but gathering was much more of a celebration for the short life of Stan Ross, a reflection of the lasting impact he has had and memories he left with us all.

Karen's work to document her brother's life and death is a unique effort that contributes to the full story of a long, controversial war that still has major impact on our country today. It is a tribute to not only Stan and Karen's family, but also to all veterans.

British poet Laurence Binyon's verse about the fallen of World War I remains as appropriate about men killed in combat and those who mourn and remember them:

They shall not grow old, as we that are left grow old;
Age shall not weary them, nor the years contemn.
At the going down of the sun and in the morning,
We will remember them.

Michael Lee Lanning
Phoenix, AZNovember, 2005

First Platoon Leader 1LT Michael (Lee)
Lanning, 1969.

Basic Training
Preparing for Vietnam

While reading Stan's letters from Basic Training, it hit me that the training he so bitterly complained about was merely dress rehearsal for the real thing: Vietnam.

Things were changing in our family. I had gotten married, Stan joined the Army, my younger sister was a teenager, and my little brother Phillip was just three-and-half-years old. I'm sure my parents felt their lives were in a constant state of change and uncertainty. I know Stan felt we were all drifting apart, losing those special bonds that connect a family and hold them together.

When Stan came home on leave that April we were able to spend some time together. I felt our relationship had changed; we were more like friends than siblings. I looked at him differently, not as a younger brother but as an equal. The knowledge that he would be leaving for Vietnam in a few days, hung over us like a dark cloud, making our time together precious, yet strained.

I had issues with the war, like many of my college friends and peers, and I was married to a man who was not in the military, which added extra strife and tension for a family already under stress. We tried to ignore it, skip over it like a crack in the sidewalk. It didn't help and we didn't discuss it.

I had returned to the Midwest after living in California for two years, where my husband fulfilled his alternative service, (1W) classification. He had been raised in the Mennonite faith and was expected to fulfill his two-year obligation to the government, but not as a combatant. At that time the government allowed for service requirements outside of the military. The length of service was two years and was mandatory. My husband was required to appear before the Nebraska Draft Board to submit his request.

It was not a comfortable situation for me. I felt pulled in two directions, feeling a loyalty to my family and my brother, and to a husband of just over two years. It was a tricky balancing act that took its toll on both relationships. It did not, however, change the love that Stan and I had for each other. I was torn between what I knew in my heart was a true conviction for my brother, as well as for my husband; I was caught in the middle.

During his months in Basic and AIT training, Stan and I would occasionally talk on the phone and he would try to make me feel better about the news of his eventual deployment to Vietnam.

The letters I received from Stan in Basic Training came to me in California and later in York, Nebraska, where we had moved after my husband's alternative service in California, and finally in North Newton, Kansas where we were attending college.

My husband and I moved to North Newton the summer of '69 to finish our undergraduate degrees at Bethel College. It was there in October that my mother called with the news of Stan's death. It is the one phone call I will never forget, Mom's voice was like a recording, strangely calm, "Karen, your brother has been killed. He's gone." She seemed surprised that I had not heard the horrible news.

For a few moments, I could not breathe, my legs felt as though they might buckle. I was numb. I wanted to scream, lash out at something or someone. It was too surreal. I wanted to yell back at her, "What did you expect, Mom?" But my heart ached for my parents, not being able

17

to comfort them and to be comforted, was almost more than I could bear. There was no one to protest my brother's cruel death, no marches for his young life snuffed out.

I know it was hard for my husband as well. He wasn't sure how to console me. The tension in my family surrounding Stan's death was so strained that my mother suggested it might be better if Phil, my husband, not come home with me for Stan's funeral. I was grieving and hurt and totally helpless to do anything about it. I knew what a scene it would cause if I insisted that my husband come home with me, so I did as they asked and took the longest train ride of my life back to Mt. Pleasant. My husband was stoic through the whole ordeal, never once confronting my parents, but it put a permanent scar on our relationship. I could never really be a pacifist, and he respected that.

I did not protest or march against the war. In fact it sickened me to see the demonstrations on campus and in the news. I knew that it hurt the guys who were risking their lives everyday in Vietnam. Students held demonstrations and rallies. Their protesting was obnoxious and rude. Their convictions seemed shallow and selfish. I felt most were pampered and spoiled. What did they know of the war sitting in their safe dorm rooms? They had no idea how the men were suffering in Vietnam, boys that were barely out of high school. Getting caught up in the fever of the anti-war movement was like a rip tide that pulled everyone along with it.

I was angry—angry with the politicians whose sons probably received convenient deferments, and disgusted with national leaders who didn't seem in any hurry to put an end to a war that was decades old, a war that showed no signs of stopping. My God! The war dragged on for six more years after Stan's death and the "military conflict" I first heard about in U.S. History class, had become personal for my family and for me.

Friendships that were made in Basic Training would be comforting to a homesick soldier. Stan's friend, Robert Rhodes from Albany, Georgia, was assigned to a different unit after a few days in Vietnam. Stan had hoped that they would be able to stay together, but Robert, being airborne qualified, was assigned to another unit.

Robert had appeared in the 8-mm film that Stan took while in training. Stan had videoed him playing a guitar while sitting on a bunk in the barracks. I had always wondered what had become of the handsome young soldier showing off his wedding ring to the camera.

It was July, 2005, that I contacted Stan's friend, and reconnected with the past. Robert survived "Hamburger Hill," with serious wounds, but came home to his wife and community to resume his life. He was very gracious when I contacted him and asked for his insight and recollections of his time with Stan. Thanks, Robert, for your kindness, support and additions to this memorial.

Robert Rhodes, Ft. McClellan, Alabama March, 1969.

Basic Training
October, 1968-March, 1969

The following letters were written during Stan's Basic Training, Specialty Training School and Advanced Infantry Training (AIT). Most of the letters are to our mother and are repetitious. Stan was very worried about her health and felt it important to write often to keep her spirits up, as she was going through some difficult physical and emotional times. I'm sure he felt by writing and encouraging her daily, he could some how make everything better. Other letters in this section are to me, friends, and other relatives.

It worried him that our little brother, Phillip, three and a half at the time, was being sent hundreds of miles away to stay with me in Nebraska. Mom was hospitalized in Minnesota, which put additional stress on our family and Stan, who was preparing to go even further from his roots. Our family, like so much of the world at that time, was in turmoil.

Stan was a caring son and brother who wanted everyone to be happy. As the letters reflect, he wanted nothing more than to come home at Christmas and for us all to be together again as a family.

Basic Training
Fort Polk, Louisiana (October 6, 1968-November 15, 1968):
October 6, 1968
9:00 a.m.
Hello Sis,

How are you? I was real happy to hear from you. You don't realize how much a letter means to a person when you're in a hell hole like this. I never thought people could be so mean! All they do is give us harassment and run our asses off! But I guess that's just part of the Army. I was so stiff the first few days I thought I was going to die. We have PT tests and exercises every morning for two hours, and then we run a mile after that. You wouldn't believe the exercises they put you through. They make you do one thing until you almost drop, then all of a sudden they make you do something else. I'm using muscles I never knew I had. (ha ha) But as far as the exercises and marching, I don't mind that. But some of this shit detail they make you do is terrible.

Like mowing and pulling weeds, KP from 3:30 in the morning until 7:30 at night, mopping and waxing floors, and a hundred other things. Every Saturday morning we have an inspection in our barracks. The drill sergeant comes in with a white glove and will rub his hand any place he wants to. If he gets any dirt on it at all, we've had it! It seems like that's all we get done is cleaning and more cleaning. It took me a week to learn how to make my bed right. (ha ha) I suppose when I get home Mom will put me to mopping the floors and making the beds. (ha ha) If I don't write very often, don't think anything about it.

They hardly ever give us any time off. I just got time to write the folks one letter last week. About the only time I have time to write anyone else is on Sundays. If we're lucky, we get most of Sunday off.

Well, Friday marked two weeks of Basic off, six more to go. I sure hope they go fast. They won't let us go to the PX (store) for a week or two yet. I sure wish I was home. I get terrible homesick. (I suppose that sounds kiddish.) (ha ha)

Last week we got our rifles and had to march four and a half miles to the rifle range. I thought I was going to die. But it was kinda fun to practice with the rifle after we got there. The food isn't too bad, but it's nothing like home cooking. You asked me about cookies and candy. There's nothing I would enjoy more than some. Warren Lane sent me some fudge Friday. It really hit the spot. Since they won't let us go to the PX or anything, my sugar content is very low. (ha ha) All I think about is candy or something sweet. But don't go to any trouble, Karen, because I can live without it.

Well, that's enough about Army life. How's everything in Bakersfield? Is it still as foggy as ever? How are you feeling after the operation? I owe you a big apology for not writing or send you a little money when you were in the hospital. I can't imagine how you felt not hearing from me. You probably thought I didn't give a damn about you or what happened, but don't ever think that! My only excuse is that when I was home I was so busy running around and having fun that I guess I forgot to stop and think about anyone. That's a fool kid for you! But I hope I can make it up to you in the future. I can imagine the trouble and hardship you're having out there. I know that when a person's in the hospital, it sure costs. Even though I didn't write, I was always thinking about you. The night you called home and said you were going in, I sat down and cried. If you don't believe me, just ask Dad, because he was the next thing to crying. I feel so bad about not sending you any money. But, Karen, I was so worried about getting my car paid for and getting everything straightened out before I left for the Army. It seemed like I was always broke. But I know that still isn't any excuse. Because five or ten dollars wouldn't have hurt me that much! Like I say, Karen, I hope you can forgive me. A person don't realize a lot of things like that until he's shut up in a place like this. When I was at home the only one I thought about was myself.

I'm enclosing $10.00 and a little gift to help you see how sorry I am. I don't need the money in here. So have fun with it or anything you want to do. It isn't much, but they don't give us much in here. Later on, if I can afford it, I'll send more to help you out.

Even though we've had our differences and haven't seen eye to eye on things, it isn't a reason for anything to come between me and you! I like you as much as any boy could like a sister and I'll do anything I can to help you!

I just hope you're not too mad! I hope you like the little gift. I thought it was nice! I hope things start going better for you, Karen. Tell Dad and Mom hello for me when you get home.

Well, I can't think of much more to write. I sure am lonesome to have someone to talk to. About the only thing I can do is write a letter. I went to church this morning. I'll bet you can't hardly believe that can you? (ha ha)

Are you still planning on being one of those bad school teachers someday? (ha ha) I'm laughing, but if you don't finish college, you're just about as stupid as I am for laughing. Education is everything anymore. I wish I had the sense to go. Maybe I will when I get out of here. Who knows?

Have you been swimming lately or anything? Have all the fun you can have. Because a person never realizes how good he's got it until someone takes it away.

Everyone has been real good to write to me from back home. I sure appreciate mail. That's about all a person's got to look forward to is the mail call. So don't forget me, Karen, and write whenever you can, and I'll do the same.

Well, I guess that's about all for now: and you're probably getting tired of reading it anyway. (ha ha)

Old Brother Stan

P.S. Thanks again for the letter and keep the good work up. <u>Thinking about you always.</u>

Don't worry about me, Karen. I'm making it. Just be sure to care for yourself. Bye for now.

Stan and a buddy mopping floor in Basic.

KP duty in Basic Training.

Karen on the beach, Monterey, California, 1968.

Special times: Karen and Stan, circa 1959.

When I got this letter from Stan, my husband and I were completing his 1W Service in Bakersfield, California. We had spent two years working in a Psychiatric Hospital, which fulfilled my husband's service obligation. I worked as a psychiatric aide while employed there. Stan, my sister, little brother, and my parents visited us there in fall of 1967. I could tell then that the draft was looming over Stan, as he seemed distant and preoccupied.

I was recuperating from minor surgery and hadn't told anyone in my family about it. With everything else they had on their plates, I didn't want them to worry about me. I waited. To my relief, the outcome was good.

Those ten dollars said much more than the amount. I knew he couldn't spare it, but that's how generous and thoughtful he was.

Our differences, stemmed from my husband choosing alternative service instead of the military. That didn't sit well with Stan. It was nothing personal toward my husband but something that he couldn't understand. Pacifism wasn't a philosophy that he nor I had been brought up with. It drove a painful wedge between us, but never affected the love we had for each other as siblings.

The gift he sent me was a satin pillow case, much like those I had seen on my grandmother's sofa that my dad and uncles had sent to her during WWII. I still treasure it. The inscription reads:

SISTER
Someone I love
I know loves me
Sister of mine
True as can be
Ever I think of the happy days flown
Remembering you always
Sister my own

October, 1968
Dear Aunt and Uncle Smith,
I'll bet you never figured I'd write. Well, you were wrong. It's just that they've kept us so busy I haven't had time until now. I've seen people keep busy before but this beats anything I've ever seen. They get us up at 4:30 every morning with not a minute off until 8:00 at night. And by the time you shave and take a shower it's 9:00, bed time.

They run our asses off and make us keep the barracks white glove clean. I always thought you had the cleanest house in the country, but it's dirty according to the way we have to keep our barracks, and that isn't running your house down any.

I was so stiff the first day or two I could have cried. I lost all the fat I had. I guess they're really trying to make a man out of me. I told Mom they've made me do stuff in here that I wouldn't think of doing at home, mopping, and waxing floors, making beds, washing my own clothes. It sure seems like hell.

Tell Francis the way they make a person rush around and run their ass off. He would be smart to put an order in to the Army for a platoon of men. (ha ha) They are better workers than those soft-assed civilians.

Thanks again for the $10.00, it sure helped out. I've still got most of it. A person can't spend too much in the Army, just for what he needs and that's it.

Well, I'd better go. It's about chow time and I've worked up quite an appetite.

Thanks for the money. Write when you can.

Nephew, Stan

Aunt Geraldine (Ross) Smith was my dad's youngest sister. She and Uncle Francis were very close to our family. She did have the cleanest house in the country. It was very large and elegant. Far different from our simple farm house with its linoleum floors and milk buckets on the back porch. She had white shag carpets which meant shoe removal was a requirement for entry. We had to mind our manners when we visited, taking care not to touch things. Her house was a wonderland of figurines, chandeliers, every modern convenience including a dishwasher which was rare in the early 60s. She was however, very gracious. I always looked forward to visiting her.

She was a terrific cook, as all my dad's sisters were. We spent many holidays together. She and my uncle were the first in our family to have a color television set and air-conditioning. We often watched the bowl games with them, and spent the day eating the wonderful meals she and others had provided.

My aunt reminded me of Doris Day. She was always elegantly dressed and appeared to have stepped out of a Hollywood set. She owned her own business—a hair salon next to the Temple movie theater downtown. She was very proud of the fact that she was chosen as Mary Pickford's beautician when she came to our town for a celebration honoring the Threshing Days. That festivity is still held as the Old Threshers Reunion every Labor Day weekend.

As long as she lived, my aunt would not be caught in anything but skirts and stiletto heels. She could match Donna Reed in the kitchen with pearls and a perky apron. She was a combination of Doris Day, Barbra Stanwick and ZaZa Gabor wrapped up in one. My aunt and uncle lived in their own home until her death.

My aunt passed away in her home, where she wanted to be, on February 28, 2006, at the young age of 90. The obvious omission of her birth date and age in her obituary came as no surprise to family or friends. The questions at the wake and funeral were not how she died but, "How old was she?"

November 3, 1968
Dear Karen,

I was sure glad to hear from you. I'm making it just fine. It's rough but a person gets used to it. We had Bivouac last week. It was three days in the woods, living off of K- rations and sleeping in pup tents and sleeping bags. It wasn't too bad. (I guess)

I'm sure glad to hear about your new trailer. It sure looked good. I guess having a place of your own is the main thing, isn't it? Like I say, I'm sure glad for you.

Well, just two more weeks of this shit. I'll sure be glad. It's been pure hell. We started getting passes this weekend. I sure was glad to get to let a little steam off. A man sure gets tired of being tied up all the time.

I guess it will be Christmas before I get a leave to go home. I'm sure looking forward to it. I suppose you heard about Mom going to Rochester. I sure worry about her. But I guess there's not much I can do.

How do you like Nebraska? I always did like those new trailers. I can imagine how nice it is. I hope you can make it to college quick. If you're smart you'll finish as soon as possible. I may even think of going to college after I get out of here. This Army sure makes a guy want to get an education.

I hear you're going to get Phillip and take him to your place. I sure miss the little fellow. Please treat him good, I know you will, If you need money for anything for him please tell me. I'll be glad to send it. I had my picture taken. It's not very good; I blinked when he snapped it. But it beats nothing. I'm sending it to you. Like I say, it's not very good. (ha ha) Write when you can.

With love, Brother Stan

Phil and I had finished voluntary service at the end of October. We moved back to York, Nebraska, where we purchased a mobile home. We located it just on the outskirts of York. Our intentions were to return to school, but the semester had already started so we decided to work that fall and winter, returning to school the next fall.

I worked at the local truck stop off of I-80, waiting tables, and my husband Phil worked at Champion; a mobile home factory. That was the coldest winter I can remember. Our pipes froze. We had snow drifts higher than our windows. My hair dryer got a real workout that winter thawing out what seemed like every pipe in the trailer. We had to dig our '64 Mustang out of the mountainous snow banks, and it rarely started on those cold winter mornings. As my dad would say, "It's a bitch out there!" Living in California for two years had spoiled us.

Our '64 Mustang was almost buried in snow the
winter of '68.

November 4, 1968

Dear Mom,

How are you today? I sure hope you're doing fine. Have they found the trouble yet? Don't worry about it, Mom. You'll be OK before you know it. I sure think about you a lot.

As far as Army life goes, it's not bad. A person gets used to it. But I sure wish I was home. A person can't beat civilian life. I get to feeling blue once in a while, but when I think of everyone in the hospitals and sick, that makes me feel better. No matter how rough I have it in here, as long as I've got my health, I've got everything, don't you agree? I'm sure you do. If there's anything I can do, Mom, just tell me. If you need any money, please don't be bashful to ask, because I've got some, and I don't need it that bad. So please, Mom, if you need it, let me know. I can't think of a better thing to do with it, than help you.

I hear Karen is taking care of Phillip. I'm glad he's in good care. I sure miss everyone so much. But Santa Claus will be here before you know it.

Don't feel bad because you can't make it down for graduation. I understand. Just as long as you get better, that's all that counts to me.

Well, just two more weeks of this Basic and I'll be able to fly out of here on that big 707 Boeing. I can hardly wait!

Time does seem like it has gone fast. When they keep you so busy, I guess a person doesn't have time to realize what day it is. They are treating us pretty good lately. I guess it's because we're close to graduation. I guess they figure we're almost soldiers. (ha ha)

I hope my card cheers you up a little, I thought it was kinda cute. (ha ha) Well, just remember, I'm thinking of you always and don't worry about me. I'm in good hands. I'm proud to be part of the U.S. Army.

With all my love,
Your son, Stan

Stan ready for graduation from Basic.

Stan knew that Mom was stewing about not being able to attend his graduation. She talked about it and wanted to be there. She and Dad were very proud of their son.

November 6, 1968

Dear Mom,

Well, I hope this letter finds you up and running. But if it doesn't, don't feel bad, because I just got in from running two miles. I'm sure bushed. But a person sure feels good when he's in better shape. This Army sure puts a man in good shape. But I wish they had a better way of getting you that way.

I got your letter today. I'm glad they are going to find your trouble. It will probably just take time. But don't worry about it, Mom, you'll be all right. A person's just got to learn to face things. I know from experience. If it wouldn't have been for the good Lord, I'd never have made it as good in here. If a man's ever going to break down or go crazy, he'll do it in the Army. But it's not so bad after you adapt to it.

Guess what I'm going to do after I get done with this letter? I've got to wash clothes. Isn't that terrible, a big Army man having to wash clothes? But that's one of the first things a man learns in here is to do everything himself. Because Mommy isn't there to clean up after their sons, like it was at home. (ha ha) But you wouldn't know any of that.

How do they treat you in the hospital? I'll bet real well. Like I say, if you need any money just let me know. (Please)

Well, as far as things here, it's just about as good as a person can ask for, for being in the Army. They're feeding us good and treating us pretty good.

The weather is just beautiful. I'm sure going to hate to leave this nice weather. But it will sure be nice to be out of Basic. Just think, November 15 and I'll be getting into that uniform and flying out in that big blue sky. I'll sure be happy!

Well, I guess that's about all for now. I'd better get to washing clothes. Write when you can. I'm sorry I don't write more, but I don't get much time. But you can bet if I write anyone it will be you!

I guess Virginia is coming down here so we'll probably go out for dinner or something. She's really a nice girl. But don't get any ideas. (ha ha) When this boy picks a "one and only," she'll be perfect! Bye for now.

With love, Stan

Stan, like other boys in the 60s wasn't required to help with the domestic chores of our house. We all had chores to do. My mom and we girls had to help with outside duties like milking and gathering eggs, but my brother didn't wash clothes or clean. I'm sure he managed to learn those skills well in Basic Training. He did however, make a mean chocolate cake when he felt like it; and he could dress and clean any game that he and Dad brought home. I was pretty good at holding the rabbits for Dad when he needed me.

November 8, 1968

Dear Karen,

How's everything in York? Have you got Phillip yet? I'll bet he's sure grown since the last time I seen him. (ha ha) Karen, if you need any money to get him something he needs, just let me know. (Please) And that goes for you too! I don't need very much money in here.

Well, one week from today I'll be flying out of here. I'm sure glad I'm almost through Basic. It's really been hell! But I'm really in a lot better shape than ever. But I wish I had a better way of getting into shape, than their way. (ha ha)

What are you doing these days? How's the weather there? It's been real nice here. I'm planning on changing from the school I had to Warrant Officer Flight Training. I will take that in Texas. But I'll probably be in Virginia until January. Flying a chopper sure seems like it would be fun, but I suppose they'll just send me to Vietnam. Oh, well. What will be will be. (ha ha)

Well, as far as things around here, it's not too bad lately. I guess they're treating us better because we're about done with Basic.

Are you planning on going to college or just taking it easy for awhile? How do you like that new trailer? It sure looked good. I just sat and looked at the picture for quite a while. It's so nice to see a civilian home. (ha ha) I get so tired of looking at Army green.

I've had quite a bit of fun the last couple of weekends. It was sure nice to get out after six weeks of confinement. I thought I would go crazy the first few weeks!

Well, I guess that's about all for now. Tell Phillip hello for me, and take good care of him, like I know you will!

I sure hope Mom gets to feeling better. I sure worry a lot about her. But I guess there's not much I can do here.

Well, goodbye for now,
Brother Stan

York, Nebraska, (left to right), Phillip, Karen and husband, Phil

November 8, 1968
Dear Mom,

How are you today? I sure hope you're getting better. I'll bet it's sure cold up there in Minnesota, isn't it? It's been a terrible day here today. It has rained all day. But I guess I can't really growl, this is just the second time it's rained since I've been here. I've really been blessed with all the good weather.

Are they still running you through a lot of tests? I'll bet you think you're some kind of walking x-ray machine by now.

Well, here I am at 10:00 on a Friday night. I've got security guard duty from 10-12. A person sure doesn't get much sleep at night. I'm sure looking forward to our three-day weekend.

Have you heard much from home lately, Mom? I haven't gotten a letter from home all week. I suppose it's because Dad is keeping pretty busy. I sure wish I was home to help him out.

I wrote Karen a letter telling her if she needed anything for Phillip, just let me know. I'll help out in any way I can. I'm pretty helpless being in here. But I can do no more than try.

By looking at that post card, that's a pretty big hospital isn't it? But if you're like me, you probably hate being in it. I remember when I had my ear operated on. Two days was plenty long enough for me. I don't think many people ever went to the hospital and got out as quick as I did!

Well, tomorrow I have a PT test. Like I said before, I sure hope I make 500.

I've got a friend in here. His wife went through the same thing you are right now. He said it just took time and patience. So don't worry, Mom, about nothing, especially me!

I'm doing as good as possible. I've got the worst out of the way. A person sometimes has to go on pure strength to keep going. But things always turn out for the best.

At church every week they have a bulletin board that says who graduates the next week. I can hardly wait till this Sunday to see my name. I've looked for eight weeks.

It will be two months next Monday since I left home. It seems like it's been a year. I sure wish it were a year, and then I would just have two years left.

I know one thing. When I do get out of here, I'm going to appreciate things more. That's the trouble with people these days. They take everything for granted. It would be good for everyone to spend a little time in the Army to straighten a guy up. I'm finally learning to make my bed correctly, Mom. It took me about eight weeks of practice, but I'm pretty good now.

Well, I guess that's about all for now. I realize this letter is probably pretty boring, but there's just not too much new going one. If there happens to be any news, you can bet you will be the first one to know. That's about all for now, Mom. Just remember you've got the whole U.S. Army behind you. (ha ha) So let's get better real quick, all right?

Your son, Stan

Stan with Friends In Basic Training At
Ft. Polk, Louisiana.

November 8, 1968

Dear Mom,

Well, here it is Friday already. One thing about the Army, a person gets to enjoy everyday for almost every hour in that day.

I'm writing this letter at 1:00 in the morning. I'm supposed to be on fire guard, but it's bad enough getting up at this hour, "let alone walking the floor." I could just kill them when I've got to get up at such an hour. But that's the way it is. So see how good you've got it! I'm just kidding, Mom.

How are you feeling today? I sure hope you're improving. But I'm sure you are. You've just got too many people that are pulling for you to do anything different.

If for no other reason, you should be happy because the Republicans are back in office again. I was sure glad to hear that.

Well, as far as what's happening new around here it's about the same. We had review yesterday on first aid, hand-to-hand combat, bayonet practice, quick-kill review and a few other reviews. They are just getting us ready for our final tests next Wednesday. We have a PT test Saturday. It's a test of physical strength. If a person makes a score of 500, the Commanding Officer will serve us dinner personally. I'd sure like to see that. (ha ha) He's a <u>First Lieutenant</u>. (I think that's the way you spell it.)

I guess that's about as far as the news goes. I sure hope they are doing you some good up there. Just remember, I'm thinking of you always. So don't let me down. Like you told me, just keep that old chin up and everything will work out. I know it sure helped me to know that people cared about me back home.

Have they still been giving you tests lately? I'll bet you sure get tired of them, don't you? But I suppose there's a reason for every one of them.

Well, I'd better close for now. It's not a big letter, but it's doing well of me at one in the morning. I just want you to know I'm thinking of you, because I sure want to keep you busy, cooking and getting me fattened up again over Christmas. But the food's not that bad, I guess. A person gets used to it. I've eaten things I never ate at home; boiled cabbage, finally liver, sweet potatoes and parsnips, and a few other things. But everything tastes good when you're hungry.

The weather has been getting cooler here the last couple of days. It sure reminds me of Iowa. I'm getting out of here just in time to beat the cold weather.

I wonder how everything is back in Mt. Pleasant. I suppose about the same.

Well, that's all for now. My fire watch is about over. I'll go back to bed for a couple of hours. Well, like I say, keep that chin up, and I'll be writing again the moment I get a free minute.

Bye for now, Stan

(Undated get well card sent to Mom)
November, 1969
Dear Mom,
I've sure been thinking a lot about you lately. I sure hope you get to feeling better, because I want to have a mom in good humor when I get home for Christmas.

Don't feel bad because you can't make it down for graduation. I understand. All I want is for you to get better. I'd go through Basic two times more if it meant you getting better!

I got six letters when I was on bivouac. I was sure happy. People have been good to write. We had to eat K-rations in cans on bivouac. It sure was hell. I thought I was going to starve. But that's the Army for you. I sure get homesick, but I guess that's life.

When I called you last night I was all by myself. I mostly run around by myself. I like to sit and just think about home.

Well, I guess that's about all for now. Be thinking about you always.

Your Son, Stan

P.S. I'm making it fine. Don't worry about me. Me and Fred Johnson got together today and went to the PX. I had my picture taken. I hope you like it. I had that simple look on my face. (ha ha) It's not too good a picture but it's me. And I can't think of a better person to salute than you.

Fred Johnson, a friend from home, and Stan.

November 11, 1968

Dear Karen,

Well, how's everything in York? How's Phillip like it there? I sure miss him. Well, today marks two months I've been in the Army. I guess time has sorta flown. I'd sure hate to go through it again. It's been hell! But the last few weekends we've had off, so that makes it better. I had a three-day weekend this week. Here it is Monday. A lot of the guys went home over Veterans Day if they had time, but Iowa is a little too far away.

I called Mom the other night. I guess she's making it all right. I sure worry a lot about her. I hope she's well before Christmas. I can hardly wait!

I hope you can make it up home for Christmas, if you can. Tell little Phillip that big Army brother sure misses him. I guess he sure hates those buses.

It seems like a year ago since I left. I guess they've got snow up home. It's been pretty nice down here.

Well, Friday I graduate and fly to Virginia so don't send me any more mail to this address. I'll let you know my address as soon as I get it. I'll sure be happy to get out of here, but then I'll just have to start counting the days over again.

What have you been doing lately? I don't suppose we'll do much the next three days. So the next time you hear from me I'll be in Virginia.

Well, that's all for now. Take care of Phillip and I'll write later.

Old brother, Stan

It distressed me that none of our family could attend Stan's graduation, but with our mother's illness and taking care of my younger brother, it didn't happen. Stan went on to Fort Belvoir, Virginia for specialized training.

It amazes me now how convenient things are for us in the 21st Century with cell phones, e-mail, and flying from destination to destination as commonplace as driving the car to work. In 1969, just making a long distance phone call took some thought.

I kept my younger brother Phillip occupied with plenty of drawing paper, blanket pup tents, and outdoor activities. He was oblivious to what was going on. Although looking back and talking with him now, he was more aware than we gave him credit.

My husband and I had one car, so I took the bus when I returned Phillip to Iowa. The ride was long and uncomfortable, but very exciting for a 4-year old. He was constantly asking questions and talking to the little boy in the seat ahead of us.

November 11, 1968

Dear Mom,

Well, here it is Monday. It sure doesn't seem like Monday. But it's Veterans Day and since I'm associated with veterans I guess we get the day off.

I sure wish I was home. The barracks sure seem deserted. Everyone that could go home went home. And everyone else is at the PX, on the phone, or something. So I guess I've got plenty of peace and quiet to write you a letter.

I sure hope they don't dope you up too much. But I suppose there's a reason for it. Do you think they are helping you yet or will it take a little more time? Just keep your chin up. It won't be long and you'll be out of there. Just think, I had eight weeks of this place and time is finally drawing to a close.

I really hate to leave my friends, but it will sure be nice to climb on that jet. I guess there's snow on the ground at home.

I called Dad after I called you the other night. He seemed like he was making it all right. I sure hope everyone can get together over Christmas. I don't want to have a dull moment. We'll really have a lot of fun, won't we?

I don't suppose we'll have to do much next week. I sure hope not! It's about time they let up on us a little bit. I sure wish I'd been able to afford the trip home this weekend. I sure got tired of messing around for three days. Me and Fred Johnson got together and went to a couple of movies, so that made things better having someone around you know from back home.

I went to church Sunday for the last time at Fort Polk. I picked up a pamphlet that they give us there. Each week they congratulate the companies that are going to graduate the following Friday, I sure was glad to see our company's name in there after eight weeks. So be sure to look in it. I circled my company. The pastor is sure nice. It sure helped going to church. (I'll have to admit.) A person has to have something to keep his chin up, don't they? I hope you like the card, Mom. I'd sure like to be able to talk to you and Dad again, but I guess a person can be thankful for a pen and paper.

Have you made any good friends in the hospital? Don't get me wrong, Mom. I've got friends in here, but there's sure a lot I can't stand.

Well, I can't think of much more to write. Don't send me anymore letters to this address. I'll let you know my new address as soon as I get it, which ought to be real quick after I get there.

Well, I guess that's about all for now, Mom. Don't forget that I'm thinking of you always, Mom. You sure helped me through Basic, so please let me help you get out of there. Will write again soon.

Your son, Stan

Chapel Number 2 used by the First and Second
Training Brigades at Fort Polk, Louisiana.

Going to church was very important to our mother. Stan knew she would be pleased to know that he had attended a church service. Later in Vietnam his faith would be tested, but it also got stronger.

November 12, 1968

Dear Mom,

Well, how's everything in Minnesota? I suppose pretty cold. The weather is absolutely beautiful down here.

I received your letter today. It sure was a nice letter. I really appreciate it, Mom. I'm glad we can be of help to each other through letters. I know if it hadn't been for your writing me in Basic, it would have been a lot worse.

You think I looked good in them khakis, wait till I come home in that uniform. I have never had it on yet, but I'll wear it when I get on that plane and to Virginia. I don't see much need in dressing up in my good uniform if I'm not going any place.

I'm sure glad they're starting to find some of the things wrong with you. Not that I'm glad there is something wrong with you, but it's just wonderful they can find it! That pamphlet I told you about, that I got at church, I forgot to put it in the last letter, so I'll put it in this one.

Well, one more training day. It sure is a nice feeling, don't forget; don't send any more letters down here. I'll let you know my new address as soon as possible. I sure hope I make it all right up there. It would have to be better than what I have gone through down here.

Mom, I want you to get that out of your head about Dad not caring. He might not be the best one to write letters, but don't ever think he doesn't care. Everyone cares. Always remember that, Mom. Dad has a lot on his mind. I can imagine how nervous he is. So please, Mom, don't ever let that pass through your mind. Dad loves you. You should realize that. He's trying to get you the best help in the world.

I called home the other night. He was anything but happy. He sounded like he had just lost his last friend. With Phillip gone and you gone, I can imagine how hard it is on him. So please don't ever think he's glad you're gone. You know better than that. I feel so sorry for both

41

of you that I can hardly sleep at night. But like I keep telling myself, things will get better. I just keep thinking of Christmas, and how nice it will be to be home with all the family again.

That's too bad about you being anemic, but that's not too bad. Like you say you'll just have to adapt to it. Do you know when you'll be able to go home? I sure hope it's soon. I can imagine how bored you probably get. I know I sure would.

Well, I can't think of much more to write. I'm also sending a post card showing the Fort. The barracks I circled, I think is ours. Anyway it's close around there somewhere. You can't imagine how big this place is. It makes the Ordinance Plant look like Mt. Pleasant against Los Angeles.

Well, I sure hope you keep improving and keep your chin up. I guess I'd better get a little sleep. Tell all those nurses hello from an Army boy. Tell them if they mistreat you, I'll have the whole Army on them. (ha ha)

Bye for now, Stan

Stan in his khakis

Dad and Mom Ross.

My mother's hospitalization, Stan being away, and the responsibility of taking care of the farm and my younger siblings, were stressful for our dad. He wasn't a demonstrative person; showing outward feelings toward our mother or his children, was difficult for him. He was from German-Irish stock; showing affection was simply a private thing. We knew he loved us, but hugging, or verbal compliments was not something he felt comfortable giving. Our mother, on the other hand, was from an Italian family where showing ones emotions was pretty much the norm. Hugging, kissing, complimenting, and pinching cheeks was as comfortable for her as breathing.

Mom felt the anxiety of being away from her family; not hearing the encouragement that she so desperately needed from Dad, didn't help her recovery. Stan, of course, wanted to make it all better, even though he knew how things really were. He was more like our mother when it came to relationships.

Dad has become softer in his golden years, especially with his grandchildren. I got my first hug and kiss from him in July of 2005. It was a shock. I was frozen for a moment, not knowing how to react. I had always hugged and kissed him goodbye in recent years, but he would refrain from returning my gesture. He'll never know how much I treasure that moment.

Time and age have a way of making the most rigid of men supple. When I call home these days, he tells me how much he appreciates me. I know he loves me.

November 13, 1968
Dear Mom,
How are you today? I really hope you are improving everyday.

I sure feel good tonight. The day after tomorrow we graduate. It seems like a dream. I thought a few times I'd never make it!

We had our last efficiency tests today. I passed everything with flying colors. I'm sure happy it's all over now. It seems like it's been just a big bad dream. But I'll have to admit when a person is in good shape, he sure feels better. I'm in better shape than I ever was. To run a mile, or to walk four or five, doesn't seem like anything. When I was home if I had to walk to the back of the pasture I thought it was bad. (ha ha)

I received my camera today. They've kept me pretty busy taking pictures. It's a good way to make some extra money. I'm going to try to find someone here who can run it so I can get a picture of myself to send to you.

Well, what's the latest word on the tests you're taking? I sure hope they're finding out all that's wrong. But don't worry, if anyone can find it they surely can. It seems so funny being so far from each other, doesn't it? They can take the boy from the farm, but they can't take the farm away from the boy. I still get terrible homesick at times. But a person gets used to it.

I'll bet you sure get lonesome at times, don't you? Have you been getting a lot of letters? I sure hope so. It sure helped me along. Like you said, each one is just like a booster shot.

I sure can't wait until I get a new address. I sure appreciate letters.

Well, I guess we're all having a little celebration tonight. Since this is about the last night in the barracks, a person just gets to where he's making some good friends and then you have to be separated. But that's the Army for you.

Well, I guess that's about all for now. It's not as long a letter as you write, but it shows I'm always thinking of you, Mom. We work together. You got me through Basic, let me help you out of that hospital.

Well, goodbye for now,
Son, Stan

I often wonder if Stan had made it home, would he have used his love for photography in some way? Our mother was a fanatic when it came to taking pictures, and I'm sure that's where Stan picked up the bug.

When we were kids our job was to gather the cows from the pasture for milking, which we did twice a day. Sometimes it was a long trek, and one we dreaded. Stan and I took turns, but the chore never got easier or shorter. It seemed those cows knew where the back corner of our property was--the longest distance from the barn. They seemed to head there in order to make us work for their precious milk.

November 14, 1968
Dear Mom,

I received your letter today. I'm sure glad you're feeling better. Just keep up the good work, and you'll be out of there before you know it.

Well, tomorrow I graduate. It doesn't seem possible. I've been so busy today packing my clothes and getting things all straightened up. They got us up at 4:00 this morning and I just got a chance to sit down now. It's 11:30 p.m.. It sure has been a long day. So I'm not going to write very much, because I'm so tired I can hardly keep my eyes open. You're the only one I've wrote for several days. It's sure been a busy week.

I'm in the front rank of my company. I sure wish you could be here to watch me graduate. It's really something to be proud of. But like I say, if you just get better, that's all I care about. I know if there would have been any way possible for you and Dad to make it, you would have come. It really wouldn't have been worth the trip for you guys to come down. I'd just been able to spend maybe half a day with you.

I guess my plane leaves tomorrow night at 12:00 a.m. It made me so mad. I was hoping to get a chance to fly in the daytime. I never have yet.

Well, what's new up at the hospital? I sure hope you don't get too bored. Well, I'll just pretend you're in that grandstand tomorrow watching me. I'll really be standing tall and looking good!

I'll write later and tell you how it was. I've just got to get some sleep now. I must be getting old. (ha ha) Thinking of you always, just hang with it. I sure miss the whole family. I hope Christmas hurry's up and comes.

Love, Stan

Stan in his dress uniform.

Fort Belvoir, Virginia (November 18, 1968-February 1, 1969):
November 18, 1968
Dear Mom and Dad,

Well, here I sit at Fort Belvoir. It sure seems different than Fort Polk. Nobody screams at you all the time. No getting up at 4:00, they let us sleep to 5:30.

Well, I suppose by the time you get this letter your operation will be all over. I sure hope it turns out successful. How long did it take you to get up there, Dad? You should have taken a plane. They go about 675 mph. They sure are nice. I ate dinner on it. They served us fried chicken and mashed potatoes and gravy, with milk and cookies. It took us one hour from Louisiana to St. Louis. I was so mad, because they wouldn't let us off the plane. It wouldn't have cost me much to call home from there. I saw the Arch at St. Louis.

Hey, Dad, remember that plane we saw crash at St. Louis that one time? Well, I saw it lying at the side, in a big ditch there at the airport.

It really seems funny, that when we stopped in St. Louis, I was that close to home. I sure got homesick. When we landed in St. Louis it was cloudy and raining. But as soon as we took off again, when we got above the clouds, it was a real nice sunny day up there.

We got on a bus at Baltimore, Maryland which is just about 40 miles from here. New York City is about 300 miles, and Washington, D.C. is about 15 miles, but that bus driver about scared me to death. People drive like crazy out here. We drove over the Potomac River. I could see the Capitol Dome shine at the far left, also the Washington Monument. I can hardly wait until I can go and take some pictures.

Make sure you take good care of the pictures I send home. I'd sure hate to lose them. I took about ten pictures for some other guys at the airport. I made a little money on it.

On the way here, we flew over the Blue Ridge Mountains and Appalachian Mountains.

How long are you going to stay up in Minnesota, Dad? Are you feeling any better, Mom? I sure do hope so. I'm thinking about you always.

Things are sorta screwed up here. I don't know for sure when I'll start school. It sure seems funny not being busy all the time. I guess when school starts, we will get off at 5:00 each night, and don't have any certain time to be in bed.

It cost 35 cents to go to a show. They had a dance last night (Sunday), I went to it. They have a bus which brings girls down from D.C. to the dance. So at least a person got to see a female.

I can hardly wait until Christmas. I'm getting so homesick to see the family. I keep that picture of the family on the top shelf of my wall locker all the time.

Well, I guess that's about all for now. I sure hope everything goes OK for you, Mom. And, Dad, thanks for the stamps. You, too, Mom. They sure came in handy.

Well, goodbye for now, Stan
P.S. Look on the backs of the pictures, I explained them.

November 18, 1968

Dear Karen,

Well, here I am at Fort Belvoir. It seems to be a real nice place. At least there's more here than pine needles and snakes. (ha ha) I spent six hours on a jet getting here. I really had a nice flight. I flew to St. Louis, then to Richmond, Virginia then to Baltimore, Maryland. I sure felt homesick when I got to St. Louis, being that close to home. I can hardly wait until I get home for Christmas.

Well, at least they don't scream at you here all the time. We get to sleep until 5:30 which seems like a dream. (ha ha) We're off at 5:30 p.m. at night until 12:00 a.m. bed check. On weekends there's no certain time. As soon as I get a little money ahead I'm going into Washington, D.C. (about 15 miles) to see the Capitol building and White House, and Washington and Lincoln monuments. This is real interesting country. There should be a few more females up here than in Louisiana.

How's little Phillip? Is he getting homesick? It seems like the family is so spread out! I sure hope things get better soon. I'll bet Phillip is sure growing. I'm about as miserable here right now as I was the first week of Basic. I just got to where I had some pretty good friends, and then a person has to leave them and start all over again.

Our graduation got rained out last Friday. I sure hated it. They really have a good parade. I'm sending you a picture. It's not real good, but it's not too bad for the source it came from. (ha ha)

Well, I guess that's about all for now. Tell little Phillip hello and I sure hope things become better quick. Hope to see you at Christmas.

Brother Stan

I did make it home that Christmas, never thinking that this might be the last one that the whole family would attend. The war seemed unreal and distant, but there was a feeling of dread none the less. We exchanged gifts and did the usual family things that were traditional with us: good food, telling stories, seeing and visiting our extended family. Stan enjoyed being with the family, but he also made the most of his leave by seeing his friends.

Christmas is one of the hardest times for our family. It took many years and grandchildren to bring the joy back to our holiday. My grandmother always said, "It doesn't matter if you have one child or ten, you can never replace the one you lose."

November 21, 1968

Dear Mom,

Well, I hope this letter finds you doing fine. I sure hope the operation was very successful. How long did it take? I sure hope it helps and you can go home before long.

When did Dad leave or is he still there? I haven't heard from anyone lately. I suppose everyone is too busy. The only one I'll forgive is you, Mom and Dad. I know you're probably not able to write yet, Mom. Don't think anything about it if you don't write. I perfectly well understand. I just want to know when you think you'll be back home. I'll sleep a whole lot better when I know the whole happy family is back together.

Well, as far as things go around here it's really boring. It's almost as bad as being too busy. They haven't said a thing about when I'll start school. This messing around every day and pulling shit detail sure gets old. Sometimes I think this Army is just a big bad dream. I sure wish I had my freedom back. But I guess three years isn't eternity. But I guess a person would never appreciate things unless he went through the service.

I sure hope Bob makes it all right in Vietnam. I sure wish this war was over. A guy doesn't have too much to look forward to in here. But I guess there are four and a half million guys in the service so I'm not alone.

Well, I wish Santa Claus would hurry and come. I think I'll get off from the 20th to the 6th, which will really be nice. Well, I guess that's all for now. Sure hope you're feeling better. Did you like the pictures?

See you in a few days, Son Stan

Stan and friend, Bob Richards, end of May, 1968
before Bob left for boot camp.

November 22, 1968
Dear Mom,

How are you? I talked to Dad last night and he said he thought the operation was going to help you a lot. I was so happy to hear it. You can't imagine how much I want you to be out of the hospital. Do you know for sure when you will? It will be so nice to think that the whole family is back together again. I sure have worried a lot about you. You can't imagine how everyone is behind you 100 %. I sure wish I was closer to you. I think I've got enough to talk about to last three weeks. (ha ha) I sure will be happy when I get on the plane to fly home. We'll all have so much fun. I don't know what to do first.

The weather was real nice today. It sure makes a guy feel good. How's the weather up in Minnesota? I'll bet it's really cold. I hope I can make it into D.C. next weekend. I'd like to get some good pictures. There's sure a lot there.

Dad sure sounded good on the phone last night. I know he's real happy about you getting better.

They still haven't told me when I'll start school. I sure wish it was soon. I get tired of messing around.

Well, I can't think of much more now. Sure glad you're feeling better, Mom. Don't let me down. Get out of that hospital quick! We'll see you soon, in about 28 days.

Son, Stan

P.S. Hope you like the card.

Reflections of a Friendship
By
Steve Klaus

Stan and I first met in the 4th grade at Elm School. He was one of the guys the teacher, Mrs. Schaefer, would pick to get a willow stick to spank someone. I remember once, it was for me. She would whip someone until they cried, so I made her work. (ha ha)

We started getting close at Pleasant Lawn about sixth grade. We enjoyed competing and having fun. By junior high, we were good friends. We stuck together, because all the city kids had already established ties and we had much in common, coming from the farming community.

In high school we did about everything together. We had other friends, but we did more with each other than anyone else. We were in freshman English class together. Certain days Mrs. Trout would look at me, smile, and say, "There is a secret admirer in my class, but I'm already married." I'd look around and Stan and Bob Richards would be laughing. It never dawned on me that they were leaving love notes for her and signing my name. Halfway though the year, they told me. Mrs. Trout never confronted me. (I received A's and B's.) To get even, I wrote letters to a real nice, but plain girl and signed Stan's name. It pissed him off because she was nice enough that when she showed her friends the letters, they would really believe he wrote them. The notes were nice, but real corny and would make everyone think Stan was a real clod. So to get even with me, he wrote this girl I really liked. I found out later that she really liked the letters I supposedly sent. They read something like, "I know you're not in my league because I'm so good looking and such a nice guy." We never got mad, just laughed and went on. It's probably good because she was really cute and the only girl that made me nervous to talk to, so that ended that. Stan and I just had fun screwing around with each other. We had a lot of fun with girls, but never messed around with the ones we knew the other person liked.

When we were going into our senior year, we had gotten some beer while driving around in his '67 Chevelle. It was summer and we decided to run to Mt. Pleasant, about 2:30 in the afternoon. As we came to Mt. Pleasant on Old 218, Stan let off of the gas with his tailpipes crackling. We drove by a local restaurant, where a patrolman was just getting in his car. Needless to say, he noticed us and here he came. I had an empty beer can so I slightly opened the door and let it roll under the car (dumb). He cited us for illegal possession of beer and also got me for littering. He took us to Judge George Means, where he fined us and then let us go. We left there, got something to eat about 7:00 or so, went back up to Wayland, where Stan went into the South Side Bar, asked for a 12-pack (quietly), drove around to the back and picked up the beer they had set out for us. We never missed a lick and doubt we ever told our parents.

November 24, 1968
Dear Steve,
How's everything back in Trenton? Is everything just dead as it was when I left?

Well, I finally got out of Basic. That was sure a bitch! I'm at Fort Belvoir, Virginia now for AIT. My school was supposed to start the 15th, but I'm still waiting to start. They won't tell a guy anything. It's almost as bad as Basic, just fucking around all the time.

Speaking of fucking, are you getting any? Don't get mad, "I'm just jealous." I sure hope I can find a little lovin' when I get home.

Have you been to Gulfport lately? I'm just 15 miles from Washington, D.C. I think I'll go there next weekend and take a few pictures. There are a lot of places a guy can go around here. I should be able to have a little fun.

Are you still planning on joining the "New Action Army?" That's sure a fucking joke. This service is a pain in the ass. One thing for sure, "Get drafted!" Two years of this hole is enough. After so long a guy doesn't care if he goes Infantry or anything else. If I could take infantry and just have two years, I'd jump at the chance. But if you want a school, you'd better enlist, because most draftees get Infantry.

If you have Bob's address, please send it to me. I'd like to know how he's making it.

How are all the chicken shits making it?

I'm Platoon guide here at AIT, so I don't have to do much. Whenever there's some detail, I'm the last to get it.

I got in a fight the other night. I done better than I thought I would. That's about all there is to do in here is get drunk or fight. I've drunk up every penny I've made so far. I've got to start saving a little for Christmas vacation. I think I'll get off from the 20th of December until the 6th of January. I can hardly wait. We'll have to have some fun.

Well, I guess that's about all for now. Write me a few lines if you have time.

Old Buddy, Stan

Stan, like most nineteen-year olds, had a healthy appetite for the fairer sex. This letter reflects that. Mothers and sisters don't like to think of their sons and siblings in that way, but I included this letter because it is who Stan was. Steve had saved several of Stan's letters and of course they all referred to their good times which included girls. As I read this letter and others that Stan had written to him, we both smiled and said, "That was Stan." Sorry, Mom!

November 25, 1968
Dear Mom,

I was so happy to hear your voice last night. You sure sounded weak, but don't worry, you'll be up and running before you know it. It will probably just take time.

As far as things around here, it's about the same. Here I sit on a Monday afternoon at 3:00 p.m. A person sure gets bored. Like I told you on the telephone, I'm a platoon guide. I never was one who liked to have responsibility. I'm getting used to it. The boys really tried to make it rough on me at first, but slowly I'm shaping them up.

I still don't know when my school will start. I sure wish it would be soon. It sure gets old sitting around. I've been going over to the gym every night to keep in shape. After all the work and exercises I did in Basic, then to come here and do nothing, I'm afraid I'll turn to fat. (ha ha)

Do you know for sure how long it will be before you can go home? I sure hope soon. I'm counting the days until I can come home. It will sure be nice. How long do you think the operation will leave you weak? I sure hope not long. I'm sure glad you liked the pictures.

Well, I guess that's all for now, Mom. Just hang on and things will work out fine. We will all have so much fun at Christmas. Good-bye for now, and remember, there isn't a minute that goes by that I don't think of you.

With all my love, Stan

November 26, 1968
Dear Mom,

How are you today? I sure hope you're improving. Are you still pretty weak or are you getting your strength back? Do you know for sure when you'll be able to get home.

I called the airport today. It's so hard to get a flight. You can't imagine. I finally called United Air Lines and got reservations. The only thing I could get was first class. It costs like hell, but if I want to get home, I guess that's the one I've got to take. It's going to cost me

$69.00 one way to Des Moines. Isn't that terrible? But it's worth every penny. So I guess you guys will have to meet me in Des Moines. I guess I'm lucky to get that. At Christmas it's almost impossible to get a plane.

Well, as far as things around here, it's about the same. I had a 20-man detail today raking leaves. It sure seems like a waste in manpower.

I heard from Karen yesterday. She said little Phillip is doing just fine. I'm sure glad to hear that. So please, Mom, don't worry about either one of your boys. We're both just fine. I've thought of putting up paper dolls and pulling one down each day until Christmas. (ha ha) I can hardly wait! Well, I guess that's about all for now, Mom. I sure hope you're feeling better and don't worry about nothing.

With love, Stan

It was a tradition at our house to cut dolls out of the Sears catalog— twenty-five of them—string them up, and then pull one down every evening before we went to bed. It was always fun to watch the row of dolls get shorter as Christmas Eve approached.

November 28, 1968

Dear Mom,

Well, here I sit Thursday night waiting until it's time to go to the show. That's one nice thing about being here; a guy can go to a different show every night. I sure like to watch a good movie once in a while.

The reason I called twice today was because the first time the phone returned all my money that I put it in. It was like a gift from heaven. It was so nice to talk to you and Dad. I sure hope you get to go home this weekend. I didn't want to mention on the phone about getting my money back. I was afraid that the operator might hear me.

Well, there really isn't too much news around here. It's about the same old thing, doing nothing. But I think I'll start school pretty soon.

I sure hope I get paid tomorrow so I can go into D.C. this weekend and take some pictures.

Well, Mom, I guess that's about all for now. It's not much of a letter, but it shows I'm thinking and behind you all the way. Just remember not to let anything worry you. Just take life as it comes and don't worry. I'll be home before you know it. So we've both got something to look forward to.

"Thinking of you always."

Your son, Stan

February 2, 1969

Dear Aunt and Uncle Franky,

How's everything back in cold Iowa and old Mt. Pleasant? I just thought I'd write and tell you that I hadn't forgot that I had an uncle and aunt. (ha ha) I can hardly ask why I haven't gotten a letter lately from you, because I've been twice as bad about not writing you folks.

It seems if I get around to writing the folks, that's about the only ones I write to. So I hope you're not too mad about me not writing more, because you've treated me about as nice as anyone could since I've been in this hell hole. It's nice to know that someone is thinking of me back home.

Have you been keeping pretty busy lately, Frank? I'll bet it's a little cold to be holding a hammer in the cold weather. If you hadn't heard, I'm down here in Alabama now. It's terrible rainy weather all the time, but it's usually warm. I'm sitting here in a laundromat writing this letter. I've been running around in a T-shirt all day. I sure hate washing clothes, but I guess it's just another Army headache.

I'm taking Advanced Infantry Training now. It's quite a switch from what I did have. I guess Mom is feeling better now. I sure hope she stays that way. If you would write and tell me when Mom and Karen's birthdays are (I forgot) and I'll send them a little something for their birthdays. I hate to write home and ask when they are. Well, I can't think of much more to write. I'll try to do better at writing in the future.

Write me when you get time, and tell everyone hello.

Homesick Soldier, Stan

P.S. Tell Frank he ought to see the WACs down here. There are about 5,000 Army women down here. "I sure hate that!" (ha ha)

After I received these letters from my aunt I noticed that she had made a note on this letter as to the dates of my mother's and my birthdays. They are both in February.

Fort McClellan, Alabama (February 2, 1969-March 1969):
February 2, 1969
Dear Steve,

Well, how do you like the big action Army? (ha ha) It's complete hell, isn't it! I finally got your address from Mom. I think you're pretty close to where I took my Basic. I was at E-4-1. Do you go to Bulldog Hall any?

Well, I'll bet you couldn't guess where I'm at, unless you've already heard. I'm in Fort McClellan, Alabama taking Advanced Infantry Training. That's right, Infantry! I knew I'd never cut that school bit. You'd better hope you never get thrown into Infantry. I thought Basic was bad, but this is complete hell. We get about four hours of sleep a night if we're lucky. But I guess I can't bitch, because I had my chance.

That sure beats the hell out of being a three-year Infantryman. I'll have to admit it, I'm getting sorta scared. I sure hope I don't get my ass shot off. But I guess if I do make it back I can stand proud. At least I'm out of that pussyfied school. I still don't believe I'm in the Infantry.

Speaking of pussy, I'll bet you're getting pretty horny. I know exactly how you feel. It's Sunday and you're sitting in the barracks. If you're lucky enough, you're writing a letter. The first week I was in Basic I never got one letter written. But it's worse here. I'll be damned, I felt sorry and thought it was sorta funny that you were starting all that shit, and here I am taking the same shit, but worse. I'm a tiger from "Tiger land." (ha ha)

Are the drill sergeants harassing you very much? We don't have too much of that here, "Thank God!" Don't let it get the best of you. Always remember that "They can't kill you!"(ha ha)

Go to the EM club when you get post privileges. I used to have a lot of fun over there. That Fort Polk ruined me. I got gung ho as hell. I wanted to be a man, someone rough. Well, I guess I got my wish. (ha ha)

When will you graduate out of Basic? We've got a good chance of being home at the same time. I'll graduate the 22nd of March, day or two before or after. I hope you get home about the same time. I don't know how much time I'll have off between AIT and Vietnam. I heard about 15 days since they need Infantrymen over there so much. I might get 15 or 7 or 30. I don't know. You'll get two weeks after Basic won't you? I start my third week out of nine tomorrow. We'll really have to have some fun if we get to see each other.

I don't know for sure, but Bill gets back sometime in March. Wouldn't that be nice if we all three get together. But I suppose that's dreaming.

The only thing nice about this Fort is that it's a WAC center. There are 5,000 or more women here. The hell of it is that 80 percent of the girls aren't much to look at. But a few beers take care of that. (ha ha) Most of them have to be back in their barracks by 9:30 p.m. But it still beats nothing.

One nice thing about being in the Infantry, no one gives you any shit. We "Tigers" are the big shits here. At least a guy doesn't have to take a back seat to anyone. I figure when I get out of this training I'll be just as good as any Marine!

I haven't heard from Bob for quite a while. I wonder how he's making it.

Well, I can't think of much more. How's the weather in Louisiana? Here in Alabama it's raining all the time, but it's usually warm. I'm in a T-shirt today. Just laying here listening to a radio. Do they let you have radios yet?

Well, goodbye for now. Write if you get time.

Infantryman, Stan (ha ha)

Steve Klaus and Bill Lane, 1968.

Stan's quick temper landed him at Fort McClellan. When he felt something was wrong, he let you know it. In this case, he should have kept his opinions to himself. That temper would be the reason he ended up in AIT (Advanced Infantry Training) training, losing his chance to work in the "rear."

Stan had signed up for special schooling at Belvoir, where he would be trained to work with air-conditioning and refrigeration (in the rear), if sent to Vietnam. That was his reasoning for enlisting rather than waiting to be drafted. Unfortunately, that never came to pass, because of his confrontation with a superior officer, who taught one of his classes. He would be sent on to AIT (Advanced Infantry Training) at Ft. McClellan, Georgia. The dye was cast; he would face the enemy head on.

Bob Richards was a childhood friend of Stan's. They hung out together, passed their time with the usual things that good friends and guys their age did back then. Cars, girls, and beer, not necessarily in that order, were probably the most serious issues in their calendar until Vietnam would change their care-free lives. Hootie and Blondie, his parents, were good friends of our family. Bob served with the Marines in Vietnam. He lives with his wife in Burlington, Iowa.

February, 1969
(A Valentine's card sent to the folks)
Poem inside
The heart that cares remembers
Good friends and loved ones too
And keeps in treasured memory
The thoughtful things they do

Mom and Dad,
Just a little something to not let you forget, that I'm still thinking of both of you always. That's the one and only thing that keeps a guy going sometimes, is just the thought of making it to home sweet home again someday.

If I never have anything, or never amount to a damn, I never can say it was my folks' fault. Because I hope if I ever have any children, I can be just half as understanding and good to them as you've been to me. It's just too bad it's taken the Army to make a guy realize how nice he really did have it.

You don't know how happy I've been since you're getting better, Mom. Like I said, we've been a big help to each other.

To the best folks ever, Stan

Stan was a romantic, a very sentimental guy. He valued and missed the home he left behind. He, like so many other GIs at that time, had never spent much time away from home. They had barely graduated from high school before answering Uncle Sam's call. Stan had never been away from home for any extended amount of time. Some kids had experienced summer camps or college. This was a very new experience for him.

February 2, 1969

Dear Mom and Dad,

Well, I'm so surprised to get three letters in a row from home. I would almost feel like a heel if I didn't write back. I'm so busy all the time here lately that I don't even realize what day it is. Time sure flies here.

We've got an inspection this Sat. by the Post Commander; she's a Major, that's right "she". A damn old lady is going to come through the barracks. So every night we get back from the field, we have to mop floors and paint to get ready for Sat. inspection. That will be one nice thing about Vietnam, they don't have inspections and polished boots all the time. I tried to call the airlines tonight, but I've got to call in the daytime I guess. So I'll do that the first chance I get.

Your letter just took one day to get here. So it doesn't pay to send air mail. We had tests today on communications, land navigation, first aide, and on weapons. I got 135 points out of a possible 150, so I guess I didn't do too bad. If it wasn't for just getting about three or four hours of sleep every night it wouldn't be too bad. I'm sending a little picture they took the other night at the EM club. I'll have to admit it, I've had worse dates. (ha ha) That's one thing, there's plenty of women around here. Some not too good looking, but that's only skin deep. (ha ha)

My turn on KP is coming up about Wednesday. So think of me. I'm dreading it already. I can take anything but that.

Hey, Dad, I got the paper today. It sure seemed nice to read it. Well, I guess that's

about all for now. I'm tired, but making it just fine,

Stan

Robert Rhodes, Stan's good friend from AIT training at Fort McClellan, recalled one of the good times they had together, "It was our sixth or seventh week of AIT (Advanced Infantry Training.) Our drill sergeant told us if could clean our rifles and have them inspected without any rejections we could have a pass to go to the main PX at Ft. McClellan. We both were so excited, because that would give us the chance to have a cold beer and maybe a hamburger which we craved. We passed inspection, Stan and I, and another guy who I can't recall. Anyway we were bused to the main PX and told they would return for us at 9:00 p.m. later that night. Stan and I asked the other fellow if he'd like to join us, and of course he said, "Yes." Stan and I ordered our hamburgers with all the things we wanted on them. We also had our beers. The waitress said we could get a pitcher for 50 cents. We got that and many more! I recall how good that beer tasted and how we talked of home and what we would do when we got out. I also remember how Stan and I felt the next morning at 4:30 a.m. When our drill sergeant got us up, it was rough! What seems so strange, as I recall, we knew we were going to Vietnam, but never talked of it. I think now we were so young at the time, it really never sunk in until it happened."

Stan in AIT training, with M-16 rifle, at
Ft. McClellan, Alabama.

Stan on Bivouac, Ft. McClellan, Alabama.

March 6, 1969, Wed. night
Dear Karen,

Well, I finally got a little time to drop you a few lines. I guess we both are kinda forgetful as far as writing a letter to each other. (ha ha)

I got the pictures you sent. The trailer looks real good. I'll bet you really like it don't you?

Well, I've just got two more weeks of this hell hole left. Believe me it's been rough. But I guess I can take two more weeks of anything. I graduate the 22nd of March. I heard through the grapevine that I've got to report in Oakland, California the 14th of April, to ship to Vietnam. So I'll just get 23 days leave. That includes travel time. I'll admit it. I'm starting to get a little nervous. It's sure not much to look forward to. But I guess I just as well learn to live with the fact, because I'm going no matter what I think.

I'd give anything to be out of this shit. It's terrible training. We eat outside, get maybe four to six hours sleep on the average, harassment constantly. After a while, a person just feels that he doesn't give a damn what happens anyway. All I hear from morning till night is some new way to fight or kill someone. But I guess there's a reason for the intense training, because a weakling or someone out of shape wouldn't make it a day in Vietnam. I just hope and pray I make it 365 of them. (ha ha) Well, that's enough of that shit. I don't even want to talk about it.

How do you like your new job? Karen, just remember and stop and think before you ever gripe or complain, because you don't realize how good you have it. You've got perfect health and you're not pushed and treated like a damn dog. Before I came in here I never appreciated anything either. But that's life. You never know how good you've got it until someone takes it away.

I sure hope to see ya when I'm home on leave. I sure hope my year goes fast. Well, I can't think of much more to write. Please write and tell me what's happening. I sure like to get letters. (ha ha) See ya in a few days, "I hope."

Write soon,
Little Brother with love, Stan

What I had dreaded all along had come true—Stan's deployment to Vietnam was almost a certainty. My brother was going to Vietnam. I knew how my parents must feel, especially my mother. It is the mothers of the world who know and feel the loss of their children in a primitive way; for they have known them before the world received them and they have felt the heartbeat and stirring of life before anyone.

I knew by being in the Infantry his chances weren't going to be good. And I also knew he would not choose the easy way out. If Stan was called on to fight, he would.

The new job for me was waitressing at the Skelly Truck stop on I-80, on the outskirts of York, Nebraska, west of Lincoln. I had worked as a waitress, but never in a truck stop. What an experience I was in for. It was hard work, but interesting because of the variety of customers that came through the café. I served everyone from truckers to business men. Interstate 80 was and is a lifeline that connects the U.S. The 60s were time of great migrations, especially to the West Coast where the weather was warm and the rules of life more relaxed. I recall hippies making their way to California in vans with wild psychedelic colors and designs and slogans that said "Make love, not war."Farmers exchanged the latest gossip and complained of low livestock and crop prices.

I waited tables, smiled as I poured the coffee, and enjoyed the experience, all while listening to songs like, "American Woman." I knew then and there I would finish college.

March 15, 1969
Dear Stan,

It's a beautiful day in Iowa. Eileen said this a.m., "Stan will be home next Sat.," the Lord willing.

Stan, Frankie Lane (the singer) is singing, "God gave me a mountain," right now on the radio. Eileen told me the name of it. Sometimes some songs have a way of getting to you. Don't they? Stanley, we can't wait for you to come home. A person shouldn't wish time away.

I got a letter yesterday from a woman who was in the hospital with me, she's doing well too, she said.

Some young boy was killed here on the highway, I don't know him.

Stan you won't know Mama. I weigh 160 pounds. I'm fat! I'm so hungry all the time, I eat like a horse.

Phillip is sitting so cute watching his Sat. programs. Remember not too many years ago you used to do the same thing.

I had a chance to go back to the Starlight, but Stan, I said no. If little Phill grows up as fast as you did. I made up my mind with God's help to stay home and be with him. The days are long, sometimes. I try to keep busy so I can't let this life overcome me. The Lord has been good to heal my body.

Daddy had to work this morning, Sat. It's the first he's had to work, and he's been coming home at 4:30 p.m. Starting next week he'll have to work until 5:00 p.m., I guess.

How's training coming? Maybe they'll give you some rest now this week. What have you found out, Stan? Anything? Listen, Stan, I write so you'll get mail till Wednesday or Thursday. Tell us about your flight times and all the details. I'll have you some good ole spaghetti made whenever you get here.

There's no more news, so be seeing you.

Love ya,
Mama

Stan with baby brother, Phillip, 1965.

Mom's letter to Stan reflects her concern over her decision to stay home with Phillip who was three-and-a-half-years old at the time. Mom enjoyed being around people and socializing; the Starlight café had provided that outlet for her. It was hard work, however, and being in her forties, a farm wife, and mother of a young energetic boy, took its toll on her. Having a baby at 42 presented new challenges for her.

Working away from home also gave her a sense of independence with a little spending money of her own. As so often happens, detours in our lives can be a blessing, and so it was with our youngest brother.

March 16, 1969

Dear Karen,

I received your letter. Real good to hear from you. Please don't worry about me. It won't do any good. Things will be the way they're going to be, and no one can change that.

How's everything in that new trailer? I sure would like to have one like it someday. I always was a trailer lover. How do you like your job by now? I hope all right. If it gets bad, just think about the Army. (ha ha) This would make any job look nice. I sure wish I was out of this hell hole, but just one more week. I'm lucky to get to write this letter. I'm writing it in a foxhole believe it or not. I've slept in one all week. It's something else! Eating cold C-rations and walking, and hunting for jack VC's all day long. I'll be so glad to get to a bed again. I haven't washed my face or anything since Monday morning. That's hard to get used to.

I'm real glad you're going to be home a week or so when I'm on leave. We'll really have some fun! I've got to have enough fun to last a year. (ha ha) I hope it's not too bad over there. But the Infantry gets the hell no matter where they go. But I'm trying not to worry about it. Because like I told you, it won't do any good.

It's been pretty nice weather down here the last few days. I'm sure thankful for that, especially when a guy's sleeping in a foxhole under the stars every night.

Well, I guess I'd better try to get a letter off to Mom and Dad before it gets dark.

So I'll see you in a week or so, "OK" like I say, we'll really have fun. The sky's the limit!

Brother Stan

Karen and husband, Phil, with cat, Tiki, in our
mobile home, spring 1969, York, Nebraska.

Greg Breeckner, Jayson Dale, and Stan in a jungle clearing, drying a poncho liner, after a rain the night before, August, 1969.

Greg Breeckner in country.

Greg Breeckner
Squad leader, 3rd Platoon Charlie Co.
Remembers Stan

Greg Breeckner recalled his Vietnam experience and friendship with Stan.

"When receiving our orders to go to Vietnam from Ft. Lewis, Washington, our C.O. said to us, 'For those of you who don't go to Vietnam, you'll miss the greatest adventure of your lives.' He was right except he never mentioned how much this adventure was going to cost.

Leaving Oakland Army Airfield to go overseas, I met Frank Leone on the plane. As luck would have it, Frank and I spent the whole tour together without any mishaps. Then one day a supply of fresh troops arrived; probably about five or six guys. One of them being a big "plow boy" from Iowa, Stan Ross. I looked at him and I think he was thinking the same thing I was, "We'd better take care of this guy. He's young and real green." Stan was put in my squad and learned quickly. He was an excellent soldier, quick to smile, did whatever he was told without any arguments. We became friends right away in a place where making friends wasn't recommended. His size made him a bit of a natural for carrying more than the others. Still, to this day, there isn't a week that goes by that I don't think of or remember that big "plow boy."

Greg has had an exciting and colorful life since those days in Vietnam. He has pursued many careers some of which include owning a motorcycle shop in the 70s, where he repaired and built custom motorcycles (choppers), and worked as a cook and kitchen manager in Bridgewater, Connecticut. He lived in an old house in an idyllic, wooded setting that was located on a stream with a waterfall, waterwheel and old papermaking shop. Greg married his wife Liz in 1982. He has two children, a son, Andrew, and a daughter, Ashley.

In the 90s he did boat repairs in Connecticut, and in 1996 he moved to Midland, Texas where he worked on oil drilling equipment and natural gas compressors.

I had the pleasure of meeting Greg and his wife, Liz, in March of 2006. I could see why Stan valued him as a friend and leader. He had that tough guy, New York accent, but a softer side that came from his Italian mother.

Greg and his wife enjoy life in South Carolina near the ocean, where he repairs boats for clients up and down the coast.

I knew Stan would make the most of his final leave before Vietnam. He looked forward to seeing old friends that were still around, who hadn't been shipped out yet.

Mom planned some times with relatives that wanted to extend their best wishes and advice to Stan; especially the men that had been in WWII, and Korea. I don't know whether that comforted him or not; probably a little of both. I know Mom cooked up a storm those few days in early April, 1969.

Stan in his dress uniform, on leave before leaving for
Vietnam, spring 1969.

Stan and Dad fooling around with their Army caps,
while Stan was on leave, spring, 1969.

Reflections
By
David Clines
Vietnam, January, 1969-January, 1970
199ʰ Light Infantry Brigade
Charlie Co. 4ᵗʰ Platoon

David Clines in country.

I was not in the same platoon as [Stan], but was acquainted with him. I have no photos of him, only memories. I can tell you what you already know, that he was a good person and one of the best soldiers I knew in Vietnam.

He was a leader and was well thought of by all who soldiered with him. I remember him smoking a pipe now and then and being a close friend to a fellow in my platoon called "Obie," Tim Oberst.

I have always had a soft spot in my heart for your brother and thought that his life was expressed in the saying, "The good, they die young." He was a good man and I will never forget him.

I have prayed for his family before and I am glad that I could finally make contact with you all. You and your family will be in my prayers in the future as well. I pray that God will comfort you and your family and that you will know that his life was observed, respected, and well spent.

By the way, the pipe he smoked was a corn cob pipe! I really don't remember if he smoked often, but I remember him in my mind's eye with that corn cob pipe.

I served in Nam from January 13, 1969 to January 12, 1970. I was in the 4th Platoon with Charlie Company. I was not wounded and came back home in good shape. I went to college after I was discharged and am now employed by a security agency in Dallas, Texas.

THIRD PLATOON, CHARLIE CO. 2/3 199TH LIGHT INFANTRY BRIGADE, (Front row, left to right) John VanDusen, Terry Wanner, Martin Specter, William Thompson, Eddie Taylor, Tom Phillips, John Self; (2nd row) Richard Sims, Tom Reed, John McCombs, Don Mazzi, James Pope, William Stoner; (3rd row) ARVN Scout, Tommy Smith, Dave Cherneski, William Perrie, Ron Parsons, James Faber, Stan Ross, Johnny Rogers, Greg Breeckner.

In Country Vietnam
(April, 1969-October, 1969)

April, 1969

Dear Mom and Dad,

Well, here I am. Vietnam at last! I've got just two things to say about this place, it's dirty and a hot-hot bastard! I've been sick from the heat ever since I've been here, but I'm starting to get used to it.

You wouldn't believe how these people live over here. It's terrible. I hope I don't melt this paper away. I'm sweating so much.

I had a beautiful flight over here. Japan and Alaska was beautiful. Guess who I've been with all day? Bill. Yes, I couldn't believe it, seeing him in a place like this! We didn't know what to say to each other. It's been so long! As soon as we got here they pulled the Infantry out and put us on 72-hour guard, here on post, or base camp. They let me off for six hours to see Bill. I haven't heard where I'm going yet. I don't suppose I'll hear for a couple of days.

We had an alert last night. I guess the VC was starting up a little trouble outside the base camp. But it wasn't anything serious. In this area a person's about as safe as a baby in a cradle. I see now why Bill stayed. For being in Vietnam you couldn't have it any better. I hope I get a place one-tenth this nice. Well, I can't think of much more to write. I hope you like your gift, Mom. I thought it was pretty. Don't pay any attention to the address on the package because I don't have any yet.

With all my love, and <u>don't</u> worry. Please.

Stan

Stan and Bill get a chance to see each
other at base camp.

*Bill Lane was a neighbor and friend of Stan's through his adolescence
and teen years. They rode their bikes over dusty gravel roads to see each
other, played catch, and hunted. They would eventually move on to bigger
toys, their cars.*

*Bill went to Vietnam a year before Stan, and as he writes in his letter,
they caught up with each other in country before Bill left. Stan often asked
about Bill in his letters home. Bill was a good friend to Stan, a friend that
was steady, unassuming, loyal, and always there for my brother.*

Bill wrote his recollections and comments to me in March, 2006,

"Stanley Ross was my good friend from childhood; he wasn't just a
friend, he was more like a brother to me. He and his family moved to the
neighborhood when he was in grade school. We lived near each other,
our homes separated by large fields, which we would cross to visit each
other. Over the years, we spent many hours telling stories, shooting BB
guns, helping neighbors with farm work, riding bikes, fishing, hunting
rabbits and pheasants. We used to enjoy going pheasant hunting up
North with our fathers. Stanley always liked stopping at the McDonald's
in Iowa City. Iowa City had the only McDonald's in the area, so that
was the big treat of the day. We liked fast cars and motorcycles, which
may have resulted in an occasional speeding ticket.

Life changed drastically after high school, largely because of Vietnam. I went to Vietnam first on March 1, 1968, and left the end of April 1969, the same month Stanley arrived in Vietnam. He and I had a chance to visit for a couple of hours at the 90th Replacement Center at Long Binh. We talked about home, and life in the Army. I am so glad I got to have that short visit with him, since it turned out to be the last time I would see him.

October 20, 1969, I was shocked and saddened to learn that Stanley had been killed. My parents, neighbors and I will always remember Stanley, and miss him."

Bill still resides in the farming community and lives in the same home he grew up in, with his wife and children. He often visits my parents, especially on the anniversary of my brother's death, October 20, and every May 13, Stan's birthday.

April 23, 1969
Dear Mom and Dad,
How's everything back in the world? They've started shaping us up a little. We run one mile three times a day, and in this heat it's terrible. I am on detail today, filling sandbags and helping build bunkers. It's sure a hot job, but there are South Vietnam women who help that could work two of me in the ground. I could just see an American woman doing half the work these women are doing. They can work all day long with a pick and shovel, and just stop for dinner, which is a little rice and old bread. I've got a whole bunch of pictures to get developed, showing the way some of these people live. I still don't have any address and probably won't have for another week. I'm going just about crazy to get a letter. I suppose about next week I'll have to go to the field. I sure hate to in this heat. In this part of the country booby traps are our worst enemy. I'm really going to watch my step.

Well, by the time you get this letter Bill will probably be home. The lucky devil! Tell him to have enough fun for both of us. Like I say, if anyone wonders why I don't write, tell them I'm waiting until I get an address.

Well, I suppose you've got the oats in by now. It's 95 and the humidity is about 110. It's hard to even keep the paper dry enough to write on.

How are you feeling, Mom? I sure hope all right. You and Dad are the main thing for me to come back to. I'll bet I think about you guys back home hundred times a day. But usually when I'm working you're sleeping in the U.S. How's Eileen's love coming? Is she driving that GTO yet?

When I do get an address, you ought to have all kinds of news. Don't pay any attention to the address I put on the envelope. It's just something to prove to the postmaster that I'm in Vietnam.

Well, I guess that's all for now. I'll be writing later. I'm trying to write as often as I can so you don't worry. So please don't worry "OK."

With love, Stan

Time was and is marked on the farm by the seasons and field work. Stan kept track of his time in Vietnam by what was going on at home. Planting oats was one of the first crops planted in the spring, a job that Stan had helped our dad with many times. It marked the beginning of the growing season and a crop to be harvested.

Stan thought of our younger sister Eileen often and loved to tease her as brothers do. He knew she was entering an important time in her life—just sixteen, when having an older brother around would have been comforting. I had gotten married two years before, and moved away, leaving her without the close bond that sisters share.

Mothers aren't as easily approached with the delicate questions concerning the mysteries of life, love, and womanhood. I know she welcomed the letters from Stan.

Stan on construction crew at base camp.

Dad getting ready to load bales in the hay loft.

April, 1969

Dear Mom and Dad,

Well, how's everything back in the world? Just another hot day over here. I was put working with a carpenter crew today. It was sorta fun for a change. That's the way it is over here. You never know what they'll put you to doing. I guess anything beats going out in the field. We loaded some sand bags last night until about 9 p.m. The sergeant took orders for beer. It was the first in about a week. It sure tasted good. It's 6% over here. They have Blue Ribbon, Hamm's, Falstaff, and sometimes Budweiser. I knew you'd be interested, Mom. (ha ha)

Well, still no address. I'm about crazy for a letter. What's Bill doing since he got home? I'll bet he's having fun. I know I'm going to have some catching up to do.

Well, like I say, not much news. I'll be writing later. So don't worry about anything. I'm getting beautiful sunburn!

With love, Stan

Stan filling sand bags.

Stan at base camp. Vietnamese women in background.

Soldiers in Vietnam always referred to the States and home as "the world." A world away, Vietnam was anything but friendly or normal.

It worried our mother that Stan had such easy access to beer, but as my Dad would say, "I'd need a little Pabst Blue Ribbon myself in his shoes!" Stan liked his beer, but he drew the line where drugs were concerned. One could argue, "What's the difference?"

Beer could not be carried while on a field mission; pot was a different story.

Michael Lanning wrote in his book, <u>Vietnam 1969-1970: A Company Commander's Journal</u>, how young and underage the GIs of the Vietnam War were in comparison to the men who fought in WWII, " Few of us had a realization of just how young we really were. It would be years before it became common knowledge that the average age of the Vietnam soldier was nineteen and a half compared to twenty-six during World War II." He goes on to say, "Perhaps the young age of the Vietnam veteran also influenced the inability of many to immediately assimilate back into the society that had sent them off to war. Not only were there no bands or parades to welcome the Vietnam vet home, but many were also still too young to enjoy the basic rights and privileges bestowed on 'adults' such as the purchase of alcoholic beverages and the right to vote for or against the elected leadership that was running the war."

Tim (Obie) Oberst left, Jayson "J" Dale, and unidentified finger enjoying some down time. Photo by Jayson "J" Dale.

April, 1969

Dear Mom and Dad,

How's things going back home? Things sure could be better over here. No letters, no cool weather, no cold beer until we get out of training. How much worse could a guy have it? (ha ha)

It will still be a while till we get an address. These Infantry units have a hard time placing you in a regular place. But just be patient. Believe me, it's terrible not getting letters. They show us a movie every night, so that sorta helps a guy out. But it sure makes him homesick.

I've wrote a few letters to Cheryl down in Burlington. I think she'll be good to write to me. If a guy can get letters, it isn't too bad. But he's got to have something to look forward to.

Well, not too much to write about. I've lost 10 pounds running in this heat. A person never stops sweating.

Well, I'll be writing later. So just hold tight until I get an address. Bye for now. "Tell everyone hello."

Stan

Stan, looking tired and leaner.

Stan didn't have a steady girl when he went to Vietnam. He enjoyed playing the field, dating girls that were cute and out for a good time. I think he knew it didn't pay to get seriously involved with anyone, since in his heart he knew he might not return. My mother often commented after his death, that she wished he would have had a child; at least a part of him would be left behind.

As I looked at the pictures of Stan taken in Vietnam, the changes in his body were very apparent. His body became much leaner, his face gaunt, and eyes sunken and dark. His face was not as youthful and carefree, but worn, and jaded. But through it all there was that smile that filled the viewer with warmth and love.

April, 1969

Dear Mom and Dad,

Well, I'm still on guard and I don't know when I'll get off of it. Today was supposed to be my last day, but they told us we'd have it for a couple more days. There's just about 20 of us out of the whole company that was here that stayed back for guard. I don't mind it; the only thing I don't like about it is that they don't give us any address.

My buddy and I from Albany, Georgia have the same bunker on guard. So that makes it real nice. I sure hope they don't separate us when we get assigned to a unit. But I suppose they will.

We got a little mortar trouble and a few snipers last night for the first time. It was sorta scary but it wasn't no way near enough to give us anything to worry about. Things are so dirty and hot! We sleep on old cots with no sheets. A person wakes up in the morning ringing wet with sweat. I'd sure hate to put up hay in this weather Dad. (ha ha)

I sure hope you're getting all of my letters. I've wrote everyday since I've been here. Has anything new happened around home? Did you like that hand-embroidered picture I sent you, Mom? If there's anything you want to know about this place, just write and ask me. There's not really that much to say about this asshole country or part of the world.

Well, I'll be writing later. Like I say, it's making it as good as possible for being over here, so don't worry.

See ya in a few months, (ha ha)
Stan

Stan on guard duty.

Karen Ross Epp

Robert Rhodes was a buddy from AIT training that Stan became very close to. He hoped they would end up in the same unit, but they did get separated.

After 35 years I located Robert and phoned him. We have talked and e-mailed since. His comments to me were, "Karen, thanks for being strong enough and having the love for your brother that you have. I understand about not being able to mourn his death until now. I recall Stan as being a fun guy who was easy to get to know and made you feel comfortable around him. We had a lot of laughs back then. Of course we were young! I had just turned 18 when I entered the Army. I was married to my high school sweetheart and needed a job badly. My only problem was that my draft classification was 1A! Back then, if you had such a classification, no one would hire you. Desperate, I signed up for the draft and I was sworn in the same day in Atlanta, Georgia. I still remember Stan's great smile! I think about him often as a lost, true friend!"

Robert wrote about their time together those first days in Vietnam, "I recall being on guard duty all day and all night. After that we were put in some tin roof buildings that had walls about head high and the rest of it was screened. We were very hot and had only fans that were located at the end of each doorway. We fell asleep but I recall waking up to incoming rounds, and the rest of the night was sleepless! Stan and I went to this club that next night, and drank several well-deserved beers."

Robert was assigned to the 101st Airborne, C Company 3rd, 187th attached to a ranger group, the 75th.

Stan and his good friend, Robert Rhodes (left), in
country, taking a break at base camp.

April, 1969

Dear Mom and Dad,

Well, how's everything back in the world? Well, I'm still on guard, but I think tomorrow will be the last day. It gets so boring a person thinks he'll go crazy, but it's pretty safe. So I guess that's all that counts. I sure wish Iowa had a little bit of this heat, but I suppose it's getting warm enough there anyway.

Have you talked to Donnie Crowl yet? I sure hate to see anyone have to come over here. I just hope and pray things don't go bad for me. A person just can't tell. If anyone wonders why I haven't written to them just tell them that I'm waiting till I get an address.

It's sure funny, here it is 7:00 p.m. Sat. and in Iowa it's about 2:00 a.m. Sat morning. If I could just get my mind off of home it would go a lot faster. It seems like a year will be forever. But I think when I start getting letters things will go a lot faster.

You wouldn't believe the food over here. It's terrible! The water has pills in it sometimes to make it pure. The only place you can get cold water is in the mess hall. Like I say, you can't imagine how dirty this place is.

Well, that's enough of that! I suppose I'd better get a little sleep. I have to go back out at 9 p.m. on guard. I just thought I'd drop a line to the people back in the world. (ha ha)

Holding on,

Stan

Bunkers provide GIs with a little more safety than being out in the open. They were constructed on corrugated metal, the kind we used to put on our out buildings on the farm, and sandbags. The bunkers provided shelter from the weather and mortar shells. Each bunker was surrounded on the outside perimeter by barbed wire and the modern version, concertina wire. About twenty feet in front of the bunkers, wire like that of baseball backstops, served as an additional screen against hand grenades or rocket launched grenades. This is not to say that men were never killed in bunkers, because they were. Bunker guard was boring and yet scary especially at night when ones imagination tended to play tricks on the mind and eyes.

The heat and humidity in Vietnam was oppressive. Our Iowa summers were known for high humidity, but from Stan's letters and other vets' descriptions, Vietnam's weather was "like being in a sauna most of the time." Stan's friend Tim Oberst recalled, "I'll never forget the smell and oppressive heat that hit my face when I got off the plane and stepped onto Vietnam soil for the first time."

Don Crowl (or Donnie, as Stan knew him) recalled many memories he had of his childhood friend. Some of the memories were of their younger pre-teen years and as teenagers, figuring out who they were.

My parents were one of the first to have purchased a color television set. Don remembered driving to our house to watch the popular show, "Bewitched" and the movie "Journey to the Center of the Earth" in our living room as our little brother, Phillip, crawled around the living room floor in his diaper and dad watched from his Lazy Boy chair.

He remembered riding a Harley with Stan while Stan stood up on the seat going at a not so-safe speed. Saddle bags on the Harley served many needs, one being a beer cooler. Donnie said that Stan had rigged up a drain hose so water could escape the leather bags. My brother was very creative when he needed to be.

Don recalled Stan as fun-loving, out-going, mischievous, and a charmer with the girls. His friends often called him, "Studly."

Don Crowl was in the 57ᵗʰ Assault Helicopter Unit in Vietnam; he was a Warrant Officer, stationed near Kon Tum, Vietnam. He went to Vietnam in May, 1969 and returned home in December, 1969, after accidentally being injured while working with explosives.

Don was employed as an EMS Helicopter pilot for the University of Iowa medical center, in Iowa City, Iowa, until August, 2005. Don and his wife, Marva, have two children and reside in Wayland, Iowa.

The following is an excerpt from a letter Don wrote to Stan, "Say the shit's been flying up here lately. The NVA have been screwing with some of our base camps. Would you believe there was an estimated 10,000 in the Ben Het area which is a few miles from here. The Air Force has been bombing the hell out of them and I think it's beginning to get to them. That's the way I like to see it! Well, I'd better sign off for now. Take care! Your Buddy, Don 'Cougar Killing Service'"

April 21, 1969
Dear Mom and Dad,

Well, this is my last day of guard. So tomorrow I'll probably go to some unit. I'll sure be glad to get my address. Is it pretty nice Honda weather at home? It sure seems funny that when it's daytime over here, it's night in Iowa. I still can't believe I seen Bill. It was really something! Tell Phillip hello. Is Eileen getting to drive the GTO yet? (ha ha)

When we were out in the bunkers last night, I could hear mortar fire in the distance. It's really hard to realize a person in a place like this. It's just like a bad dream. It's so damn hot, it's hard to sleep. A person wakes up sweating, but you get used to it. It hasn't rained yet here. I figured it would be raining all the time. If it ever does I'm going to lay in it.

Well, that's about all for now. I'll feel more like writing when I get an address. See ya in 360 days. (ha ha)

Stan

Before Stan left for Vietnam he purchased a Honda motorcycle at an unbelievably cheap price. Dad was skeptical about the bike's history. His feeling, that it was too good to be real, turned out to be just that, too good! Dad's suspicions were confirmed by the local authorities. The cycle had been stolen.

We all took turns riding it that April, Stan's last leave before heading to Vietnam. Stan took movies of us riding it, and being the daredevil he was, he performed for us by doing crazy stunts around the yard, scaring Mom to death. His daredevil nature would be tested in the months to come.

April 23, 1969

Dear Mom and Dad,

Well, I finally got assigned to the 199th division. That goes to prove you can't count on anything. I figured for sure I'd get in the 1st Infantry division. The 199th is a real small division. They say it's always located around Saigon, or in that vicinity. In other words, we more or less protect and keep the peace around Saigon. The VC has been giving the Infantry a little trouble around Saigon. I sure hope it settles down before they take us to the field. I guess it will be another week before I get an address. I sure wish I could get mail. Please write me often. That's the only thing a guy's got over here.

Like I figured, me and my Albany, Georgia buddy got separated. That's what's the hardest on me. Here I sit and don't know anyone. A guy's got to have a friend over here or he'll go crazy. But I'll just have to make new friends, I guess. I've already lost track of the days. Every day is the same over here. I guess the war stops for nothing. I've never sweated so much in my life. If a guy ever walks around, he'll be soaking wet with sweat.

Well, Bill starts home tomorrow. I can imagine how happy he is. Have you seen Donnie yet? I put in for a machine gunner on a helicopter. I hope I get it, but I probably won't.

How's little brother? I've got all my pictures of the family in my pocket all the time. I'll bet I look at them ten times a day. If I could just get my mind off of home, things would go better I think. But a person can't help it, I guess.

I got some more jungle wear today. So I'm just about fixed up. I seen a boy that I went to school with up in Fort Belvoir. He said all of them came over here, too! Over 600 a day come into the replacement center. It's sure a sad bunch. War is hell, that's all I can say. A guy thinks he's going to lose his mind. But a person's just got to accept the fact. If I get to stay around Saigon somewhere, it'll be a lot better than up by the DMZ somewhere.

So I keep saying these little prayers, Mom. Someone may hear them. The first thing a guy will tell you, that's been over here awhile, is to have faith in the man upstairs, and things will go a lot better. Well, I feel better already. Writing a letter can sure help at times.

How's everything been going for you, Dad? Are you riding the Honda very much? The VC over here have a lot of them. Well, I can't think of much more to write.

When I get an address, I'd better get some pretty thick letters, because you've got some catching up to do. (ha ha) Well, I'll be writing later, and don't worry.

Stan

Stan out on his first mission after
being assigned to the 199th.

BMB Headquarters, Long Binh, Vietnam, 1969.

Part of the Old Guard Compound.

Just follow the signs "Home!"

The 199th Light Infantry Brigade (Light) (Separate) "Redcatcher," which Stan had been assigned to arrived in Vietnam from Fort Benning, Georgia on December 10, 1966 and departed to October 11, 1970. Pressed for a rapid buildup of United States ground forces in Vietnam in 1966, the Army built a separate Light Infantry Brigade around four elite Infantry units with a glorious past. Redesignated on March 23, 1966, the 2nd Battalion 3rd Infantry, 3rd Battalion 7th Infantry, and 4th and 5th Battalions 12th Infantry, and Troop D. The 17th Cavalry was assigned to the newly formed 199th (Separate) Light Infantry Brigade. Their motto was, "Light, Swift and Accurate."

The "Old Guard," as it was also known, traces its lineage back to 1784 when it was constituted as The First American Regiment by "resolve" of the Continental Congress. In keeping with its esteemed tradition and glory, the 1st Battalion of the "Old Guard" holds the vital assignment of guarding our nation's capital and serving as the Army's official ceremonial unit in the Washington D.C. area. They are the soldiers that guard the Tomb of the Unknown Soldier.

Karen Ross Epp

    Robert J. Gouge describes in his book, <u>These Are My Credentials,</u> *how the 199th was formed in Vietnam,* "In early 1966, orders came down from on high, specifically from General William C. Westmoreland, to form an independent and light, separate Infantry brigade that was to be utilized specifically for Vietnam service and which was to guard the Saigon/Bien Hoa/Long Binh area. Since the city of Saigon and the surrounding areas were known as the vital organ center for the American involvement in Vietnam, its safety and protection were of the utmost importance. The new unit was to be charged with this mammoth task and would sometimes be called, the 'Palace Guard.'

    The terms 'Light' and 'Separate' meant that the new brigade would not have all the heavy equipment and excess material that normal Infantry units contained and it would not be under any divisional or similar control. In short, the baggage and personnel would be cut in half, the new brigade's artillery firepower would consist of M102, 105mm Howitzers (Towed) and the unit would be placed under the command and control of the Military Assistance Command Vietnam (MACV) and II Field Force.

    The 199th was to become the 'Orphan Brigade,' the only such one to serve in Vietnam. Its mission was to be threefold: 1) Upgrade the Army of the Republic of Vietnam (ARVN). 2) Pacify the countryside and win the 'hearts and minds' of the civilian population. 3) Eliminate the enemy.'"

Redcatcher insignia.

Robert Rhodes, today, with one of
his hobbies—racing.

Robert Rhodes, Stan's buddy, commented on the circumstances that led to his being separated from Stan. "Stan and I sat there watching the convoys of buses coming by with banners on the sides of them saying '1st Calvary going home.' After a short time, others would go by with signs that named another unit going home. As they continued, we both noticed that some units' buses were empty as others were full! I recall the 101st Airborne convoy going by with only five to ten guys on three buses! I told Stan, 'I hope I'm not assigned to that unit,' knowing that I was Airborne qualified. The next day a chaplain showed up at our guard post and asked for me by rank and name. I was told I was to join him and others that were being sent to the north of South Vietnam near the Cambodian border with the 101st Airborne Division. That's when I lost contact with Stan, and was later told that he had been lost in a fire fight. I was truly upset, but didn't have long to mourn, because I had been hurt on Hamburger Hill and was in no shape to do anything."

I know Mom and others at home kept the prayers going for Stan and everyone with him. She didn't "offer up" just her son to the Lord, but other sons and daughters whose families worried about their safety.

When I went through Stan's pictures, the ones he kept with him in Vietnam, I noticed how worn and frayed they were around the edges. The family pictures were well worn, I'm sure, from Stan's frequent handling of them and showing his buddies. They were stained with his sweaty fingerprints, and probably absorbed a tear or two. It was like holding a rare treasure, part of someone I knew and loved so long ago.

Dad, Mom, and Little Phillip. (One of the family
pictures Stan carried.)

Eileen with Phillip in our front yard, summer 1969.

April, 1969

Dear Mom and Dad,

Well, I'm still here. (ha ha) How's everything at home? I'm so lonesome for a letter I can hardly stand it! Friday I should have an address. It's Wednesday now, I sent $125 home. Make sure you tell me if you received it, because mail can get lost.

How's Bill taking civilian life? It started to rain; I guess the monsoon has come in. I've had wet clothes on ever since it started. The tents leak and you wake up wet. This place is the ass hole of the world.

Has anyone wondered why I haven't written? Please write me often, Mom. That's all I ask for; a guy has to have something.

I guess we head for the pineapple fields Sat. The biggest enemy there is booby traps. Charlie or (VC) doesn't bother us too much, but the bastards really give the booby traps hell. Don't worry, I'm too good an Infantryman to let anything happen.

Anything been happening new lately? Tell everyone hello. I don't know much more to write. Like I say, when I get in the field, I don't know how often I'll be able to write, so please understand if I don't write as often as I have been.

With all the good old Ross love, Stan

The foot soldier in Vietnam was referred to as legs and grunts. To carry their loads was to hump it. Most all the GIs carried photographs of a girlfriend, parents, sisters and brothers, grandmothers, pets, pin-ups, you name it—anything to feel that connection with home and sanity.

Mom did write often, almost daily, as she knew it would help Stan's morale and keep her from thinking too much about the danger he faced. Even in her eighties she still writes letters to me weekly. Her letters kept Stan going when he felt lonely and full of despair.

May 2, 1969,Friday

Dear Karen,

Well, I finally got an address, so I figured I'd write to you, because I sure hope you write to me.

I don't really know how to describe this place, because a person would have to be here to believe it! It's so hot all the time; a guy sweats 24 hours a day. I was sick for about a week from the heat. The whole place is dirty and dusty. It's impossible to keep clean. We have been living in sorta like tents, but tomorrow I go to the field. I sure hate to. Our worst enemy is booby traps. We work mostly around Saigon. I'm in the 199th Infantry division, and their main mission is to protect Saigon.

How's everything in Nebraska? I'm so anxious to hear from home, I can hardly wait. That's about all a guy's got over here is a letter. I've thought about that night me and you went to Gulfport a million times. We really had fun didn't we! (ha ha) A person sure misses things like that. But I'll have it again sometime.

Like I told the folks, I don't know how often I'll get to write when I'm in the field, so please try to understand if I don't write often. Some guys say they're out in the field eight months at a time. I sure hope I don't get out there that long at one time!

Well, Karen, I don't know much more to write. All I can tell you is just thank God you live in the U.S. You wouldn't believe the way these people live over here. The women over here can out work three American men!

I guess Bill is home now. I'll bet he's happy. Well, that's all for now. If there's anything you want to know, I'll try to answer you.

With Brother Love, Stan

The following are Donald E. Stephen's comments from his personal war experience, about being in the field in his book, Bait, Vietnam 1971, "After being in the bush for a few long weeks, I had decided that we, the good old American draftees, were the bait. Whether we were nibbled on, chewed, or swallowed whole, depended on where we were dropped. Every twenty-one days we were pulled out, healed up, fattened up, patted on the back, and then dropped in a new place."

My husband and I moved to York, Nebraska after leaving California in late October of 1968. We purchased a trailer. In those days mobile homes were affordable for young couples just getting started, and for us, a good way to move without the hassles of finding new housing. We lived at the Elms trailer court just outside of York, Nebraska.

I went home that April to see Stan, his last leave before departing to Vietnam. He and I spent a lot of time just talking. That weekend, I think it was a Saturday, we went to Gulfport, Illinois, which was just across the river from Burlington, a river town on Iowa's Southeastern border. It was the place to go in those days. You could buy liquor by the drink and get into some cool clubs. It was the one place we never told our parents about when we were young and underage. We went to a dance club, where we saw some of his friends. He seemed on edge most of the evening, trying to pack into one night as much fun and living as was possible. He danced with several girls, using his charm to get them on the dance floor. I remember the band playing "Proud Mary," a great song to dance to. Whenever I hear that song I think of that night and Stan, and how for one evening the war and all other problems were forgotten.

Toward the end of the evening he engaged in a shouting match with a couple of guys that were in the National Guard; the Guard was considered an easy way out of the draft and Vietnam in those days. Stan didn't have a lot of love for the Guard or the guys in the Reserves. How different that is today, as the Guard and Reserves are the ones serving in Iraq, and of course, the draft no longer exists.

That weekend was the last time in this life that I saw Stan alive. There were so many things I wanted to say, but it didn't seem like the time to bring up anything "heavy" as we used to say. He had enough on his mind, and I didn't want to add to it.

Our youthful optimism gave us hope that everything would turn out for the best; being that young, life appeared endless and our bodies indestructible.

May, 1969 Sat. morning
Dear Mom and Dad,
Well, Mom, you remember when you said you were going to do something about my feet? Forget it, because they put me in the hospital this morning (Sat.). It seems like they get worse all the time. I went on

sick call this morning, and the doctor told me to go straight to the hospital. So here I am, television, radio, air conditioning, and food brought to me. I've got it made, (ha ha) for a couple of days anyway. Best of all they can give me an address so I could write you. So please write me a fat letter! I'm dying for a letter, but remember, don't write to this address for more than two days, because I won't be here. I figure about seven to ten days for me to get a letter. It takes about three to get to you and likewise. I hate lying in a hospital, but it's all good time everyday I'm here. It's one less day in the field.

Now remember not to write to this address for more than two days, OK? But give it hell those days! (ha ha)

Now don't worry about me. I've got all the comforts of home in here. The doctor said he was going to keep me off my feet a couple of days to see if they would harden up. They can't figure out what's wrong with them.

There's sure some sad cases in this hospital. I feel sorry for some of these guys. I could cry. There's one in here, a chain saw got loose from him. It almost cut his leg off!

Well, I'll be writing later. I'll be looking forward to a letter or two.

With love, Stan

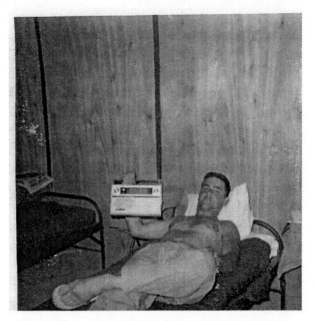

Stan in the hospital, suffering from "immersion foot,"
enjoying his radio.

Like so many other GIs in the field, Stan's feet became a real problem for him. He was often in his boots for days, walking through muddy rice paddies, never getting a chance to dry out his feet. This condition, referred to as immersion foot, resulted from feet being submerged in water for a prolonged period of time, causing cracking and bleeding.

Their jungle boots were constructed of canvas and leather, which were better than the typical all-leather boot but no matter what they wore, foot problems were a constant aliment of GIs in the field. Robert Gouge talks about the jungle boots in his book, <u>These Are My Credentials</u>, "One of the most enduring trademarks of the Vietnam War was the Tropical Jungle Boot that was issued to nearly all the soldiers who served in Vietnam. The jungle boots had OD green, canvas tops and a black-leather bottom, with eyelets on the inside of each foot to allow for proper drainage when wet. After constant use and abuse for a year by grunts that had waded through endless rice paddies, steamy jungles, rocky mountains and hills covered with razor sharp elephant grass, the once shiny black-leather bottoms of the boots turned into a dirty-gray, cut and scratched bottom layer."

When everything else had rotted away, or been lost, a GI's boots would be the one he understood—the thing he held on to with pride. It was his badge of courage, a symbol of survival.

Donald E. Stephen writes in his book, <u>Bait, Vietnam 1971,</u> "A rain could last for days with no let up. Immersion foot was a constant problem; at least two or three men were in the rear area at all times correcting foot problems."

When I met with Arrol Stewart in August of 2005, he related many of his war experiences to me and my brother, Phill. One of the many things that stayed with him from Vietnam was the memory of being wet so much of the time, fatigues clinging to his body in the humid jungle. His comment to me, "Even to this day, I hate to be wet!"

Lt. Arrol Stewart, January, 1970 FB Maze.

May, 1969
Sunday afternoon
Dear Mom and Dad,

Well, here I still sit in the hospital. It's real nice in here, but you know how I like lying and sitting around. Times go so slow. We have ice cream, pop, and everything in here. They put some medicine on my feet last night. I hope it does some good. My feet sweat so badly in this weather.

By the time you get this letter I'll be out of this hospital. I sure hope you got my last letter, telling of my temporary address. But like I say, don't send any letters to it over about two days, because I won't be in the area. I'll sure be glad to get a permanent address.

How did all the movie film turn out, especially the one of Dad riding on the Honda? How did the one of me getting on the plane turn out? I don't think I ever had a more empty feeling in my life, as when that plane took off! I sure hate this place! This country has nothing. I can see why people lose their minds over here. Some of these guys in the hospital, you can't imagine!

Well, what's new at home? Have you seen Bill quite a bit? I'd give anything to be back in good old Iowa! It's hard to imagine how far from each other we are! Like they say, "We're a world away." Here it's Sun. afternoon; at home it's Sat. night. That really hurts. (ha ha) Everyday is the same over here.

How's little Phillip? I sure miss the little guy. I have his picture and the family's in here on my little table. It sure helps to look at them.

What have you been doing lately, Mom? Are you putting in a garden? Just try not to worry about me. I'm trying to write every day so that you won't worry. I'll make it all right. Well, I can't think of much more to write. I'll be looking forward to a letter, and I'll be writing later.

With love, Stan

The family after Karen's graduation from high school.

Our mother always had a large garden (or truck patch) and put up lots of vegetables for the winter months. We also had an orchard that provided us with wonderful canned peaches, cherries, and apples. Canning and butchering was a part of our family's tradition. I'm sure Stan could picture Mom out in her garden pulling weeds or picking the ripened produce. He would have gladly traded the battlefields of Vietnam for her garden, where just a few years earlier he complained about pulling weeds for her.

The garden plot that once filled a major portion of my parents' yard is now a lush, grassy lawn where the grandchildren play catch and chase each other, screaming with delight as they tumble to their knees and repeat, "You're it!"

May 3, 1969
Dear Mom and Dad,

Well, I guess they're going to let me out of the hospital today. I'm glad, because this place was driving me crazy. It's real nice, but time goes so slow. They said if my feet didn't get better they would have to take all the skin off the bottom of my feet so new skin could grow. I sure hope I don't have to have that done!

This Friday I'll get an address so…if you haven't stopped writing to that temporary address, stop now, because I probably won't get the mail.

I'll be going to the field by the time you get this letter. I don't know how much I'll be able to write, but if I don't write as often as I've been doing, please understand! I sure hate to go out there. I guess it's water and mud two-feet deep out there, but I'll make it. Please don't worry!

With all my love, Stan

When I went through Stan's trunk, I found the Army-green flip flops he had worn in the hospital, and probably most often to the showers. As I looked closer and ran my hand over them, I could still see the impressions of his foot print on the surface. I don't know why Mom kept them with his other belongings that were retuned after his death, but I have a feeling she ran her hands over those impressions many times herself.

May 8, 1969
Dear Mom and Dad,
Guess what? An address, finally, here it is!

PFC Stanley D. Ross
RA 680 69633
Co. C 2nd BN. 3D INF.
199th INF. BDE
A.P.O. San Francisco, California96279

Isn't that wonderful! I'm so anxious to get a letter. I can hardly wait! Make sure you tell Karen and Phil. I guess we go to the field Sat. They gave us our rifle tonight, but don't worry please. I'll be all right. I got with a couple of other good buddies, but I sure miss the one from

Albany, Georgia. I'm sending a money order with this letter. I'd write more, but I've got a lot of people to write to now. So I'd better get to it.

Be looking forward to a letter (big fat one). (ha ha)
Stan

May 10, 1969 Saturday
Dear Mom and Dad,

Well, by the time you get this letter I'll have more than a month in country. Eleven more to go. It sure seems like a long time, but it will pass. The first month has flown. I sure hope it's the same for you.

I got my first letter today. It was from Cheryl. It was sure good to have a letter from home. I hope I get one from you guys tomorrow.

What's Bill been doing? Is he in jail or anything? (ha ha) They brought our mail in by helicopter. I haven't seen anyone or any shelter for one week now. Sometimes I think we are in the country all by ourselves. We are still setting up ambushes every night.

How's everyone back home? Tell little brother hello. I sure miss him. If I ever think for one minute he'll have to come over here, I'll personally take him to Canada.

It's so hot and there are so many mosquitoes here. It's terrible sleeping weather. We found a booby trap yesterday. It was a homemade grenade. You wouldn't believe the things those VC try to pull. A guy sure has to stay awake.

Cheryl says it's been real nice weather back home. I'll sure be glad when summer's over back there. Then I won't think so much of what I'm missing.

Are you starting to plant corn yet?

Guess what? Three more days, I'll be an old man. (ha ha) I sure wish I could get back to a base camp so I could have some fun on May 13th, my birthday. But that's dreaming.

Like I say, not much news. Just thought I'd write to let you know I'm thinking about home all the time. I always just think that, "I'm over here for little Phillip!"

God Bless for now.
With love, Stan

The rituals of Vietnam became mind numbing for GIs. Doing the same thing over and over, preparing to kill or be killed ate away at the soul. Tim O'Brien speaks of this in his book, <u>The Things They Carried,</u> "If you weren't humping, you were waiting. I remember the monotony. Digging foxholes. Slapping mosquitoes. The sun and the heat and the endless paddies. Even in the deep bush, where you could die any number of ways, the war was nakedly and aggressively boring. But it was a strange boredom. It was boredom with a twist, the kind of boredom that caused stomach disorders."

Phill on the job for Amtrak.

My brother, Phillip, didn't have to go to war as Stan did. Without the draft, he like so many men of this generation, elected not to serve in the military. He had a choice. My younger brother has always felt a debt to Stan, although his memories of him are scattered, being only four when Stan was killed. There is a deep connection to Stan that will never be lost.

Phill attended Mt. Pleasant Community High School, graduating in 1984. He went on to Iowa State University where in 1988 he received his degree in Journalism.

Phillip worked as a sports editor off and on over a five-year period after college, but his love for the railroad and dissatisfaction with the long hours and low pay as a small town journalist made the decision to become a railroader an easy one.

He is currently a locomotive engineer for Amtrak, running passenger trains from St. Louis to Kansas City. He has a daughter, Emma. My brother Stan would have to look up to his little brother if he were alive today. Stan was six foot two, but the "Little Man," as Stan called him, is six foot five.

As Stan mentions in this letter, he would turn the ripe old age of 20 on May 13, 1969. It would be his first birthday away from family and friends.

Tim Oberst's birthday was May 12th, he and Stan enjoyed that connection. For Tim, it is a bitter sweet reminder of a special friend and comrade in arms.

Stan with his good friend, Tim Oberst, sharing some
downtime in a hooch.

Charlie Co. 2ⁿᵈ BN, 3ʳᵈ INF, 199ᵗʰ LIB,
walking in the sunshine on a
tank trail. Photo by Jayson Dale.

May 15, 1969 Thursday
Dear Mom and Dad,

I can imagine how worried you are, since I haven't written the last few days. Please believe me, I can't help it! We've been out on a mission for about a week now, and I'm still out here. Today is Thursday the 15ᵗʰ, and I don't know when I'll have the chance to send it.

You can imagine how hot and sweaty I am. I can't even keep this paper clean. This last week has been hell! We've been on the move every day. They bring us water and C-rations by helicopter. Talk about being out in the middle of nowhere. This is it!

Everyday we have been going through these small family huts out here in nowhere land. We have an interpreter with us. He talks to the people about where the VC is. Sometimes we find VC in the huts, and usually they come out fighting.

I sure hope we get back to a base camp some of these days. A person never gets to shave, wash or change clothes out here.

We had to go through rice paddies yesterday with a full pack and walking through mud in this heat. It's not fun, but I'm not alone.

I sure got letters on my birthday. You couldn't have timed it better. I got every birthday card right on my birthday.

Today I guess we won't be moving. We're just setting up ambushes near by. So I thought I'd write. But like I say, I don't know when I'll get to send it.

Well, how's everything at home? Well, less than eleven months. (ha ha) I sure wish it was April, 1970.

Mom, I sent $125.00 home and $40.00 home. If you still don't have the $125.00, please let me know.

You asked what I needed. If you can, please buy me a radio. Now remember not to buy a big one, just something little, a 6-transistor or something. It would sure help out. A guy doesn't have anything out here, so a little music once in a while would kind of take off the tension and boredom. Pay for it out of the money I sent home.

As far as for anything else, I can't think of anything. It would just be more to pack, unless I gave it away. If you can think of anyway to send my camera over here, in something that can keep water out, do it! Because when we cross streams, if a guy doesn't have plastic over his billfold and pictures, they will all get wet. Maybe you can think of something air tight to put it in. But don't send the light and take the pistol grip off, because the smaller I can make it, the better off I am. Maybe you can think of something, I don't know. It would be better if it was in something hard too, so that it couldn't be crushed. But most of all, make sure it's water tight.

If you can get the radio with a leather case around it to help protect it, and please make sure it's not bigger than pocket size. Well, that's that.

I'm sure glad you like the picture I sent. I can imagine it in the living room.

Too bad about that girl getting killed at the R&R crossing.

That's too bad about your GTO boyfriend Eileen, but that's life. (ha ha)

Yes, I've got a sun tan that's clean to the bone. It feels like cowhide. The worst thing I hate is sleeping on the ground all the time. And then rice paddies have mosquitoes and rats bigger than dogs. It's hard to get used to waking up at night with rats running within arm's distance, but I'm usually so tired to pay any attention.

Well, I can't think of much more to write. Like I say, I can't help it, that I haven't written. I write every possible chance I get.

"OH," I almost forgot to tell you, guess who I ran into over here the other day when we were crossing a road? Mike Kitch. He's a truck driver over here. Isn't that something? (ha ha) When he seen me he really hit the brakes. I was so surprised I didn't believe my eyes. We sat and talked for about an hour. It sure was good to talk to someone from back home. He's got four and a half months in. I was with him the night before he left to come over here. We really had fun. He's got it made over here, just drives a truck.

Well, goodbye for now, and keep the letters coming. They're just like a shot in the arm.

With love, Stan

It's a small world! Stan's chance meeting with high school friend, Mike Kitch.

Vietnamese child outside FB Marge near Cam Tam.
Photo by Jayson Dale.

Stan beside heavy rucksack that
weighed over 60 pounds.

Walking with a heavy pack was hard on the body and made getting around extremely difficult. Stephen, in his book, <u>Bait, Vietnam 1971,</u> describes his experience with the rucksacks GIs had to carry, "The sergeant and I laid out all the equipment on the bed, and I told him there was no way it was going to go in that little rucksack. But Sergeant Cuevas just popped the top of his beer and said that it would. There were three days worth of C-rations (9 meals), 10 quarts of water, a poncho and liner, an air mattress, 10 hand grenades, 150 feet of rope, a personal can, and lots of small items. I crammed them into the ruck and tried to pick it up. It weighed between eighty and one hundred pounds. I told him that I couldn't carry it all day in addition to my weapon and ammunition. He popped a top on another beer and told me I would."

I first contacted Mike Kitch by phone. He was surprised to hear from me, and we caught up on family and hometown news. While Mike and I talked, I told him that I had pictures of him and Stan standing in front of a truck. I had been puzzled for a long time, as to the identity of the soldier standing with Stan. But like everything else in my research, Mike's name appeared in the above letter and the mystery was solved. He did recall spending time with Stan at Fort Polk, Louisiana while on leave during Basic Training. Mike said he had visited Stan's grave Memorial Weekend, 2005 and that he thinks of him often.

Mike and his wife, Wanda made a special trip to Mt. Pleasant to see my parents and the rest of the family Labor Day Weekend in 2005. We talked about Stan, Mike's war experiences, and the incident that lead to the pictures of him and Stan. Mike explained that he was hauling supplies for a new fire base camp being built down in the Delta region, when their paths crossed. He went on to tell me the story, and this is his recollection of that day, "It was sometime in mid-May, 1969. I don't remember the exact date. At the time I was in the 446th Trans Co. stationed in Long Binh. It started out a typical day for an Army truck driver. I was in a ten- to twelve-truck convoy headed out of Saigon, all hauling concertina wire for the perimeter of a new artillery fire base camp. We were driving down a dirt road 30 or 40 miles out of Saigon and as happened on a lot of convoys. We came up on Infantry soldiers patrolling the road ahead of us. As usual I started scanning every face I could and all of a sudden there was my good friend from home, Stan Ross. He was talking to another guy and didn't look up at me. He was right there, ten feet from me and I couldn't stop. About one half mile up the road we started turning into the fire base; I had one truck and the gun jeep behind me. Shortly, the sergeant walked back and said we brought too much wire and they were sending the last two loads back. I told him about seeing my friend and asked if I could go back to see him. He said I would be well protected with those guys so go ahead and be ready to fall in line when they started back. As I started back I could already see Stan's squad walking toward me so I started trying to pick him out again. I saw him on the left side so I started straight toward him and blew my loud air horn. Several of the men headed for the side of the road. I hid my face with my hat and stopped with Stan right out my window. I looked down and said, 'How the hell do you get to Iowa from here!' He got that big Stan smile on his face, shook his head and said, 'I should have known it would be you with a steering wheel in your hand.' We spent about an hour talking mostly about home, our cars, and the pretty girls we knew, but couldn't reach from there. I met a couple of his buddies and some pictures were taken that I had forgotten about until I just saw them recently. Then the trucks started coming and it was time to say good bye. It never crossed my mind that I would be the last person from home to see him. I would gladly have given that hour away to his family, but I guess it was meant for me to have it. It is an hour of my life I will treasure for the rest of my life."

Mike Kitch currently lives in Hannibal, Missouri, with his wife, Wanda. He operates a trucking company.

Mike Kitch with his truck, summer of 2005.

May 18, 1969

Dear Mom and Dad,

Well, another day in Vietnam. Not much news, just sitting here on the bridge watching traffic go by. If you haven't figured out some way to send my camera over, send it anyway. There's certain ammo cans that are water-tight and will protect it pretty good. So send it as quickly as possible, and also send five or six rolls of film with it, because I never get around where I can buy any. And it's awfully hard to get a hold of color film over here. And when you send my radio, send some extra batteries for it, "OK!" Now pay for all of this out of my money. There sure is a lot of traffic going into Saigon today. When I get the movie camera over here, I should be able to send back some real good movies.

How are you feeling, Mom? I hope you're not worrying, please don't! It won't do no good.

Well, that's about all for now. I just thought I'd remind you that I'm thinking of the good folks back home all the time. (ha ha)

With love, Stan

Stan finally got the 124 Instamatic and his movie camera that took 8-mm movies. He took many movies which Dad later converted into a VHS tape. In 2005 I converted my tape to a DVD.

My children were amazed at the quality and amount of movies Stan took. It was interesting to share Stan's image and experience with them. It gave them a greater respect and understanding of what their uncle went through. Their comments during the film were quiet references to how handsome he was and how he smiled even though he was under such difficult conditions. I could tell it was hard for them to comprehend such a place, and the pain that our family experienced. The jerky footage displayed a much different generation, my generation, the "baby boomers."

We still have the original 8-mm tapes. How Stan would have enjoyed today's technology. He would have been the first one in line for the latest photo or recording devices. I'm so glad that he took the movies and still shots for us to revisit him from time to time. I am also thrilled that Dad had the foresight to preserve them for all of us.

May, 1969

Dear Mom and Dad,

How's everything at home? I'll bet it's real nice weather. Well, I finally made it to my base camp out in the field. They had to take us by boat. It's really out in the boon docks. We are right along a stream. The mosquitoes and rats are unbelievable. I had to go out on ambush last night, we slept on air mattresses. The rats make as much noise as the people walking. I just about went crazy. The rats run across your legs and around the area. Can you imagine trying to sleep around that?

Some of these guys out here haven't seen anybody but the people in their squad for more than six months. They just laughed at me and really got a kick out of the way I acted. I guess a guy gets used to it. These guys out here in the field live like animals. One sure thing, they're men, and they will do anything to help a person out.

I guess there hasn't been too much action lately. It's mostly setting up ambushes and going out on patrols. It's so terrible hot out here in the boon docks. Like I say, it's hard to explain the way it is. Just thank God you're in the wonderful U.S.

How's Bill doing? I sure hope I get a letter pretty soon. I can't think of much more. Just don't worry, because I'm all right. After a few days I'll get used to this, then time will start going by fast. It sure seems funny; out here a guy calls a captain by his first name. It's just like one big family. Like I say, don't worry, I'm in a good group. Be writing later.

With all my love, Stan

Cam Tam FB, some of the guys in Stan's squad,
(left to right, front row) Stan, Jayson Dale,
Greg Breeckner;
(second row) Elden Rasmussen, Dave Cherneski,
Mike Yusko, Tom Reed, unidentified , John
VanDusen, Don Mazzi, Terry Wanner.

Pests of all kinds plagued GIs in Vietnam, but as Stan said, the rats were a big problem. In his book, <u>From Classrooms to Claymores</u>, Ches Schneider relates his experience with the over-sized rodents, "When on guard in the bunker, we saw rats whenever an illumination flare popped. They would be right there slightly beside you in the dark, and when a flare brightened the area, they would dive for cover. It was disgusting. Sometimes in the middle of the night rats jumped on your chest or stomach while you were asleep."

As Edelman writes in <u>Dear America,</u> Chapter 2, "For months on end, they lived in the bush, eating C-rations, bathing rarely, sleeping without comfort, filled with fears of the shadows in the night that only the dawn could dispel. They might return to base camp for a few days or a few weeks to 'stand down'—take a breather from the bush. But the boonies was their home, and they spent the bulk of their tour in the thick of it, humping."

May 1969

Dear Mom and Dad,

How's everything at home? I sure miss all of you! But I'd just as well get that out of my mind.

Well, there's not much new around here. We've been going out every night, on ambush. I'm sorta getting to where I'm not quite as scared as I was. But a person still can't let his self get too assured. One sure thing I'll have to give the Infantry credit for,

they'll get us cold beer, no matter where we are. These guys drink 24 hours a day. Anyone else but Infantry has certain hours to drink.

We had to go out today and cut Nippo palm. It's sorta a bamboo. They took us by helicopter. The mud and water was waist deep, but it was actually cool. I haven't taken a bath for over a week now. We're really a grubby bunch of men. We don't wear underwear or shirts most of the time.

We ran into a little sniper fire last night. But nothing bad, these guys take it with ease; the only thing that worries me most is booby traps. They're bad news! My squad leader, Greg, has been here seven months, so he knows his business. I'm glad of that.

I'll bet the weather is getting real nice back home isn't it? Well, I can't think of much more. I'm getting so anxious for my first letter. It ought to be here any day. Well, don't worry. I'm making it as good as possible.

With all my love, Stan

Unidentified GI, obviously without underwear.

Most GIs didn't wear underwear, especially the grunts in the field. Stephen writes in his book, <u>Bait</u>, "Most of us didn't wear the OD green underwear in Vietnam anyway. And we weren't really worried about our mothers finding out. Everyone's arms and faces were brown from the jungle sun, and everyone's asses were white as sheets. If Uncle Sam had seen us, I would have gotten a real skinning."

Tim O'Brien writes in, <u>The Things They Carried</u>, "They carried the standard fatigue jackets and trousers. Very few carried underwear. On their feet they carried jungle boots—2.1 pounds…" *Stan was referring to SGT Greg Breeckner, his squad leader. Breeckner and Stan became very close and Breeckner encouraged him to become a squad leader later in his tour. Greg sent a heart-felt letter to my parents after Stan was killed. He also signed a sympathy card that had the signatures of Stan's entire platoon.*

Michael Lanning's recollection of Greg Breeckner was that, "He was a top notch soldier, leader, and a tough guy!"

I got in touch with Greg on January 25, 2006. He was very gracious and was surprised to hear from me. He remembered Stan with fondness and admiration.

Chinook, supply bird. Photo by Jim Faber.

Sgt. Greg Breeckner.

May 21, 1969 Sat.

Dear Mom and Dad,

Well, finally got helicoptered out of the jungle. I've had it! I'm so tired of mud waist deep and rice paddies, and mosquitoes. It's really tiring, but they brought us to Bin Dinh Bridge. It's about four miles South of Saigon on Highway 4. We guard the bridge, and send out ambushes at night. It isn't too bad on duty.

I should have a lot more time here to write you. I hope you got my last letter, telling why I couldn't write for a few days. All I can say is that I'm real glad we're out of there. It's pretty nice here. We can buy cold beer and eat hot meals. I was really getting sick of C-rations, but things like this won't last. We'll be going back to the rice paddies in about three weeks. So at least for the next three weeks we won't have it too bad.

I didn't take a good a picture for the paper did I? (ha ha) Well, I'm glad things are going pretty good at home. I get so homesick sometimes. What's hell is the fact that's no recreation at all! A person never sees a base camp. There's not even an EM club or something, and like I said in my last letter, send me my movie camera (if you can find something) or buy something that would protect it from water.

Did your ever get that big map I sent home? It should have the bridge on it. Well, there isn't much new. I'm just sitting here drinking a cold one, looking down the river and getting homesick.

Well, I'll be writing later and, Mom, please don't worry! I'm OK. Like they say, I'm too ornery to get hurt. Take care and tell everyone hello.

With love, Stan

Stan with his rucksack in the rice paddies.

Like most of the grunts in Vietnam, Stan was faced with days and weeks in the field with no relief. If they weren't fighting, or setting ambushes, they faced dull routines filled with loneliness and boredom.

In The Only War We Had: A Platoon Leader's Journal of Vietnam, *Michael Lanning writes, "Boredom and fear were my two constant companions in Vietnam. Loneliness was a strong third."*

Tim Oberst explained why they kept men in the field so long, "It was because you wanted men that were experienced and knew what to do. The new guys were noisy and green." Tim later joined a Hunter Killer Team. He said he felt safer with that team than when he was in a line company. These teams were small in number, five or six men, who relied on stealth and experience.

May 22, 1969

Dear Mom and Dad,

Well, how are things at home? I hear it's been pretty rainy. Boy, it sure is a hot one here today. Over 100, I guess. I hope I can keep from washing the paper away. I'm still here at the bridge. We have to set up ambushes each night. Last night we went out and stayed in a barn instead of out in the rice paddies. That's one nice thing about my squad leader, if he can get by without doing something, (creating more hassle) he will. That was the first night since I've been here that I had shelter. I never thought it was so nice to sleep in a barn. (ha ha)

Did you get the corn in dad? I wish it was time to pick it, but it will come. I got some more pictures back, so I'll be sending a few at a time. Like I say, don't lose them!

I really appreciate it, Dad, that you have written. I sure look forward to letters. Guess what my nickname is? "Hercules." Because I'm the biggest in our platoon. I'm down to 185, and all muscle, (ha ha!) (Bragging now ain't I?) but eating these C-rations all the time, and humping for miles some days with 30 pounds of gear and ammunition on your back, really builds a guy up!

Mom, if you send anything send me some of those home-made chocolate chip cookies. Some packs of pre-sweetened (grape) Kool-aid and little cans of fruit. I like apricots best! Now don't drop everything and run to send this off. It's just if you want to sometime (no hurry). I hope my radio comes pretty soon. Have you sent my camera yet? Well, I can't think of much more right now. Every day is the same. Tell everyone hello!

Bye for now, Stan

Stan was 6 ft. 2 in. and one of the bigger guys in his unit. Taken at Fire Base Marge.

It was rare that our Dad wrote to anyone, so I know how much his letter meant to Stan.

When Stan mentioned sleeping in the barn, I recalled him getting caught smoking cigarettes in our barn at home when he was younger. Needless to say he was punished for it, and our Dad explained (not just words) how fast a barn full of alfalfa would burn. I smiled when I remembered that incident so many years ago.

Walking through the same barn over the 4th of July weekend in 2005, the memories came back; the warm familiar scents of the hay, kittens scurrying about, and pigeons cooing. My mind became flooded with past images of cows in the stanchions, and milk fights. Stan and I would spray each other, stretching the poor cow's tit so we could get the right angle on our shot; usually aiming for the face.

Mom kept Stan supplied with goodies from home, and even got a little carried away at times. Like most Italian mothers, providing her kids with plenty of food would cure all ills. She still likes to spoil her family with goodies, Mom wrote the book on "comfort foods."

May 23, 1969 Friday

Dear Mom and Dad,

How's everything at home? I received two letters from you today. They almost get mad at me for getting so many letters. (ha ha) Mom, don't worry about me not getting the mail. I probably get it all. It's just that sometimes I get no letters, and then the next day I get two or three. You can't imagine how much I enjoy getting a letter. So please keep up the good work. I'm really looking forward to my radio.

Now don't worry about me drinking too much. (I'm not a fool.) But, Mom, a person's got to have some fun. I thought we might be able to go to Saigon sometime, I get so nervous! It's really hell the way they run things over here. The guys in the rear at the base camps get EM clubs, movies, PX's, USO shows, and what do we get...not at damn thing! Eat out of a damn can, and fight, but that's the messed up Army for you.

We had a guy get hit from a booby trap the other day. It messed him up pretty bad. But when he realized what happened he smiled about the whole thing. We said we really felt sorry for him. Guess what he said? "You guys are the ones I feel sorry for, because you've got to stay here in this hell hole. I'm getting out!" It sounds foolish, but most guys could care less if they get hit. Now don't go jump to conclusions. I'm sure as hell not going to get that bad! But you can realize how a guy's morale and spirits would go away after days and months of fighting without any kind of recreation. I just think of when I get out, my nice car, and how I'll make up for this hell!

Our mail comes about 1 p.m. each day. That's about 9:00 p.m. at home the day before. So when you're sitting there watching television at 9:00 p.m. you can think of me reading my letters. (ha ha)

So Eileen's getting pretty good on the Honda? I suppose it will be worn out by the time I get home. (ha ha) Has Dad or Bill ridden it any lately? Can Eileen change gears yet? Tell Dad to check the oil every now and then.

Well, that's about all for now. Tell me when you receive my pictures.

With love, Stan

Mail call at Blackhorse, a lifeline
for GIs to the "world."

Still with a smile, Stan stands beside his poncho liner,
which serves as shelter.

As I read Stan's letters, read the books by Vietnam vets, and talked with them, it became clear that there was a lot of resentment toward the guys in the rear.

Stephen writes in his book, <u>Bait</u>, "At noon we rucked up again. Another platoon was unloading at the same time. One of the men in the other platoon mentioned the common expression heard many times a day in Vietnam: 'War is hell.' And the familiar return from one of ours was, 'It sure is, but contact is a real motherfucker.' The familiar peace and victory signs were exchanged. For the real grunt fighting in Nam, these were familiar happenings and the sincerity was ever-prevalent. The REMFs [rear-echelon motherfuckers as a whole could not understand all that was in those exchanges. Only a grunt knew. Not that the REMFs were never shot at or wounded. But they didn't hump a hundred pounds every day, or fight the insects and the jungle, and the lonely feeling of being nowhere with only twenty or thirty men to rely on."

In Edelman's <u>Dear America,</u> *GIs express their feelings about being in the field too long. In a letter from Delta Company to then President Nixon, they wrote,* "You can't imagine how disturbing it is to have a friend with just days left before he goes home lose his life. As a man nears the end of his tour, he becomes tense and nervous and cannot properly function in the field. He hesitates to act in situations where he once would have acted instinctively. He becomes so concerned about his own welfare that he neglects the well-being of others."

Letters from home kept Stan going as Bernard Edelman writes in <u>Dear America</u>. He felt Army Sergeant Michael Kelley said it best in a letter to his parents, "I feel like some 13th-century peasant trying to conceive of the place called heaven. Letters from home are like Bibles: they tell of tales so distant from this reality that they demand a faith before one can actually believe them. Is there really such a beautiful place, and such a good life on that distant island or is my memory based only on some childhood myth that I was awed into believing?"

One of the men that served with Stan was Eddie Taylor, he wrote a sweet letter to my sister Eileen, while in Vietnam. A connection to the states and home and what waited at the end of their tour gave GIs strength to go on. My sister answered Eddie's letters. I found this one among Stan's letters home. Mom had saved it. Eddie's letter...

Eileen,

I have received a couple of letters since I wrote you last. I thought maybe it would be better if I didn't write since hearing about things from here would just bring about bad thoughts, but I am happy that you continued to write. I didn't want you to write just because I kept answering the letters.

I did receive a Christmas package from Mr. Lane and although I didn't find a return address, the outside was messed up; I will use same address as yours with his name on it. I'm sure it will reach him in a rural area. He sent a beef roast and the complete squad had a feast. (Ha)

We are getting a lot of new men in now, as the platoon is bigger than it ever has been. I finally got an R&R on the 17th of Feb. I want to go to Hong Kong but they offered me Tokyo, so I took it. Any form of civilization will be great. From all I hear, it's similar to the states, so

I may get homesick. I will have four-and-a-half months left when I return, and maybe to see what I am missing, will make the rest of my tour go faster.

Well, we have our re-supply, and getting ready to move out, so I will say bye for now. I hope you haven't gotten disgusted and decided not to write, I promise to answer sooner than before. Give your family my best wishes and keep smiling.

Hoping to become a better friend,
Eddie

Eddie Taylor.

May 24, 1969 Sat.
Dear Mom and Dad,

Well, another day in Vietnam. Not much new, but as I said, if I get any time off at all I'll write you, because I figure you worry (even though I wish you didn't).

Boy, it really rained hard last night. I got so wet on ambush I almost washed away. But that's about the only way a person can get clean. (ha ha) I sure hope my radio comes pretty quick. My camera too!

Not much action lately. They are talking about working with the 9th Infantry division. I guess the VC is really giving them hell! I sure hope we don't have to help them out.

Some asshole went to sleep the other night on ambush not far from here, when he was supposed to be on watch. The VC snuck up on them and killed six out of eight. The guy that fell asleep and one other guy made a run for it and made it. I wonder how he feels, being responsible for six dead! But that's the way the VC is. They sit and watch for someone to mess up so they can have their fun.

How's the corn coming, Dad? It sure would be nice to see good black soil again. This place doesn't have shit! I never seen or heard of anywhere like this damn place.

I see Jim Burns is going to Quarter Master School. I hope he doesn't have to come over here. Have you seen Steve any? He sure got screwed on leave didn't he? I've written him twice and haven't heard from him yet. Tell the little devil to write. (ha ha)

Well, I guess that's about all for now. Tell everyone hello.
With love, Stan

You too, Warren (ha ha)
Like you say, it is boring and hard to make carbon copies.

P.S. Now remember, Mom, if you don't get a letter sometimes for four or five days, it's because they've pulled us out on a mission, and it's impossible to write when you're on the move all the time. (But don't worry!)

Staying awake while on guard was hard when the lack of sleep wore away at a GI's alertness. Stephen writes in Bait, *about his experiences. He explains some of what Stan was talking about,* "With so few men in the field, it was easy to make a mistake. Everyone was taxed to the limit of endurance. Army perimeters became smaller and smaller. Night watch became longer and longer. It was only a matter of time before we would all be dead."

May 25th, 1969 Sunday

Dear Mom and Dad,

Well, I just realized it's Sunday. Unless someone actually told you, you'd just figure it's another day. Sometimes you might have to ask ten different people before you can find out what day it is. I almost hate Sundays over here, because I know it's Saturday night at home.

When does Steve have to report to Oakland to come over? Tell him to take an extra week or so, because they won't do anything to him. You've got a year to serve over here so they don't really care if you start it the day you're supposed to. I wish I'd have taken an extra week or so.

Not much new around here. We had a real nice quiet ambush last night. So that's something to be thankful about. I've heard rumors that we might get airlifted out today to the Pineapples. It's mud up to a guy's ass out there. I hope we don't have to go.

Well, I'm doing pretty good at writing ain't I, Mom? But like I say, I could miss a week at time writing, because it's impossible to write when you're on the move all the time. Here at the bridge we haven't been too busy. So there's nothing to do in our spare time, but either sleep or write letters.

How's Eileen and the Honda coming? I can see them now, around and around the house. I remember how Dad used to cuss when we'd made tracks around the house! (ha ha) Well, tell everyone hello.

With love, Stan

New recruits headed for Vietnam.

The Honda on the sidewalk in front of our home,
1969.

When we were kids we did make tracks around the house, and it became a virtual race track for our tricycles, toy trucks, and doll buggies. Nothing's changed, but these days it's the grandkids that run around the two-story farmhouse. The dirt track has been replaced with a sturdy sidewalk. When I visit my childhood home, I can almost see Stan running around the house with that mischievous grin on his face, daring me to catch him.

Stan's high school buddy, Steve, would ship out to Vietnam, but he would not see Stan in country.

May 26, 1969 Tuesday

Dear Mom and Dad,

Well, how's everything at home? As far as for here, I guess not too bad today.

I'm still here at the bridge, but yesterday was a day to remember. They thought there was some VC along this river about 30 miles up north. The 9th Infantry division was up there, so we went up to help them out. They took us by a sort of barge about five miles up stream in the thick of things. As soon as we got there, and they lowered the big doors, they started calling air strikes in and that's something to see. Those guys in those jet bombers really can fly. Then they called artillery in. It was just like on television. It was hell on earth, and then after that was all done we had to go in and clean the place up. "You can't imagine!" I think that's the most scared I've ever been, but that's all over, and here I am back at the bridge.

Boy, that really shocked me about Art Roach! Isn't that something the way this old world goes? A person never knows. You'd think he would have lived for 100 years.

I got a letter from Fred Johnson. He says he's really got it made. He works a regular day, ten hours. I guess he works on helicopters. He says he doesn't ride in them. All he can write about is getting married when he gets home. The poor devil; that's what women will do for you, (ha ha) but I'm happy for him, that he's got a good job over here.

Well, I'll bet the weather is really getting hot at home. I sure would like to have a big '74, and ride down the road at home, but I will someday.

Have you sent my radio and camera yet? I sure hope so. It would be nice to listen to a radio again. How's work going Dad? "Not worth shit!" Ha.

Well, I'm sending some checks in this letter for you to put away for me. Well, I'll be writing later. I'm all right, so don't worry!

With love, Stan

Huey helicopter used in Vietnam.

Bin Dinh Bridge.

Lewis "Snake" Ruth, a friend of Tim Oberst, and a member of a hunter killer team with the 199th, recalled Stan guarding the Bin Dinh Bridge. He didn't know Stan well, but the image of him taking pictures while at that post stayed with him.

In his May 26th letter, Stan mentions Art Roach, who was a cousin of my dad's. Death happened in the "world" too!

Fred Johnson, a childhood friend of Stan's, lived in what was known as White Oak, a hilly, rural part of our county. In those days, rural communities named their schools after trees, patriotic symbols, or animals. Some that I remember were, Eagle, Richwood's, Elm, and finally Star, where Stan and I first attended school. I remember riding the school bus and stopping at Fred Johnson's small farm house that sat on top of a hill. The bus rides were long and felt like roller coaster rides in our part of Iowa.

Dad and I often take rides through the countryside when I'm home. He likes to reminisce and talk about the old days as we drive by familiar landmarks. We drove by Fred's old house on one of those drives recently. It looked the same. It was comforting to know that it was still there perched on that hill.

Fred made it back from Vietnam, and resides in Burlington, Iowa, where he works for Case, an implement manufacturer.

May 26, 1969

Dear Mom and Dad,

I got some of my pictures back, so I'm sending them home. Now try not to lose them or anything, OK. I'll write on the back of them what they are. Most of them are just of Vietnam from the air. I've got about 60 more coming.

Mom, if you can send me some <u>color</u> film for the Instamatic 124. It's so hard to get a hold of any over here, and especially for me. Take it out of the money I sent home.

Bye for now, Stan

I remember my first Instamatic camera. It was quite an improvement over the more cumbersome Brownie or Box cameras we were used to. It opened up a whole new world, where anything and anyone were fair game for a casual photo op.

As I went through the pictures that Stan had sent back, some of the negatives were undeveloped. I tried taking them to the usual places that develop film, but none of them could help me. I finally found a professional photography company in Wichita, Kansas. They were equipped to work with my negatives. The pictures turned out crisp and clear and the color was as bright as the day Stan took them.

May 27, 1969
Dear Aunt Geraldine,

Mom has been writing me and saying you are in the hospital, or were at least. I'm sorry I didn't write sooner, but believe me; it's hard to find time to get letters off to my folks. But you have been extra good to me, and I really appreciate it.

If I could have gotten to a place where I could have found a get well card, I'd have sent it. But the only way I can even get a hold of writing paper, is to have someone get it for me back at the base camp. I haven't been out of the field yet. It really gets miserable out here at times. But like I tell everyone, it's hard to explain how it is over here, or the way the people live. One thing sure, I'm thanking the good Lord every day that I can return to the wonderful U.S. after my time's up.

Well, enough of that. I sure hope your hand gets better. I suppose it will just take time. Those old hospitals can sure get boring, can't they? How long were you in the hospital? Do you think that this operation will fix you up pretty good? I sure hope so. I can imagine how painful it is.

Tell Uncle Frank hello for me. I'll bet now that the weather is nice, he's real busy. I'd pound nails 18 hours a day if I could come home. (ha ha) But that's dreaming.

That was too bad about Art Roach, wasn't it? A person never knows, does he? At least I've got good health. But sometimes I think it's a wonder, after eating C-rations all the time.

Well, I can't think of much more. Actually there's not much new that ever happens around here. Like I say, I'm sorry I didn't write sooner, and I sure hope you're coming along fine.

With love, Stan

Uncle Frank owned a construction company. My aunt kept the books and did the payroll for him. He was a hard worker and skilled builder. His business was very successful, and he eventually brought his son, Robert, into the partnership.

Stan kneeling, Jayson Dale behind him with locals,
south of Saigon. In May, his first mission, displaying a
cache of weapons found on a sampan.

May 30, 1969

Dear Mom and Dad,

Well, I suppose you thought I'd forgotten your address. (ha ha) But like I say, we never know when we'll be sent on a mission. And we just got back from five days out in the field. It sure was nice to get back to where a person can shave, and wash his hands and face.

Yes, I received my radio. I'm listening to it right now. (It's wonderful.) It sure helps out. I'll bet we listened to it until 3 a.m. last night! We always do a little celebrating when we come in from the field. We played cards and must have drank 100 beers (ha ha) and listened to the radio. That's about the only fun we have.

It wasn't too bad a mission. It was tiresome and hot! But no one was hurt, and that's the main thing. We called in artillery and gun ships on some VC in the real dense jungle. We went in later and tried to find any strays. But artillery pretty well messed up their day. I'm looking for my camera in the mail today.

Yes, Mom, you've done better than I figured. I just wish there was something I could do to repay you. But I'll be home someday. Then we'll have the fun of our lives!

So Steve and Diana are through! That's a woman for you. (ha ha) I suppose he and Bill are having quite a bit of fun. All I can say is for Steve to have all the fun he can. Because over here your day consists of getting up, eating when you have time, getting shot at, and going to bed.

Well, I'm glad the garden is coming OK. I get so sick of eating out of a can all the time, I don't know what to do. But if a person's hungry he'll eat it!

You asked who has written, Karen, the people in California, the ones in Kansas City, the woman at Sears, John Lane and others. I've heard from a lot of people. Believe me, it sure has helped.

Hey, Mom, you know that three-fourths of the squad I'm with are Italian! Right up my line. Right, Mom! (ha ha)

Well, I can't think of much more to write. I had helicopter rides when I was out on the last mission. I'm sending a clipping of my Army report. It tells of the first contact I had. Boy, was I scared! But I guess everyone done all right. At least we got a body count!

Write next time I get a chance, Stan

Stan in the field on a mission.

A soldier's first contact or firefight was something that was never forgotten. Stan was no different. It was a baptism into the bloody waters of war. In his book, From Classrooms To Claymores, Ches Schneider recalls his first firefight, "I crawled into my poncho liner that night to ponder the day. It was at such times that I analyzed what had happened during the day. I had been in my first firefight. I had not run. I had not panicked, wet my pants, or fainted from fright. I had not gone crazy…I had kept my head and used my military training properly. I had not played a major role in the firefight, but that was okay, too. I had not been shot in the back, I was not crippled or maimed. I had a second war story to tell."

SPC Stephen M. Klaus was a member of the 25th Infantry Division 2/27th Wolfhounds, Co. C. Steve served in Vietnam as a sniper with the 27th INF, from 1969-1970. He was stationed outside Cu Chi usually about two or three miles from Cambodia. He went into Cambodia April 1st of 1969 and came out April 7th of 1969. During his service Steve earned 2 Bronze Stars, two Army Commendations, one with V device. Other medals included a CIB, and several campaign ribbons. Steve said he would be in the field for a month at a time; when he came in his rifle would be torn down and cleaned and then he would be reloaded and sent back in the field for another month.

Steve's missions typically consisted of fifteen men with the Infantry, five or six with the Rangers, a sniper team would consist of him, a radio man, and one other sniper. They would go out at dusk and return at dawn. Steve did suffer shrapnel wounds during one of his missions when a booby trap exploded near him.

I asked Steve what the fear was like for him, and he said he didn't dwell on it, but when he had time to think he would get the shakes. His recollections of combat were very similar to the other vets I talked to. He said that Hollywood's version was not always accurate, and that things that are done during war are not pleasant, but necessary.

Steve and his wife, Diane, married when Steve returned from Vietnam. They still live in the area. When I went home in the summer of 2005 he and I reminisced about his friendship with Stan and his time in Vietnam. Steve also shared some of the letters that I have included in this writing. Since Stan wrote these letters to his good friend, the contents are that of a typical nineteen-year-old guy filling his friend in on his latest romantic conquests and bar experiences. Stan and Steve shared many escapades during their high school years. Steve shared many memories he had of Stan, some which were more private than others. Steve got a twinkle in his eye and a mischievous grin on his face when he recalled a few of their teenage adventures.

Stan was proud of his Italian heritage. Our mother was a first generation Italian American. He enjoyed the guys in his company who shared that culture and background. Greg Breeckner was one that shared that heritage, his mother was Italian.

Steve Klaus served as a sniper, 25ᵗʰ Inf. 2/27ᵗʰ
Wolfhounds, in Vietnam, 1969.

Diane and Steve Klaus, 2005.

May 31, 1969

Dear Mom and Dad,

Well, here it is Memorial Day. Did you get to watch the 500-mile race? About all I heard was who won. Well, anyway, I wish you a good day. That's just one more holiday out of the way for me. I can't wait until those Christmas cards come.

Well, about ten more days and I can chalk up another month. We should get paid today; (BIG DEAL) there's nothing to spend it on but beer! I sure wish I could get to a PX sometime. My worst problem is never having the chance to let off a little steam! If a person could go to Saigon to a dance and have a little fun it wouldn't be too bad! But they won't let the Infantry units go there. I could just imagine an Infantry unit that's been in the field for six months, get turned loose in Saigon. We'd tear the town down! (ha ha)

It will soon be two months for me out in the field. It sure gets old. Same faces every day. If I didn't get along as well as I do in the squad, I'd go crazy! They say I'm the life of the squad.

We had a little contact one night on ambush. The VC were shooting green tracers. A person would swear every one of them was missing you by two inches. I told the squad leader to kick me in the ass so I could get it lower to the ground, everyone started to laugh right in the middle of all the shooting. (ha ha) It's hard to believe that people would laugh when you're getting shot at. But there's always something funny in every fight. All a guy can do is pray no one gets hurt.

That's too bad about John Guffey! But malaria is really bad over here. I've seen two guys catch it. But most of the time it makes them happy, because they get out of the field. Well, that's about all for now. Keep the letters coming.

With love, Stan

Stan and his buddies playing cards down in the Delta, south of Saigon. (Clockwise from bottom) Medic (unidentified), Mike Yusko, Dave Cherneski, Rick Sillanpaa, Stan, Vito Lavecchio, Jayson Dale, Elden Rasmussen.

Tim O'Brien writes in his book, The Things They Carried, "For the most part they carried themselves with poise, a kind of dignity. Now and then, however, there were times of panic, when they squealed or wanted to squeal but couldn't, when they twitched and made moaning sounds and covered their heads and said Dear Jesus and flopped around on the earth and fired their weapons blindly and cringed and sobbed and begged for the noise to stop and went wild and made stupid promises to themselves and to God and to their mothers and fathers, hoping not to die. In different ways, it happened to all of them. Afterward, when the firing ended, they would blink and peek up. They would touch their bodies, feeling shame, then quickly hiding it. They would force themselves to stand." *He goes on to write,* "Awkwardly the men would reassemble themselves, first in private, then in groups, becoming soldiers again. They would repair the leaks in their eyes. They would check for casualties, call in dustoffs, light cigarettes, try to smile, clear their throats and spit and begin cleaning their weapons. After a time someone would shake his head and say, No lie, I almost shit my pants, and someone else would laugh, which meant it was bad, yes, but the guy had obviously not shit his pants, it wasn't that bad, and in any case nobody would ever do such a thing and then go ahead and talk about it."

Stan probably did some of the same things that O'Brien talks about in his book. He would, however, try to see the humor in the situation to lighten things up.

Ches Schneider, in this book, From Classrooms To Claymores, relates his fears and anticipation of contact, "Still, I understood that I hadn't faced the real test yet. The real test would be when I experienced my first firefight. How would I react when someone was shooting at me? Would I run? Panic? Freeze? Could I shoot another human being? Humans are not the rabbits and squirrels I hunted in my native Missouri woods…Luck had been with me, so far. But the reality of my situation kept coming back to me. Sooner or later, somewhere, somehow, the first firefight would come. Would I be able to conduct myself appropriately? Would my next trial end in honor, or disgrace?"

Stan was the life of the party when he was with friends and family, and as our mother would say, "He was a cut-up!" *It probably helped to keep everyone laughing, other wise I'm sure the daily stress of war would have been too much! Many of Stan's buddies recalled how he would make them laugh even in the most serious situations. The one thing they all remember was his great smile!*

Men at Blackhorse Mess Hall, (left to right) Greg Breeckner, Stan, Frank Leone, Jayson Dale.

Stan with two of his buddies at BMB, Long Binh, (left to right) Dave Cherneski, Stan, Jayson Dale.

Buddies at Blackhorse, (left to right) Jayson Dale,
Frank Leone, Greg Breeckner, and Dave Cherneski.

June 6, 1969

Dear Mom and Dad,

Well, what's it been, six days since I last wrote? We just came
in from a mission. I'm writing you before I clean my rifle. It sure
doesn't seem like I'd been in the field six days. But time really flies out
there. But it was six miserable days. The monsoon is in full swing.
You wouldn't believe the way it rains over here, and sleeping in it at
night (it's hell)! And that's when the VC like to hit, is when it's raining
hard. So a person has got to stay awake most of the night. But as far as
trouble with the VC, it wasn't so bad. There's always a sniper here and
there, but that's not much to worry about.

Has Phillip got the little jacket I sent him? I thought it was kinda
cute. Tell him the material it's made of is what I sleep on every night.
That's my bed! I guess they figure it's hard to see in the jungle and
underbrush.

Hey, Mom, I haven't forgotten how good you've been to write. And
remember, I said if I could I'd try to show my appreciation.

Well, all I'm going to tell you is to watch the mail for a little present. (ha ha) I had to order it, and it's the best I could buy! And you deserve the best, Mom. I've been so depressed at times I could almost cry, but I can always look forward to that letter. So I hope you like it, Mom. I know you will. Like I say, it's the best I could get and it's got everything. I'm giving you too many hints. (ha ha) You should be getting it in about a week after you get this letter. Well, enough for that.

Dad, don't think I'm forgetting you. But it's just that I never get any place I can buy anything. The only way I get anything is if some salesman comes around, or if I send for it. I haven't been to a PX or to a base camp for six weeks now. Bill wrote and said I'd probably been to Saigon by now (Big Laugh). I sure wish I could go to Saigon a day, or even get back to civilization. Anything just to let off some steam!

Well, the 15th is Father's Day, "Happy Father's Day, Dad." Now that I think of it, your birthday too, Dad! The first chance I get to get you something, I will. But right now I can't even get a card. I sure wish Mom's birthday was here. I'll be practically home then.

Well, almost two months gone, ten more, "Damn." I suppose Steve is getting ready to come over. I'd sure hate to say goodbye again. That just about killed me, when I had to get on that airplane and leave.

I got a letter from Bob. He said he is going to extend six months for a possible early out. He said he'd get a 30-day leave before he started his extra six months.

All I can say is, he must not have it too bad, or he'd never put in for extra time. I wouldn't spend one minute extra in this hell hole!

I haven't received my camera yet. I'm starting to wonder. But I guess sometimes it takes quite a while. So don't worry. Well, I think I'm catching up a little on writing. "Ain't I?" Well, that's about all for now. Bye for now. And, Mom, watch the mail.

With love, Stan

P.S. Hey, guess what? The mail just came. I got my camera and the box of film. (Finally)

Thanks a lot! And don't worry about me taking chances with the camera.

"Little Phillip," saluting in the jacket that Stan sent
him

Phillip, 2005, Memorial Day weekend, holding the
jacket Stan gave him in 1969.

Stan's high school friend, Marine Bob Richards.

Reflection by Bob Richards
April 25, 2006

Stan and I became friends in school when we were about 10 or 11. We both grew up on farms and had chores to do; that was what we had in common at first. We both also liked baseball. We would stay at each other's houses, and after chores we would play baseball until dark.

As everybody knows by now, time goes so fast that you go from being a kid to a teenager in no time. Here come the cars and freedom. Stan had the first car and his generosity was like not other; what was his was yours. Many times we would go to Mt. Pleasant or West Point to the dances. Just having you there along was the most important thing to him. If things were dull, he would come up with something to make them lively. You know…a little drink, maybe a fight or two, drag races. He had a way of always keeping things going and keeping things fun—with Stan, there was never a dull moment.

As a friend, Stan was the kind that no matter how tough the situation was, he would be there for you. You always knew things were going to be okay; he wouldn't have it any other way.

This is just a little part of what our friendship was like growing up. If you really knew Stan, you knew what honesty, loyalty, and bravery was supposed to mean. I can't write about a lot of the things we did, because it's "classified information."

I had just flown to Australia to start R&R when I found out about Stan's death. I was sad, but I know God takes the special ones early. I don't know why, but he does. We had talked and talked about the war and about death. I know Stan was trying to save someone.

I'll miss all the years we could have had watching our families grow up. Friends like Stan don't really die; they live on in your heart until you can see them again.

Stan loved to give gifts and he wanted to show Mom how much he appreciated all the letters she so faithfully sent. He was more than certain she would love what he had sent to her; finding it hard not to spill the beans about what the gift was. Our mother, a very spiritual person, lived her faith everyday, and prayed that the good Lord would protect her eldest son from harm.

Stan's friend Jayson Dale recalled how they came to purchase the Bible that Stan was talking about in his letter. As it turned out Jayson also bought a Bible for his mother. Jayson recalled that he and Stan had purchased the Bibles from two Korean men that were selling different items along the road.

My brother, Phill, still has the small jacket that Stan sent him. When I took pictures of him holding it Memorial weekend, 2005, I felt a twinge of déjà vu. Thirty-five years earlier Mom had posed my younger brother in that jacket, in the same yard. I feel so fortunate to have a family home to return to. It is comforting to know that it will always be there to welcome me home for whatever reason.

June 7, 1969 Sat.
Dear Mom and Dad,

Well, how are things back in the world? I sure get homesick for it sometimes. I received my camera, film and batteries all in fine shape. Thanks a lot! I'm really proud of you, Mom. You did an outstanding job of packing my camera. And like I said in my last letter, there's something on its way for you. I just know you'll love it. It even interested me! There I go again giving you hints. (ha ha) Well, it's Saturday here. I was just thinking about Steve. I'll bet he's leaving today. I sure hate to see him come over here. He wrote me a letter. I guess he's really been raising hell, (ha ha) I don't blame him! After a couple of months in this place, a person feels like pulling his hair out!

Well, things are pretty dull around here. We're still out on ambush every night. It hardly ever fails to rain every day. It can really get miserable. It would be so nice to sleep under a roof again.

Like I say, not much new and Happy Birthday again, Dad!

With love, Stan

P.S. Tell me how many pictures you received. I've already taken a roll of film. Were there any bad places in those rolls from Belvoir? I'm sure glad about you getting those.

Stan with his 8-mm movie camera and a lap full of
film, which he used!

The Bible, with its thick, tooled-leather cover, did have everything, maps, a concordance, beautiful Renaissance style pictures and a dictionary. You name, it had it!

Mom still has the Bible. It is displayed in my parent's home in a prominent spot in the living room. I looked through it when I visited my parents. Tucked away in its many pages, were pictures of Stan, newspaper clippings, poems, and a pressed flower from one of the many bouquets at my brother's funeral.

The Bible that Stan sent to Mom. It's a little tattered and taped up, but it still remains one of her prized possessions.

June 8, 1969
Dear Mom and Dad,

Well, I hardly know how to write what I want to tell you without scaring you. But I'll try. Today we were out on a mission, and we spotted some VC. Well, like always we had to go after them. I no more than got off the LCM, (armored barge that carries Infantrymen) and we got hit. The VC was giving it all they could. Well, anyway I got hit (shrapnel in the right arm). Now don't get all excited, I'm still as good as new. They didn't even have to take me to the big hospital. They fixed me up back at the aide station at camp. The C.O. (Commanding Officer) told me a quote, "You're a hard fighting man." I couldn't help but feel proud! They say I'll get a Purple Heart. But since I didn't go to the main hospital I'll probably have to wait for a while before it's presented to me. I sure feel like a "hero," Mom. (ha ha) They just don't realize what kind of fighters the Ross's put out.

Well, enough of that. I just thank God it wasn't any worse than it was. I wasn't even going to mention it to you, but they took all the details down and will probably send it to the newspaper, so I figured I'd better try to explain. They may even let you know before I get this letter to you. Like I say, I don't know how they work it. But most of all, Mom and Dad, please don't get all stirred up. I'm OK! And most of all don't go telling anyone. Just wait and let them read it in the paper. (Please promise me that!) Just watch the paper and it will probably be in there.

Well, I suppose you're too shook up to read anymore so I'll close. I hate it that I even wrote this letter, but I figured it would be best. I think I'll get a little sleep. I feel a little sore tonight. (ha ha)

With all my love, Stan

The "Third's Rough Three" (left to right) Don Mazzi,
Dave Cherneski and Stan.

That shrapnel wound, I'm sure gave Stan a feeling of pride and relief. It would be a badge of courage if he made it home. Most of the young GIs hadn't achieved any greatness in their young lives, as Ches Schneider would relate in From Classrooms To Claymores, "In real life, back in the World, I'd never made a winning touchdown or a game-winning base hit. In Nam, one of my greatest fears had been that I would get injured or killed before I ever did anything even semi-important. In the back of my mind, I reserved the thought that I might endure a whole year and have nothing to show for my efforts. People back home would ask, 'And what did you do in Nam?' My reply would be a sad and forlorn, 'Nothing.' Now at least, I would have one war story to tell my kids and grandchildren."

My parents have Stan's Purple Heart in a nice case with his other medals. Dad and Mom were proud of his commendation, but they would have traded it for their son's safe return home. Maybe that wound took some of the war jitters out of Stan. He had survived a fight and come out of it scared but alive.

Stan, like other soldiers, didn't want to upset his family. His comment, "I'm OK," was repeated in some manner in every letter. He didn't like to talk about the fire fights or the ambushes because he knew how it affected everyone at home. I've asked some of the men who knew Stan and served in Vietnam, what that fear was like. They each had different explanations. One said "it was like waiting for a fast ball. You'd either hit it, or you would strike out!" Others said they only thought about being afraid after the fighting stopped. For most, they only thought about the next moment.

June 10, 1969
Dear Phyllis,
I was sure glad to hear from you, and sure hope you write me often. Sometimes I think I'll go crazy over here. This place is hell. It's hard to explain the way this place is. It's hot, dirty; a person sleeps out in the open all the time.

As you probably know, I'm in the Infantry, and they catch all the hell. It was sure hard to get used to killing and seeing people suffer, but that's war. I just hope and pray I make it out all right. Believe me sometimes a guy thinks, "That's it!" Well, enough of that. No one wants to hear about killing or things like that.

Well, how are things down at the plant? I sure wish I was back down there working. Those were the good old days. (ha ha) Are you still working days? I know now why they are so busy down there, the way we shoot up ammunition.

Well, I can't think of much more to write. Like I say, I was sure happy to hear from you. It does me great good to know that someone back home cares.

With love, Stan

This letter was written to our Aunt Phyllis. She was my dad's sister-in-law. My Uncle Dale had passed away before Stan had gone into the service. He was one of my brother's favorite uncles. He and Aunt Phyllis had no children. Stan was very close to them.

Aunt Phyllis worked at the Ordinance Plant just on the outskirts of Burlington, Iowa. The plant covers hundreds of acres, and is enclosed by a formidable fence topped off with razor wire. Over the years it has employed many in the surrounding communities and in my family. This munitions plant is still there turning out war materials employing hundreds of people, as it has for over sixty years.

When I was a child it wasn't uncommon to hear about explosions at the plant. It was, and is, a dangerous place to work. It always gave me a chill when I drove past it and imagined how serious its purpose was.

Several of my aunts found employment there during World War II. Their safety was always in the back of our minds. I loved to look at pictures of my aunts, standing with their hands on their hips. They stood with a new found confidence, in their coveralls and bandanas, looking every bit as empowered as the popular war poster featuring "Rosie the Riveter." It sure beat doing dishes and cleaning the house.

Though the job was distasteful and dangerous, it helped clothe and feed many families during those difficult years. The plant still churns out needed war materials for our nation's military.

June 10, 1969

Dear Mom and Dad,

Well, I haven't heard from you for three days now. They say that people eventually start writing less and less. I guess it's happening to me now. I'm just kidding. (ha ha) I suppose the mail is tied up somewhere.

Things sure haven't been the best around here lately. I've been walking point the last three weeks. Every new man has to until someone else new comes in. I've been walking point for two squads (18 men). It really gets scary breaking through the path.

Boy, I really got a treat last Sunday. They let me go to the PX in Saigon. It was the first time I've been out of the field since I got here.

It's really something the way some people have it made over here, especially the Air Force. They have it better than the Army back in the States. But that's the breaks, at least I got a couple of hours of fun. I took some movies while I was riding in the truck. I've taken two rolls already (some real good ones)! Don't worry, I don't mess with it unless it's safe.

I just thought, Mom, by the time you get this letter you'll have received your present. I hope you like it!

I got a letter from John Guffey. He said he really hit it lucky. (He caught malaria.) That sounds funny, but after a few days out in this shit, a guy would almost do anything to get to the rear. But I've made up my mind I'm not going to let it get the best of me. I fight my best and that's all I can do.

Well, almost two months in. Ten more months of hell and I can come back to heaven! I sure miss everyone.

I hear old Nixon is going to withdraw 25,000 troops. But not a damn one will be Infantrymen. It will be some pussy in the rear.

Well, I can't think of much more to write. I suppose we'll be moving to some other area in a few days. I guess we're headed further north. I hope it isn't too far! But what will be, will be.

I sure hope I hear from you tomorrow. It's really a let down when I don't get a letter.

Tell Warren thanks for writing. And I'll drop him a line the first chance I get.

With all my love, Stan

"Humpin" on a trail.

Stan's comment and opinion regarding the Air Force was one that many in the field held of those in the rear. Lee Lanning writes in a June 15, 1969 journal entry, "The rear troops gave us a wide berth. The next day, the entire Battalion would arrive at BMB and for a few days field troops would fill the clubs and PX's. None of the REMF's would be welcomed or, for that matter, easy to find."

"Walking Point" was a very dangerous position to have in the squad. It meant walking ahead of everyone else and clearing a path through the jungle with a machete while carrying your rifle in the other hand. Point men were the most vulnerable. If anyone was going to get hit, it would usually be them. Tim Oberst, one of Stan's good friends in Vietnam walked point many times while he was in country. He said, "It was hell being that tense all the time. Walking point was usually given to the FNG's (Fucking New Guys) until the next new guy, 'Cherry', came along."

Many of the abbreviation's, slang, and acronyms that GIs used in Vietnam became defined for me after reading <u>Dear America</u> *by Bernard Edelman, and Michael L. Lanning's books,* <u>The Only War We Had: A Platoon Leader's Journal of Vietnam,</u> *and* <u>Vietnam, 1969-1970: A Company Commander's Journal.</u>

Lanning writes in an August 22, 1969 journal entry, "At the lead of the company was the point man. He not only had to make the initial break through the thick foliage but also, as the man most vulnerable to an enemy ambush, had to constantly watch for booby traps and signs of enemy activity. The Point man was followed by the soldier called 'the slack' whose sole purpose was to guard the lead soldier. Frequently the men in these two slots traded positions, allowing the point a little rest and ensuring that the most alert man was first."

Stan and his good friend and platoon member, Jayson Dale, took turns walking point. They watched out for each other.

Edelman writes in <u>Dear America,</u> *Chapter 1, "Cherries": First Impressions, "…we were trim and eager, jaunty and scared. But mostly, we were young. White, Black, Hispanic, and Native American, Guamian and Hawaiian, the majority of us were not yet out of our teens. 'Cherries' we were called and 'Newbies.' And 'FNG's'—'Fucking New Guys'—by troops hardened and made less sanguine, perhaps, by just a few months in the bush. Like them, we would age—bust our cherries—quickly."*

Robert Gouge, who's father Jack Gouge served in Vietnam with the 199th, writes about the stress of humping through the Vietnam jungle in his book, <u>These Are My Credentials,</u> *"The heat and smell of decaying plants and animals hovered over the jungle floor, permeating the area like an invisible force. The Redcatchers would hack and cut through the dense, seemingly endless jungle vegetation. It was always a slow and nerve-wracking endeavor."*

June 15, 1969
Dear Mom and Dad,

I received the box of apricots and Kool-aid (June 14th) thanks a lot! But I haven't received a letter in about three days. What's wrong? I sure miss letters.

Well, how's everything at good old home? I've got almost four rolls of film taken. I've really got some good ones. We got air mobiled by helicopter to our ambush sites. So I had a few good chances to get movies of the type of terrain we work in. It looks pretty flat from the air—but those swamps will wear a guy down in about one hour. But we move up north to the jungle the 18th. I sure hate to go up there. But at least it won't be swampy up there. But the jungle is hot and most of it you've got to chop your way through. But it's hell no matter what or where we go. Pretty soon a guy could care less. I get so damn disgusted sometimes I don't know what to do. I sure hope I can get a job in the rear in a few months. But I suppose I'll be out here for ten months like some of these other guys.

You asked about snakes. I've been real lucky so far, I haven't seen any. But in the jungle they're thick! I just hope I never run into one. It's bad enough being around mosquitoes and rats all the time! What a feeling when you wake up at night feeling four feet run across your chest. (ha ha) I don't think there's any discomforts in the world a man doesn't go through over here.

Well, I suppose Steve is over here by now. I wonder what unit he'll get into. I hope he lucks out and gets to stay in a base camp.

I guess not much new around Mt. Pleasant. Have you received your little box yet, Mom? I sent Phillip a little jacket. I hope he got it. I thought it was kinda cute. Well, I can't think of much now. I guess it's just one mission after another around here, some scary and some a push over. I sure hope I get a letter from you tomorrow.

With love, Stan

Huey UH1 Helicopters like this one, air-lifted GIs.

Many of the front line Infantry spent long months in the field because of the short supply of new recruits, and the fact that many of the GIs were sick or had foot problems causing the squads to be short in numbers. As soon as they recovered they were sent back out into the paddies or jungle.

In Edelman's <u>Dear America,</u> Chapter 4, a letter from Delta Company 3/21, 196th Light Infantry Brigade of the Americal Division to then President Richard Nixon reads, "We feel that there should be a system set up that allows men to obtain jobs in rear areas for the last three or four months of their tour. Officers and Medics only spend half of their tour in the field. We have men with 11 months and days in the field who have seen five platoon leaders come and go. Why can't we get the breaks that officers do? After all, we are all men…"

Tom Phillips, 3rd platoon member wrapped up in
his poncho, after being injured in the leg. Photo by
Jayson Dale.

Tom Phillips passed away in November, 2004. He suffered from Ocular Melanoma (cancer of the eye). Cathy, his wife, said that Tom was diagnosed in 2000 and had undergone radiation for the tumor, but it returned and eventually claimed his life.

Tom was hesitant to speak of the war. He was injured, shot in the ankle while in Vietnam, and spent several weeks in the hospital there. He came home in 1970. Cathy and Tom were married in 1972 and had three children. Tom worked as a welder for many years. Both Tom and Cathy are native New Yorkers and she still lives there.

June 17, 1969
Dear Mom and Dad,

Well, here I am back at base camp. It's the first time I've seen this place since I got in the country. These guys have really got it made back here. We'll just be here for three days. I've got to admit, they have really showed us a good time. Last night our captain fried steaks for the whole company. We had a wagon load of ice and beer. All you could drink free! Then after all done eating, they had a stripper and a wild band. The stripper took <u>everything</u> off! I thought everyone would go crazy! But, Mom, I didn't look! (ha ha)

They should show us a good time, especially for having to go up north. One thing about the jungle, it's dry. These damn swamps drove me crazy. But in the jungle a person has to dig in each night. (Sleep in a foxhole) I'm sure not looking forward to it.

Hey, Mom, I really heard something today that really made me sick! You know that Sergeant Tilley, the one I went through AIT with? The one you saw on the film! Well, he got killed already. I don't know when it was that he got killed. Mom, I just happened to have his address at home. I'd appreciate it if you would try to get a hold of his folks and give them my deepest sympathy. It really tears me up to think he got killed in this son-of-a-bitch of a place. Here's the address:

His name -- H. Samuel Tilley Jr.
2727 Waughtown St.
Winston Salem, NC 27107

Please try to call his folks for me. The Lord only knows what they're going through. I had seen him over here before I got assigned to my unit. He was telling me then how hard it was on his mother when he had to leave. Tell his mother I thought a great deal of him and that he was one of the best soldiers I'd ever been around.

Well, enough of that. I can't believe that Dad's fishing. I'll bet that really tickles Warren. First he converts to motorcycles, then fishing. (ha ha) That pisses me off about that Honda. But like you said, that was the right thing to do. And we got $50.00 worth of good out of it.

Hey, Dad, I ran into something today that I think I'll get you since I've gotten something for about everyone now. I know you'll really like it. I hope you liked your gift, Mom! It should be there by now. I haven't received the cookies yet. I sent home a whole box of films. So you'll have plenty to see. They won't let me take my camera to the jungle. So I put it in a safe here at base camp. Hey, about that car, "I knew it. "As soon as I leave, you trade cars. (ha ha) I know I'm going to have one the first minute I get home. I'm not getting a new one. I don't want big payments. I can't believe how nice it will be to get home. I'll kiss the ground when I get off the plane. (ha ha)

About those films I'm sending home. I know what it's going to be, just a bunch of questions. Bill can probably explain some of the shots I took in the village. I got a lot of them when I was on the helicopter. Most of the men in it are of our squad. I never took any pictures where it wasn't safe. Be sure and send me a picture of the car.

So Dorothy is working in town. If you happen to know Carl Burkey's address, send it to me. I'll drop her a few lines and surprise her. But don't say anything to her. We did have quite a bit of fun together! (ha ha) Well, I can't think of much more.

With love, Stan

Philipino band and stripper entertaining
during stand-down.

Stand-down entertainment.

Steaks grilling at stand-down.

Stand-down was quite an event for GIs, especially when they had been in the field for days without clean clothes or real food. Our family was pretty easy going when it came to joking and talking about certain taboo subjects. Stan got a kick out of teasing Mom about the strippers. She wasn't a prude, but she took her faith seriously and she worried about her son in ways that most mothers do.

As I read the books and journals of veterans' experiences, I was enlightened on how a soldier's physical needs were met. At first I was offended and repulsed, but the more I read and grasped the conditions that these men, many 18 and younger, were under, I comprehended their loneliness, the craving for physical contact and warmth, in such a hopeless and bleak environment. The knowledge that they may never live to see another day would be enough to send anyone into the arms of a willing partner. Donald Stephen describes this in his book, <u>Bait</u>, "There's a place where all the village women come to. The MPs keep them in a confined area…The concertina wire is three layers high and there's an MP station on each end. The grunts line up on one side of the wire and the women line up on the other. The men look them over and when they pick one out, they walk down to the MP station and turn in their ID badges. Then they're free to do as they wish until the women's curfew."

Ches Schneider talked about short-time, "Sex with a Vietnamese female. Paid or unpaid." *I don't know what my brother did or didn't do, but I can not judge him or anyone else, as I've never been in their shoes. War, throughout the ages, has never been kind to women. Soldiers in Vietnam were no different than Vikings or Romans before them.*

Lanning describes a stand-down at Camp Frenzell-Jones in a June 16, 1969 journal entry in The Only War We Had, "The party continued. More steaks were grilled. Beer by the trailer load continued to arrive. A Filipino band played popular music on an outdoor stage. Songs about homecoming or any tune that mentioned a hometown or state were well received. The Vietnamese stripper took it all off to show us what we were fighting for. She seemed embarrassed at first…I convinced the officers in charge that it was 'Infantry only' night. The REMF's could go one night without their beer. We were doing them a favor anyway; their presence would only have gotten their nicely pressed uniforms and shined boots a little rearranged by the field soldiers."

It seemed the "F" word was attached to most of a GI's vocabulary in Vietnam. It became the only word strong enough to explain the war, the country, and the dying.

Dorothy Burkey still lives around our hometown area. She remembered Stan with fondness when I last saw her at our parent's 60th wedding anniversary celebration.

Vietnamese women were beautiful and Stan
appreciated that beauty.

June 18, 1969

Dear Karen,

Well, I finally got around to writing. I'm sorry I haven't written before this. But believe me I hardly find time to write the folks. As far as for over here, it's just about the same hell hole over here. Old Charlie Cong has been giving everyone a hard time.

Well, we're going up north tomorrow. I sure hate to. It's thick jungle. But it will be good to get out of these swamps for a change. It doesn't make much difference any more where I go. I get so damn disgusted and depressed sometimes. It's hell, that's all I can say.

Well, enough for that. How's everything with you? Are you in college now? I think I'll try to go to some college after I get out. College life and running around sounds like a winner to me. I'm sure going to catch up when I get out of here.

So little brother is out with you? I sure miss him. I'll bet he won't even know me when I get home. I guess Eileen is coming out too! I sure wish I was back in the picture again. (ha ha)

Well, I can't think of much more to write. Thanks for writing, Karen.

With love, Stan

The swamps of Vietnam were dreadful. Lewis "Snake" Ruth and Tim Oberst described one hellish night spent in just such a place, "We got lost," *Ruth said,* "rather our leader got us lost. We had to sleep in the swamp all night. It was pouring down rain, so we tied ourselves to trees along the bank so we wouldn't drift downstream and drown." *Tim recalled,* "It was the most indescribable feeling, trying to sleep while your body was half submerged in water, knowing there's nothing you can do but endure it until dawn when you could search for safety." *Ruth went on to say that the 199th was a good outfit despite the fact they were one of smallest units in Vietnam. Their reputation was one of Light, Swift, and Accurate. There wasn't a large arsenal behind them. They were on their own most of the time. The men would be loaded on dump trucks and taken to a designated area, where they would remain until air-lifted out.*

"Ohio Boys," Tim "Obie" Oberst and Lewis "Snake"
Ruth, at Blackhorse fire base.

Men getting ready to head out to the field in the
dump truck.

*Phillip came to stay with me and my husband while Mom was
hospitalized. It bothered Stan that we were all in different places, but he
knew that I would take care of our little brother.*

*Phillip was more like my child than my brother, because of our age
difference. I was a sophomore in college when Mom, at 42, gave birth to
him.*

*I tried to make my home a place where he felt safe and loved in
those uncertain days. Phillip was a very bright child who had a vivid
imagination and was very active, which made our trailer seem even more
crowded than it was. Like so many children who have older parents, he
entertained himself. He was, in a way, like an only child. Phillip spent a
lot of time drawing, reading, and flying model airplanes around indoors or
wherever he decided it would be fun.*

*When you're four years old, as my younger brother was, family dynamics
are over your head. But the effects of Stan's death would imprint and nag
my younger brother as he matured. Stan's death impacted Phill more than
he or any of us would realize.*

*Revisiting Stan's life and death gave Phill and me a sense of peace and
closure by connecting with those who knew Stan and were with him in
Vietnam. He was able to ask questions that had haunted him for a long
time. Living up to a big brother that was larger than life and a hero in*

everyone's eyes was difficult, to say the least. Stan's boots would never be filled by any of us. He was and will always be a part of us that represents strength and a link to our best and worst traits.

Phillip doing some art work at my kitchen table in York, Nebraska.

June 18, 1969
Dear Mom and Dad,

I'm enclosing some pictures and money. We take off for the jungle tomorrow. I guess we'll spend 15 days at a time out there, come in for five days rest, then out for another 15 days. So, Mom, if I don't write every so often please understand. We can't have any beer, radios, cameras, no nothing!

I don't know how a person's going to keep from going crazy. But just pray for us, Mom. That's all anyone can do. You've been wonderful. I'll never forget you and Dad for the way you've written and please keep them coming. For the next three or four months it's all I'm going to have. After 15 days out in the field at a time a person will probably turn into a complete animal.

Well, enough for now. I haven't got my cookies yet. Don't send any more Kool-aid. I've got it running out my ears. (ha ha) But thanks for what you have sent.

Bye for now.
With love, Stan

Charlie Co. 2/3 Operation, humping in the jungle
around the village of Cam Tam. Photo by Jayson Dale

Mom did pray for Stan. I'm sure her knees ached from doing so. She knew her son was worth no more or less in God's eyes than any other mother's child, but she prayed for him daily. Sometimes our prayers are answered, but not with the results we'd hoped for. Mom's belief has always been that, "God makes no mistakes, only men do." I always felt that was a simplistic statement, but it has sustained my mother and given her peace.

She looks forward to being reunited with her son one day. That has been her source of strength all these years.

The loss of a loved one does strange things to a person's outlook on life and the here-after. Some become more spiritual, while others lose faith and ask why a loving God would permit wars and the death and destruction that follow. I found that was the case with Stan's friends who returned from Vietnam. Faith became stronger for some while others felt the opposite.

167

June, 1969
(Note written in a Birthday Day card)
Dad,
I don't know if I'm early or late. (ha ha) But I did remember that your birthday was this month. If you're like me, I never want to have any more birthdays. Twenty is old enough. (ha ha)

Things have really been going strong the last couple of weeks. I'm sorry I haven't written, but we've been so much on the go.

I guess they're going to ship our asses up north now. I guess it's all jungle up there. At least we'll be out of the damn swamps. They are hell to fight in.

Well, enough of that. I sure hope you have a good birthday, Dad. I'd give anything to be there.

With love, Stan

Stan's comment, "I never want to have any more birthdays," was not meant to be taken literally. But it made my heart ache to read it. Maybe Stan knew that he wouldn't see another birthday. Each day spent in the field increased the chances that the next bullet might have his name on it. I know what he meant; he enjoyed his youth so much!

The verse written in a Father's Day card:

Dear Father
I want to thank you
For your counsel and advice.
Your patient understanding,
Your help and sacrifice.
I have so many memories
Too special to forget,
Of the love you've always given
The example you have set.
I want to wish you happiness
Today and always, too,
Because it means the world and all
To have a Father like you.

June, 1969

Dad,

We'll have to make up for this year that we're both suffering through, won't we?

I'm really going to enjoy life and the privilege to live in the U.S.A. when I get out of this hell hole. One thing for sure, I'm doing my part for that privilege. But I figure it's all for the family.

Best Dad Ever, Stan

Whether one agrees with the purpose of war or its honorable motives, one thing that has become clear to me, the soldier on the front lines does what he feels is right and good. Young men, barely out of their teens, will not be judged for the killing. They were forced to participate. Judgment will fall on the leaders that made the decision to sacrifice the nation's youth on the altar of expansion and greed.

Stan, seven years old, sits on Dad's lap during
Grandpa Joe Ross's 80th birthday gathering, Grandma
Kate (Hyde) Ross in the middle.

Steve Klaus (right) assigned to the 25th Inf. Div.

June 20, 1969
Dear Mom and Dad,

Well, we got moved to the jungle. There is a lot more NVA up here. But not mud to your ass like in the rice paddies. It's almost pretty country, if a guy could just drive through it.

Hey, Mom, have you got your present yet? You should have. Boy, we really had fun at base camp. I'd give anything to stay in the rear.

I got a letter from Steve. He's in the 25th Infantry Division. We're just about 25 miles apart, but I'll probably never get to see him. I can imagine how he feels. Those first few nights on ambush I thought I'd go crazy. I sure hate to see anyone come over here.

I heard there were over 350 men killed last week over here. It makes me so damn mad, words can't express it! I wished to hell every one of those high-filluting government men would come over to this hell-hole one day. They're the ones who ought to be killed. These guys over here have a full life ahead of them. I don't know how I'm going to stand it being around some people back home.

Have you called that Tilley woman yet? I'm still sick over that. He was such a good guy and had to die for no fucking reason at all.

How's everything at home? I looked at the family picture the other day. It's terrible to be separated. You should be getting a whole box of film. Well, there's not much news.

How's that new car? I'm looking forward to a picture of it. Like I say, I'll bet Dad fits in that real well. (ha ha) Will it peel rubber? I'd sure like to tear the guts out of it. Remember what I said about the Chrysler. (ha ha)

With love, Stan

P.S. Don't send any more Kool-aid! Hey, Mom, guess what? They just brought in the mail. Cookies, too, now! (real fresh) not broken either. Thanks a lot! I got both cans.

In 1969, the news media reminded us daily that we were in a desperate situation as a nation. Many, under the age of 30, were suspicious of anything the older generation said or did. We thought of ourselves as the enlightened generation and only we knew what was best for the country. That was especially true on college campuses. When I was with college friends or classmates I did not talk about my brother, the soldier. I knew I would be judged as unenlightened, and he with disgust. I only knew that I wanted Stan to make it home safely. I took one day at a time, sighing with relief, that he had lived to see another day.

It did, and does, trouble me that leaders in our government, who send young men into combat, do so without the input of its citizens. Presidents and congressmen would do well to spend a week at the front, in the field, and get a taste of what they send the troops to do. Our leaders might think better of their decisions if this were a requirement before taking office.

As the death toll reached two thousand in Iraq in October of 2005, I heard the same words of anger and discouragement as our nation tries to cope with another war. Those of us, who remember Vietnam, worry that this war may drag on with fruitless results.

My prayers go out to those families that are reading letters and e-mails from their sons and daughters, holding on to the hope that they will return safely. My heart aches for those parents and wives who open the door to the messenger who delivers the news of their fallen soldier.

June 28, 1969

Dear Mom and Dad,

I suppose you're worried because I've not written, but believe me it's not my fault. We came out in this jungle ten days ago and haven't got to go back in yet. They say we'll be out here for ten more days. I don't know if I can stand ten more days out here. The only people we see are the ones that bring our supplies in by helicopter. Eighty-five percent of this jungle a person's got to cut through. Me and this other guy are still point men. We take turns cutting through; it sure wears a guy down.

They keep saying we'll go in the fire base camp, but we keep making contact with the NVA and they won't let us go in until things calm down out here. I wished I could kill all these damn NVA. It's hell just waiting around until they hit, and they hit hard when they hit. (Believe me.)

You asked about me wanting a job in the rear. I'd give anything to have a job in the rear. A person thinks he'll lose his mind out here. Right now I'm sitting in a foxhole with three other guys. I'll just have to take some pictures when we finally get out for a little rest. My whiskers are an inch long. (ha ha) We really look terrible. My shirt is almost rotted off. Like I say, you can't imagine it. Well, I'd better close. Some other guys want to get a line off. I'll write the next time I get a chance. Don't worry!

With love, Stan

P.S. I got a letter from Robert Rhodes, the one from Albany, Georgia. He's home. He was on Hamburger Hill and got all messed up. He said he tried to call at home, but didn't get an answer. But at least he's out of this hell hole.

Fire Base Marge. Photo by Jayson Dale.

When I spoke with Robert on July 25, 2005, he recalled his ordeal on "Hamburger Hill," In a soft southern drawl he explained how he was wounded (ironically on my brother's birthday) May 13, 1969. Robert was on that hill from May 7ᵗʰ though the 13ᵗʰ, where he sustained six wounds. After being injured so many times, he was air-lifted to safety and medical attention. Robert recalled being placed on top of dead soldiers already in the helicopter, to be airlifted to the nearest hospital. He remembered his wish at that moment, "I prayed, 'Dear God, if I'm going to die, let me die at home, not here.'"

Robert explained that it has taken a long time to heal emotionally from the war and his injuries, and that he suffered from PTS (Post Traumatic Stress Disorder) for years before he sought help. He, like many other vets was haunted by dreams, dreams of blood, men screaming, the same dream over and over. Many things that happened during his tour he has blocked out. Watching movies or documentaries about the war was equally difficult for him until recently. His comment to me was, "The day you called, and since, have been a big help to me in finding myself and what I have hid for years." *Robert went on to say,* "My main objective, when I got out of the service, was to put everything out of my mind, to move on. But it remained there and continued to bother me. I do remain proud of my service as an Airborne Soldier who was lucky enough to serve with the Long Range Patrol (known as the Lurps) in Vietnam. We saw a lot of action. They were the best I served with!"

Robert was sent back to the States for rehab, where he spent four months at Walter Reed Hospital. He worked as a heavy equipment operator for thirty years at a marine base near his home. Robert now owns his own landscaping business.

He stated in an e-mail about his service, "We were taught in our training that not many of us would come home. And the ones who did would be wounded or disabled with wounds for life. But Stan and I, we were young, strong, and believed in the United States of America, and felt like it was a just cause for our time to defend the country with pride as our forefathers had. I find a lot of times, if I get on my Harley and ride for a long way, I can make myself feel that what we fought and died for was for some good, somehow. Maybe it was good just for making America appreciate its heroes more, like your brother. But I also know this did not stop the pain for you and your family."

Robert has a daughter who lives in Texas, and two granddaughters, ages seven and eight. The death of his wife, Carolyn, his high school sweetheart, to cancer in 2000, was difficult. She was a great source of strength and comfort throughout their marriage. He recalled a visit to the Wall in Washington, DC, "I visited the Wall one time, and I had thought of leaving my Purple Heart and my Bronze Star for Stan. I was so emotional at the time my wife had to lead me away, and we sat down on the grass. She was so wonderful for me and to me. I was so fortunate to have been able to share 33 years with her."

Robert's name not only came up often in Stan's letters, but he was in films that Stan had taken in Basic Training at Ft. Polk, Louisiana. Our family had always wondered what had become of the handsome young soldier who played his guitar and cut up for the camera with my brother. I promised to send Robert a copy of the DVD made from the original tapes. Communicating by phone and e-mailing with Robert has been a healing experience for both of us.

We discussed the war in Iraq and the similarities to Vietnam. He expressed great sympathy and compassion for the troops serving in Iraq and empathizes with their families.

Early days in Nam, Robert Rhodes left, and Stan
enjoying a drink at the EM Club.

Medivac helicopter.

Jayson Dale, Stan's good friend.

Jayson Dale and Stan looking more fit, May, 1969,
southwest of Saigon, rice paddies location.

Reflections
By
Jayson "J" Dale
199ᵗʰ ²/3, Charlie Company

I first met Stan at Redcatcher in April, 1969. This was the training camp for new arrivals. We were restricted to the area. Stan and I left for the EM club. Had a great time and, yes, we were caught coming back. The First SGT. said we should be a little quieter, but not in those exact words. Our punishment was extra PT.

Stan and I were assigned to Charlie Company 3ʳᵈ Platoon. We served together from Redcatcher through the Mekong Delta to the jungles and around Saigon. He was a friend who became my brother. People speak of Duty, Honor, and Country. Stan was all of that and more. He believed it was his duty to be in "the Nam" and do the best that he could. I always knew he would be there for me. The word Duty personifies Stan.

> Duty is the sublimest
> Word in the language.
> You can never do more
> Than your duty.
> You should never wish
> To do less.

Robert E. Lee

April through part of June we were south and west of Saigon in the paddies. Being the two new guys, we rotated "walking point." We knew if one of us tripped something, both of us would be hit, always hoping it would be a Chicom grenade and not a 105 round or "Bouncing Betty." Since we were new guys we were also the outcasts. We were not expected to make it. This changed over time, but it also brought us closer.

June of 1969 we moved north to the jungle and worked out of Black Horse and a village named Cam Tam. In July came "Butterfly Hill." The carnage was incredible, especially with all those butterflies flying around during the fighting. Stan said, "I don't care if I never see another butterfly." To this day I am startled whenever I see one. That day we also witnessed and were part of American troops not caring about themselves, but only their brothers.

Stan and I talked after the battle. If we were hit badly, we hoped it wouldn't hurt for long. The biggest concern was our families. How they would take it. We both came from families with Midwest values. Our fathers taught us how to be men and our mothers spoiled us. We both had brothers younger than us. He had two sisters and I three. Stan was born on May 13th and I have a brother born on that same day. Stan and I humped the boonies, slept, ate, cried and laughed together. We shared letters and care packages from home, dreamed of visiting each other homes, and talked about what our mothers would cook for us.

Stan lived by "I am Third," God, you, then me. He was a Christian and was not afraid to show it. We prayed together many times. He put everyone ahead of himself. In August we were both made "Acting Jacks" (Sgt.) Naturally his men came first.

We were fortunate to have learned from leaders like, Sgt. Melvin Ploeger, Captain James McGinnis, Lt. Norm Sassner, Lt. Arrol Stewart and Lt.Tom Fallon, and Sgt. Greg Breeckner. Sergeant Frank Leone and many more were offered battlefield commissions (which they declined).

We called Sergeant Ploeger, Top. They got his title right! I remember when Stan and I were trading off walking point, somewhere in the paddies. The day before, one of our other platoons tripped a 105-round (artillery) in an AO (Area Operation). It blew the hell out of three guys! Needless to say, Stan and I were a little shaky.

Well, that day we heard on the horn (radio) that two guys were needed back at the road. It was about one-fourth to one-half mile away. Guess who had to go? The two new guys, Stan and I. It took Stan and I about an hour to get there. Well, Top is with three or four clerks (typists) and maybe a cook. You could tell they were scared to death. He had brought us "Hot Chow". He walked point with Stan and me, behind him, and the clerk's way behind all of us. It took about 15 minutes with him leading to get the food to the platoon. He didn't have to do that, but did. His "grunts" always came first. I learned more about leadership and how to treat people from him and Capt. McGinnis than I ever did out of any psychology book in college. You lead by example, and you don't ask anyone to do something you wouldn't do yourself—very simple.

We won every battle, but in the end, Vietnam was taken by the North. Was it worth it? I believe it contributed to the fall of communism years later, but it cost us a very high price. This country lost many men like Stan. The ones that returned lost their youth. We would never look at the world the same way again.

Until Desert Storm, I was always bitter about losing a brother like Stan. As I watched Desert Storm take place, I realized the reason we were taking so few causalities was these troops were led by Vietnam veterans. The country may not have learned, but we (the veterans) did. When I think of Stan, which is almost every day, I remember his grin and laugh, but above all, his love for his family.

I leave you with this thought, "I am not afraid of tomorrow, for I have seen yesterday and I love today." I just wish I could share today with Stan.

"Old Guard Sir"
Jayson Dale

July 1, 1969
Dear Mom and Dad,

Well, we finally got to come in to the fire base camp for about two days. We were out in that damn jungle 14 days. I tried to get a camera to take some pictures of us when we came in, but they don't allow us to have cameras up here. But believe me, we were a sight! My clothes were torn, so muddy they weren't even green anymore. I'll say one thing, it was an adventurous 14 days.

We really made the news. We discovered a NVA Base Camp on hill 335. This means we were 335 feet above sea level. Anyway, it was really something. You wouldn't believe the way the camp was. I've got to hand it to them for having nothing to work with but the land. They can really work wonders. Most of it consisted underground. They had kitchens, beds, and tables made of bamboo. Like I say, it was really something. We even got a body count, four gooks. But even if they are our enemy, I still don't like killing people.

The way it all started was, we were sweeping this path of jungle when all of a sudden we got ambushed. We were real lucky. Just one guy hit while we were in contact. But nothing serious, he got hit in the cheek. Went in one cheek and out the other. (Real lucky!) Anyway after it was all over we figured they would head for the nearest hill. We were right! The next morning we headed for the hill. I have to admit it was scary! Sometimes I really get the shakes. We even discovered a printing press, which they use to write up fake ID cards. Like I say, it was really something. One thing sure, time really flies out there. But a person never has time to do anything. We're always on the move.

We are headed for war zone D when we go out again. I guess the 1st Cav. is up there. So we'll probably be working around them. Boy, I sure wish the rain would stop. A person can almost count on a rain between three and five o' clock, and living out in it can really get miserable. It seems like I'm always wet.

Well, here it is a half an hour later. I just went to protestant services. I guess it won't do any harm will it, Mom? (ha ha) Yes, I want a picture of that car. Hey, speaking of cars, you know that old women with the Caprice Chevy across from the diner? If she ever sells it, I'd like a chance at it. Why don't you stop and tell her sometime to let you know if she ever does decide to sell it.

Tell Eileen thanks for writing. If you see Paul again, thank him for the peanuts. They were outstanding. This is about the only letter I'm going to have time to write. We move out again in the morning. It seems I never have time off.

I'm sure glad you like the Bible! There's not supposed to be one any better. It's the most complete, and best, and that's just what you deserve! Everyone here says I get bigger letters from my Mom than anyone ever saw. I just smile and say, I've got folks that don't forget.

About Warren's land he bought, I knew about it when he bought it. He just never wanted me to tell Dad, because he figured he'd laugh. (ha ha)

Well, I can't think of much more at the moment. All your cookies got here in fine shape. Thanks!

Your letters take about four or five days. Well, I hope this makes up a little for not being able to write sooner. Like I say, I can't help it! I know you must worry. But I'm all right.

With love, Stan

In a jungle clearing, Jayson Dale (right) and Stan,
wait with their squad, for a supply bird.

P.S. No sense to keep spending money or stuff to send to me. I'll
tell you when I need anything, because out in the field I don't need
anything. And I know postage is higher than hell. I can hardly believe
Dad's fishing so much! I've sent a $110.00 money order and a $180.00
money order home. Please tell me when you get it. Mom, when you
want to ask me an important question just put them at the end of
the letter, that way I'll know where to look to see the question. Hi
Phillip…Tell Eileen to wait until I get home before she gets married.
I'd like to go to her wedding. (ha ha)

    With love, Stan

*In Lanning's June 26th entry from <u>The Only War We Had,</u> he makes
reference to the soldier Stan refers to as being hit in the cheek,* "Sassner
guided each platoon into sector. Little's platoon was the last to return,
his medic half-carrying a rifleman who had taken a round through the
lower face. Apparently the soldier had his mouth open when the bullet
entered. Its exit took out some teeth and part of the jaw and cheek."

One of Stan's friends, Steve Klaus, a sniper with the 25ᵗʰ Infantry Division, explained to me how the "shakes" that Stan talked about could be paralyzing at times. Steve said, "I would get the shakes if I had time to think about an upcoming mission or one that I had been on. Fear was always worst when there was time to think about it."

Our Uncle Paul, Dad's older brother, sent Stan the peanuts. Paul was a colorful character to say the least. He was a WWII veteran, rough around the edges and intimidating. I never cared for him as a child; he frightened me. Kids seem to sense things that adults miss. He was full of war stories from his own experiences and had an opinion on everything from religion to why women were put on the earth to serve men.

Paul and my Aunt Geraldine, Dad's youngest sister, would accompany my sister and me to meet our brother's body which had been flown into the Moline / Quad Cities Airport. My parents were too distraught to go; it was one of the longest car rides of my life. My sister and I sat quietly in the back seat, not speaking, staring out the windows, occupying our minds by biting our fingernails or playing with the buttons on our coats.

(*Written on small note pad*)
July, between the 4ᵗʰ and the 10ᵗʰ, 1969
Dear Mom and Dad,

I don't have too much time to write. The supply chopper is coming in, in a little while, so I'll try to get a few words in. This makes the fifth day out here. We should be going in, in about five more. (I hope.) This jungle is so damn thick a man walks in it for days and never knows where he's at.

We've been working with a Hunter Killer team; we have dogs and everything, German Sheppard's. They sure hate the VC. (ha ha) But it really gets hairy at times. I've never seen the like, if we don't run into trouble, we go looking for it.

We had quite a fight the 4ᵗʰ of July. We lost nine men. You surely heard about it on TV. But we cleaned house on the NVA, approximately 35 dead. But they were costly. I'll never understand this war. It sure gets me. Well, enough of that. Nobody wants to hear the bad.

I received both letters and pictures the same day. And, Mom, you're the greatest! I don't know what I'd do if it wasn't for those letters. Everyone says they don't know how you do it. Everyday I just tell them, I've got #1 folks. (ha ha)

The pictures were real good, in fine shape. They bring tears to my eyes. Don't think they do me harm, because it really helps out. I look at them ten times a day. No matter how much of a man they say we are, I'm still a kid at heart. I never want to grow up.

What really got me was little Phillip. I miss him so much. I can't ever write about him without almost crying. It's hell being so far away, but time will pass. Just as long as I make it out of here alive, that's all I care.

Robert Rhodes, the one you asked about, is home. He got hit pretty bad over here. He said he tried to call the house but no one answered. Well, here comes the bird from somewhere in the jungle.

Love, Stan

Hunter Killer Team at BMB prior to mission, led by
Greg Breeckner. Front, (left to right) Tom Phillips,
Greg Breeckner, Nelson "Baltimore" Berryman, Back,
Tim "Obie" Oberst, Elden Rasmussen, Jayson Dale.
Photo by Greg Breeckner.

Eileen, Little Phill, and Mom salute for Stan in one of
the many pictures Mom sent to keep his morale up.

This letter was emotional for me to read, not only for the content, but because it was written on a small note pad 3x5 inches with the red mud of Vietnam smudged over it.

The fight that Stan was writing about took place on what GIs called Butterfly Hill. Two of Stan's friends, Jayson Dale and Tim (Obie) Oberst recalled Butterfly Hill with mystic reverence. It was a horrible place to be, but at the same time, beautiful with the butterflies hovering around them. Tim recalled, "It was hell. We were pinned down, bullets whizzing over our heads and all around us."

Michael Lanning describes that day's fighting and the butterflies in his journal and book, <u>The Only War We Had: A Platoon Leader's Journal Of Vietnam</u>*. His July 3rd entry reads,* "As I look back, two other things seem locked in my mind. The first is the large swarm of yellow, purple, and black butterflies that had stayed around us all that day, oblivious to the fight."

He (Lanning) also wrote of that day, "Crawling quickly over the downed trees, we reached the bodies of the Delta dead. The nine were in an area the size of a small room. They were so close that some lay on top of others. Off to the side was the RTO's blasted body. His radio was at his side. We lay among the dead as we continued to pour fire into the bunkers we could now see just ahead. We paused long enough to confirm we had found all nine bodies and to set the safeties on the dead men's weapons so that our crawling over them would not accidentally discharge a round. It soon became obvious why the enemy had fought so hard. Weapons, food, medicine and supplies of all types were being found and brought to the center of the perimeter."

Although Mom was hesitant to say too much about the fun times at home, Stan, like other GIs, loved hearing about the family and the "world". It gave him something to look forward to, knowing that there was some degree of normalcy somewhere, especially after a day like the one he'd just had.

Stan and Tim Oberst enjoying a beer while in the
Delta region.

July 10, 1969
Dear Mom and Dad,

Well, they finally let us come in for two days. We go back out the 12th. They don't let us sit around long.

How's everything at home? I'll bet the weather is fabulous isn't it?

I guess I'm telling you too much, aren't I, Mom? The way your last letter sounded, you're going to end up making yourself sick worrying too much. Like you said, "There's nothing you can do," So don't worry, I'm making it all right. I realize sometimes I write too much of the bad. I know nobody wants to hear that. But in the Infantry, nothing happens that isn't bad news, either someone gets killed or hurt. That's all a person ever sees. Believe me, it's hard to write a letter of good news.

I saw a helicopter crash yesterday and had to help cut away the jungle to pull them out of the mess. It was some sight. I just hate it when I've got to help bring in the wounded or dead. It just kills me! But a person has to not let it bother him.

When I think of you back in the world (the States), everyone friendly, no one trying to kill you, or the constant worry of getting it next, it's almost hard to believe anymore that there is such a wonderful land. The funny part of it is that 80% of the people over here don't even pack a weapon or even see the action. I won't know how to act, when I get home, and won't have to carry a weapon. (ha ha) I sleep with it, eat with it, and carry it everywhere I go. I'd feel naked without it.

I got a letter from Donnie Crowl, the lucky shit! That's the best job the Army got—flying choppers. Some get shot down, but there's thousands over here. And all they do is fly around. It was a real treat when I first got over here to ride in them. But the only time we do ride in them is when there's trouble some place. So I'd just as leave stay out of them.

Well, guess what? I got awarded my CIB badge today. Big deal! (ha ha) But one sure thing, no one can wear it unless they've been in the Infantry and been in a fire fight and mortar fire. I'll send my paper home. Don't throw it away.

I had a notion to tell them to keep their badge and awards. I don't want to see any more field action. (But I didn't say it.) Well, like you say, "another day". Boy, I really get homesick at times.

I got a letter from Bob. I guess he's just got five months left, but he's coming back again for six more. I sure can't see that.

You asked about my feet. I've been to the doctor three times since I've been out of the hospital. I've faced the fact that they will never be better until I get out of this messed up place. Everyone's feet is bad, but some worse than others. Sometimes I never take my shoes off for two weeks at a time. I've just got to send a picture home sometime of us when we come in from the field. I'll bet you won't even recognize me. (ha ha)

I haven't received the package with the ham yet. I suppose it's tied up somewhere. Tell Eileen thanks for the letters. If I ever find an extra minute I'll write her. I've never seen such a hassle all the time. Whenever we do get to come in, they make us get new ammunition and everything else just to take up our time.

Hey, Dad, guess you had quite a birthday. Don't even remember much of it do you? (ha ha) But try to get your strength back before I get home and celebrate my 21st birthday, and get out of this hell hole, then we'll both lie on the porch. (ha ha ha) I'll get 45 days leave when I get home. That will take in my birthday. What a day that will be!

I really like the car. It's better looking than I had figured. Have you opened it up yet? Unlock the air conditioner and it will probably go 150 MPH. (ha ha)

Hey, Mom, have you received my two money orders yet? One was $110.00 and one was $180.00. I've kinda worried about it getting there. Please don't forget to tell me.

Well, I can't think of much more to write. But I'll try to catch up a little on writing when I do have time. Well, I guess I'll close for now. Keep up the good work writing, and try not to worry.

With love, Stan

Don Crowl, one of Stan's friends from home, beside
the helicopter he was trained to fly.

When I read letters like this one, I thought of how Stan explained the horrors he witnessed during his days in Vietnam, like he was talking about taking out the trash. We at home could only imagine the hell he was going through. Tim O'Brien wrote in his book, The Things They Carried, how soldiers generalized what was happening to them,

"How do you generalize? War is hell, but that's not the half of it, because war is also a mystery and terror and adventure and courage and discovery and holiness and pity and despair and longing and love. War is nasty; war is fun. War is thrilling; war is drudgery. War makes you a man; war makes you dead."

The awarding of the CIB badge is one of the most treasured of medals presented to a soldier. It means he earned the respect and dedication of his men for his courage and valor during a fight. Most of the vets I talked to said they valued the CIB above all other medals. It meant they had been through the "fire" and survived!

Michael Lanning writes in his July 1, 1969 entry of his first journal, The Only War We Had, "CIBs were awarded somewhat loosely in Vietnam. Many an Infantryman wearing the badge, especially senior officers, saw little combat. Personally, I felt on that day at Black Horse the same way I feel now; I have received no higher award or honor than the rifle and wreath of the CIB."

Vietnam veteran and former English teacher, Ches Schneider, writes in his book, From Classrooms To Claymores: A Teacher At War In Vietnam, "I was the most proud of the Combat Infantryman's Badge, because it told the world that I had humped and fought."

Stan continued to suffer from immersion foot. I can only imagine how painful it was. He, along with his buddies, managed to go on despite the condition.

Our dad seldom drank to excess. He usually had a few cold ones during hay bailing or a little whiskey once in a while with friends. A whiskey bottle would sit under the kitchen sink for months before it was empty. Mom would make us an occasional "hot toddy" when we were sick. Dad probably drank too much on his birthday to help him forget about his son so far away and in such danger. Knowing Mom, she didn't feel a lot of compassion for him, leaving him on the porch to sleep it off.

He tried not to frighten us with details, but we knew the peril he faced, and the bullets he's dodged again to live another day. Mom and Dad lived one day at a time, letter to letter in the summer of 69.

July 14, 1969
Dear Mom and Dad,

Well, how's everything at home? Got less than nine months left. Beats twelve all to hell!

Well, we've been out for three days now. We've set up a perimeter around a village. There are over 500 Infantrymen around it. Now there's a company sweeping through the village checking for NVA, while we set outside so none can slip through. It's not too bad. Beats humping the whole day long, and after that 4th of July deal! It's sorta nice to sit and take it easy. That really shook me up! A person could fight these people for 40 years and never get it over with. The jungle is so thick they can hide forever. You talk about it getting dark at home when the moon isn't out. You should be in the jungle. It gets so dark a person can't see his hand no matter how close it is. I've had to touch it with my tongue sometimes to make sure it was there. That's the scariest time of all, at night. Every sound you hear, you don't know if it's some kind of animal or the NVA. We haven't had any trouble since the 4th. Thank God for that!

Hey, Mom, you remember that night you said you couldn't sleep? Well, I asked our sergeant if he remembered what we done that night, and he said we got hit, and then I remembered. (It was quite a night!) You moms are really something! This best buddy of mine, Jayson Dale from Seattle, Washington, his mom reminds me a lot of you. Me and him have been through everything together. Matter of fact, he's sitting on the other side of our nice made foxhole fixing up some coffee for us. (ha ha) I wished you could see us. If they told me back in the States I'd be living like this and eating out of a can all the time, I think I'd have went to Canada.

It's a good thing you're storing away a lot out of the garden, because if I catch you opening a can of food, I'll scream! (ha ha) And lay on white sheets again. (It will be heaven!) Well, that's enough dreaming.

Hey, would you please send me another radio? That one you sent didn't last for shit! I wished I'd have saved the guarantee, because it just wasn't right. Get one about the same size as the one you sent, OK! Now pay for it out of my money. No sense in you buying it.

I got a letter and pictures from Karen today. I'll send you the pictures, because the only place I can keep something dry is in my helmet.

Well, I guess that's about all for now, the supply bird will be in pretty quick, and I'll get this letter on the way.

With love, Stan

P.S. Send me Steve's and Bob's addresses. I lost them, and don't worry about me.

Stan's good friend Jayson Dale and Elden Rasmussen
fishing with grenades. Photo by Jayson Dale.

The absolute darkness of the jungle was something that all GIs talked about who were in the field and in the jungle. In Tim O'Brien's book, The Things They Carried, one of his characters explains how it was, "They'd sleep away the daylight hours, or try to sleep, then at dusk they'd put on their gear and move out single file into the dark. Always a heavy cloud cover. No moon and no stars. It was the purest black you could imagine... the kind of clock-stopping black that God must've had in mind when he sat down to invent blackness. It made your eyeballs ache. You'd shake your head and blink, except you couldn't even tell you were blinking, the blackness didn't change. So pretty soon you'd get jumpy. Your nerves would go. You'd start to worry about getting cut off from the rest of the unit—alone, you'd think—and then the real panic would bang in and you'd reach out and try to touch the guy in front of you, groping for his shirt, hoping to Christ he was still there. It made for some bad dreams."

I sent Jayson Dale a copy of this letter after I had contacted him in March, 2005, along with a picture that Stan had taken of him. Jayson and Stan had shared a lot together as the letter states. Getting in contact with Jayson after so long, was helpful in putting some of the puzzle pieces together about Stan's time in Vietnam and of the circumstances that lead to his death.

In my many phone conversations with Jayson he talked about the things that stayed with him after the war. He explained what it was like on Butterfly Hill. In a strange and surreal way, it was beautiful as the butterflies floated above them, and the fighting raged on all around. The imagery of nature's beauty against the backdrop of war was hard to imagine. He said he still thinks of it when he sees a butterfly; it startles him.

When Jayson spoke to me about his experiences in Vietnam, he explained how his son, at the age of five, wanted to go camping. Jayson had no interest in camping, it would only bring unpleasant memories of his time in the wet rice paddies and dark steaming jungles of Vietnam, where camping out under the star was anything but pleasant. He did eventually take his son camping and he learned to enjoy it again.

Jayson returned home in April of 1970. He lives with his wife, Linda, in Washington State and has retired from the Postal Service as Postmaster.

July 17, 1969

Dear Mom and Dad,

Well, another day in VN. How's everything at home? Things haven't been too bad over here. I hardly believe the fighting is slowing down over here. It just runs in spells. A person might not make contact for a month then all of a sudden the little bastards will hit everyday for a week at a time. A person never knows. I'll be so glad to say, "That's my last fire fight." What's this about Steve getting a job on a chopper? I sure hope he did. That's a good job, and most of all, you're out of the field. I get so tired of sleeping on the ground.

Now for the questions you asked. Those kids in the film were at a town called Claudette. It's a fire base camp where they let us come in for one or two days rest out 15 or so. But that was down south in the rice paddies, and that picture of me stirring something, that's right (It's shit)! I've had to burn shit more than once. (ha ha)

Yes, I've received my pictures, they're in my helmet. I look at them almost every day. Yes, I wrote Burkey just for the hell of it. She still loves me. (ha ha) The letter was so mushy, I had to laugh. Cheryl writes about once a week. I write her about every month, to make sure I keep in touch. She'll be a lot of fun when I get home.

Well, that's all the questions I can think of to answer for now. Why don't you tell me if you received my two money orders? I've sorta worried about them. One was for $110 and the other $180.

So it's sorta wet at home? You don't know what rain is. (ha ha) You can almost set your clock by the rain over here. It's terrible at times, wet every night. We've been setting up ambushes at night in these rubber plantations. It gets wet and darker than you can believe. One nice thing about up north here, you don't have to worry too much about booby traps.

Hey, Mom, you wouldn't believe what we done the other day. We ran across a corn field. My eyes got as big as silver dollars! It really made me home sick. Anyway, I picked about ten ears and carried them in my pack until we started setting up our ambush. I got some water in my steel pot from a nearby stream and boiled the corn, took some grease from inside a can of C-rations and had corn on the cob! Tell me that isn't living off the land! (ha ha)

Yes, all the Italians are still with me. We really get to going at times. They really like their booze. (ha ha) Well, I hope the rain don't bother your crops too much.

Well, I can't think of much more for now. I'll write next chance I get. Bye for now, and tell everyone hello.

With love, Stan

P.S. I found out for sure how much time difference between here and Iowa. We're 11 hours ahead of you. If it's 6 a.m. here it's 5 p.m. at home.

Stan took his turn at burning human waste from the
latrines. He had a smile for the
camera in spite of his task.

Vietnamese mother and children near FB Claudette.

When we were kids we always looked forward to that time of year when the sweet corn would be ready and we could stuff ourselves with the juicy ears dripping with butter. I had to think of those times when I read how Stan had made a meal on corn in a Vietnam field. The Iowa farm boy was right at home fixing the corn they happened on.

The steel pots (or helmets) as GIs referred to them, had many utilitarian features in the field. As Stan mentioned, he could keep his pictures dry in his helmet, used it as a stool, boiled water in it, and it served as a wash basin.

Lanning writes in The Only War We Had, *August 18, 1969 entry,* "We all hated the damn steel pots. Heavy, hot, and uncomfortable, mine was the first thing I took off every opportunity I had…We used the helmets for much more than protection. We sat on them and carried our cigarettes in the webbing at the top of the inside liner—the only place we could keep them dry. The elastic bands securing the pot's camouflage covers served as convenient holders for P-38's, insect repellent, and crosses. Peace signs adorned some of the helmets. They were not statements of protest against the war but rather expression of desire for a real peace that only soldiers can appreciate."

Robert Gouge gives more examples of the utilitarian uses for the steel pot, "The helmet shell was enclosed in a camouflage cloth-cover, and on the outside, an elastic band was used to secure such things as a plastic bottle of insect repellent, cigarettes, LSA gun lube, matches, casualty cards, or anything else the soldier wanted to keep dry or readily accessible." Helmets became graffiti boards for the GIs that displayed such statements as, 'Re-up and Throw-up,' 'War Is Hell but actual combat is a Motherf---er,' 'Don't shoot. I'm short,' 'When I die bury me face down so the world can kiss my ass,' 'LBJ's hired killers,' 'Home is where you dig it,' 'When I kill the only thing I feel is recoil,' 'When I die I will go to heaven because I've spent my time in hell.'"

The picture of Stan holding a long stick, stirring something in a large barrel, puzzled me for a long time. I couldn't figure out what he was doing. Then I read the previous letter and it made sense. He was stirring human excrement doused with diesel fuel. It wasn't one of the most pleasant tasks, but everyone had a turn at it. Stan was far from squeamish. When we were very young we had an "outhouse" as many farm families did. Stan often helped empty the manure loader from the barn lots and livestock pens. We weren't required, however, to dabble in our own.

Lanning writes of this dreaded duty in a June 11, 1969 journal entry in The Only War We Had, *"In a fire base containing well over one hundred men, human waste disposal was a constant problem. The solution was small wooden latrines, platforms built over 55-gallon drums cut in half. When containers were nearly full, diesel fuel was added and set aflame. The smell of the burning shit dominated the air of the fire base. Shit-burning detail was a great threat to even the most malingering soldier."*

Steve's job with the choppers turned out to be a short lived assignment, as he was eventually picked to be trained as a sniper.

July 22, 1969
Dear Karen,

Sure glad to hear from you. I'm sorry I don't write anymore than I do, but I hardly get time to write my folks. It seems like we're on the move all the time. We haven't been having too much trouble with the VC lately. But you never know when the little bastards will start again. But I'm making it as good as possible. A person can't ask for more than that.

Too bad about the trouble you're having with the colleges. It must be disgusting to not know where you're going next.

Thanks for the pictures. They were really good. I sent them home to Mom. Well, I can't think of much more, Karen. Nothing seems to be worth writing about over here. But thanks again for writing, and I'll try to do better than I have.

With love, Stan

When I wrote to Stan it was hard to know what to say. I didn't want to dwell on things that were unpleasant, yet I was afraid to talk about the good times too! I didn't want him to feel more miserable than he already was. I felt guilty for enjoying the simplest things.

He was sleeping on the ground, often in the mud. I had a comfortable bed and white sheets. I had someone to lie with, to comfort me, to dream with, to make future plans with. I had warm, nutritious meals; he was eating C-rations and drinking fowl tasting water mixed with Kool-Aid. I was enjoying my youth, dancing, making love, wearing clean clothes; he was trying to survive another day, living in rotting fatigues, and dreaming of the day he could hold a girl in his arms again. I could call my family, hear their voices; Stan waited for mail call, when a letter might come. I wanted to be optimistic, but when I watched the news, I felt cold and uneasy. Would someone call me today or tomorrow to say that Stan had been killed?

Robert Gouge writes about the importance of mail to a GI, "Perhaps the most important aspect and highlight of every soldier's day in Vietnam was to receive mail or care packages from home. The day would be judged good or bad depending on whether you received any letters or not."

After reading this letter, I felt guilty. Stan was apologizing to me for not writing. I should have been the one apologizing, instead of complaining about getting a late start on school that fall. Oh…the mind of the young, how fickle and self-centered it is!

July 22, 1969
Dear Mom and Dad,

Well, I finally got some good news. (I'm in the hospital again.) Now don't get all excited! It's just a bad case of the flu. They thought it was malaria but it turned out to just be the flu. Man, I'm lying here in an air-conditioned room watching television. I even got to watch the space walk, and believe it or not, I slept between white sheets last night. (ha ha) I'll have to admit I was sick for awhile, temperature was 104. But it's almost normal again.

The only way to get a break over here is to get sick. I'll probably be here two to three more days. So by the time you get this letter I'll be back beating the bush!

Hey, Mom, you said you talked to a guy who was in heavy equipment over here, and that he really had it rough. Well, maybe he did, but just don't believe everything you hear. All I know is that I've been around almost all kinds of people with all kinds of jobs over here. I've yet to find one that gets half the action and shit on, the way the Infantry does. Sure everyone has their war stories, but believe me, a man who has seen the shit fly doesn't want to talk about it!

Just like the artillery, they set back in a fire support base and we go out in the damn jungle and hump maybe three to five miles in an afternoon. Then we come back to the fire support base, all tired and dirty, and then they bring out hot meals to the artillery, and what do we get....C-rations. Tell me that isn't hard to take. Well, enough of that!

I guess it's a little wet at home. I can imagine how you feel, Dad. That's really too bad about Ralph. It seems if they can land a man on the moon, they could find something to get rid of cancer. Cancer is a damn shame. But to see young boys killed I believe is worse! I've felt so bad at times, I wanted to scream! Because in every fire fight, when someone calls "Medic" a million things go through your mind.

Things have been pretty calm lately. We ran into six VC about a week ago, by surprise. They were smarter than most damn gooks. They surrendered! Me and two other kids had to guard them until a helicopter came and got them. The captain said, "Shoot them if they move wrong!" I had my rifle on full automatic. I almost prayed for one of them to move, so I could pump about twenty rounds in him! You think that sounds cruel, but after you see a few boys cut down, it kinda turns a person.

Well, I can't think of too much more. It's sure nice to hear the rain on the roof instead of lying out in it.

Hey, Mom, ask Mary Kay if she ever received a get well card. I sent one almost ten days ago. But all I put on the envelope was Mrs. Allen Gerick, RR Wayland, Iowa, so I don't know if that was enough.

Well, bye for now. I think I'll go eat some ice cream. (ha ha)

Love, Stan

Huey Medivac lifting injured, what was known as
"dust off."

Tim O'Brien writes in The Things They Carried, *"Men killed, and died, because they were embarrassed not to. It was what had brought them to the war in the first place, nothing positive, no dreams of glory or honor, just to avoid the blush of dishonor...They crawled into tunnels and walked point and advanced under fire. Each morning, despite the unknowns, they made their legs move. They endured. They kept humping."*

It sounds terrible, but we were all glad when we heard Stan was in the hospital, at least he wasn't in the field being shot at.

Mary Kay Gerick was a dear friend of my mother's. They shared many days visiting, baking, and gardening. They were a great support for each other, sharing of their summer produce and advice on child rearing. They were hard working farm wives that made fun out of their rural lives by caring for and supporting each other. They are still friends, but due to their age, they don't get to see each other as often as they'd like.

I remember watching the space walk in our trailer in York, Nebraska, thinking about Stan viewing it a world away. He was so excited about seeing such an event. Those of us who grew up in the 60s felt a certain pride in getting a man to the moon. It was a challenge handed down by President Kennedy to our generation. I think we all felt part of it somehow.

Reading of being ready to "pump rounds" into his captors was pretty unsettling for me when I first read his words, but then I had never been in a life-and-death situation as he was. How small and safe my world was.

July 23, 1969
Dear Mom and Dad,

Well, here it is 10:30 a.m. so I thought it was about time to crawl out of bed and write you a few lines. A person just can't beat this hospital life! Only bad part about it is that they take blood from me about four times a day to make sure there are no signs of malaria. It seems like I feel just fine in the daytime, but then at night my temperature goes to about 102-104 degrees. So they say I'll stay here until it completely goes away. I hope it stays that way for six months. (ha ha)

Well, I can't think of much more. Like I say, don't worry. I'm safer than I've ever been. I don't even have to sleep with my rifle. I suppose Warren is on his vacation now isn't he? Did Bill go along? Have you sent my radio yet? They're really a lot of company over here. Well, pretty soon it will be August, another month marked off.

Well, tell Dad I hope it dries a little for him. Bye for now.
Doing fine, Stan

Karen Ross Epp

Dear Karen   July 24

Well I'll bet you could never guess where I'm at. The hospital. "Thats right." nothing serious. they thought it was malaria but I guess it isn't. actually they don't know what it is. I wrote and told mom it was the flu. As far as I know it could be. HA. All I know is that my temp hasn't been down under 100° for over 4 days. But its funny. I don't feel bad at all. matter of fact this hospital life is great. TV, hot food, play games all day. HA. I even slept between sheets. HA. HA. Most of all I've got to watch all the moon pictures on TV. So In a way, I hope I'm here 6 more months.

Its a wonder a person isn't sick all the time. living like a rat, sleeping in the rain. but thats the way it is.

200

well its almost @ 1AM and the capsule is supposed to be down any time. So I guess I'll go listen to it. I shouldn't be staying up this late. becau I want to get up in time for dinner tomorrow. HA HA. I'm sure going to hate to go back out to the field after HA life like this. HA.
never had it better HA

Stan

Brother

P.S. "don't worry

I had heard that Stan had put a match under the thermometer to raise his temperature reading. I'm sure he's not the first to think of such a trick to further his stay in the hospital. He would return to the field soon enough.

In Vietnam the water that the GIs drank was not the purest and could cause illness. Each soldier was required to put tablets into the water that made it safe to drink. Malaria pills were also handed out for them to take so they wouldn't come down with the disease.

Most would have welcomed it, over the alternative.

Ches Schneider writes in <u>From Classrooms To Claymores</u>, "I had come down with a cold. Maybe it was from the nights of seventy degrees that were chilly compared to the days that registered one hundred plus. The cold wasn't in itself a big thing, but piled onto all the misery, it was the last straw."

July 24, 1969

Dear Mom and Dad,

Well, another fine day in the hospital. But I think about tomorrow will be the end of my vacation. My temp is almost normal so I suppose they'll be throwing me out. (ha ha)

Mom, you made me so mad and disappointed when I read the last letter and realized you hadn't sent me a radio. But, I don't stay mad long. (ha ha) Do you realize how far I was from the nearest post office when that radio blew up! I sure as hell wasn't going to pack it for two or three weeks until I had a chance to send it home! When a man's humping the jungle he doesn't pack anything he doesn't need or that doesn't work! Well, enough of that.

BUT PLEASE SEND ME A RADIO AS QUICK AS POSSIBLE! I'll bet you think I was kidding about singing to myself. OK, a person gets so damn bored and nervous at times, it's terrible, and I ran out of fingernails a long time ago. (ha ha)

You remember the fight we ran into the 4th of July, I mentioned a couple of weeks ago? Even though nine men got killed I had to laugh at one instance, but this was before I heard of how many got killed. But anyway, right in the middle of the fight, and I mean the shit was really flying, the Jocks and RPG rockets, machine guns, but anyway, the log I was lying behind wasn't very big and I could hear the rounds hitting the other side. I saw a big rock to my right so I thought I'd better try and get behind it. A bullet sure as hell wouldn't go through that! (ha ha) Well, I started low crawling over to it, and believe me, a man can make his ass about half the size if he wants to. But when I got there, I had to laugh. There sat a big black guy, and I'd have sworn he was a preacher, because he was praying at the top of his voice and crying at the same time. I guess he just had 50 some days left, and he thought that was the end for him! I said, "Hell, you're so damn ugly. They want someone they can stuff!"

Well, I guess that's all for now.

Doing fine, Stan

P.S. Hey, Dad, if you ever get in a pinch or need extra money sometime, feel free to use mine, because I sure as hell won't need it for a few months. No sense you paying high interest on money when you can use mine.

This was the 60s. My brother's interaction with African-Americans in his 18 years was limited before he entered the military. Our town was a typical Midwestern community with a small number of black families who stayed on their side of the tracks and in their part of town, tolerated by indifference. We got to know them through school activities and by just seeing them around. As most blacks in those days, they held unskilled jobs that white residents of our town would not do.

My brother harbored some prejudices. He held views that most white boys did in the 60s, mainly out of ignorance and learned prejudices passed down from generation to generation.

In the military he was forced into integrated living conditions with many different minorities. He got along for the good of the unit. I am not saying that he was a champion of civil rights, but he respected the men he served with and those under his supervision regardless of color as long as they pulled their weight and did what was good for the safety of the squad. I'm sure Stan saw the best and worst in men while he was in Vietnam. It was a different world in 1969, but the military deserves credit for desegregating their ranks. Whether it made men more tolerant of each other is a question only they can answer. Racial tensions in Vietnam were beginning to be a problem. It was a situation that mirrored what was going on at home. Ches Schneider concluded that the Black soldiers had gotten the idea that Vietnam was a white man's war.

July 25, 1969
Dear Mom and Dad,

Well, another fine day in the hospital. Boy, it's going to kill me to leave to go back to the field, but at least I've had a few days rest. If I'd have had a female I could have almost called it R&R. (ha ha)

There's not much new since I wrote you yesterday. I won a monopoly game. Ate three hot meals, played cards, and watched TV. Sounds like a busy day, doesn't it!

They still haven't gotten my temperature down to normal yet, but the last reading was 99.6 so they're gaining. I suppose I'll be here for two more days at the most. Well, like I say, not much news. Hurry up with the radio!

Doing fine, Stan

Stan loved music. He enjoyed the rock & roll of the 60s as much as anyone. His transistor radio came back to us with the rest of his belongings. As I looked at it for the first time in years, I was struck by how similar it looked to today's version, the iPod. It had the small ear pieces that allowed only the listener to hear music, like the newer technology we enjoy today. I'm sure Stan would have enjoyed them all.

July 26, 1969
Dear Mom and Dad,
   Well, another fine day in the hospital, but the weather outside is nice too! During the rainy season it's not near as hot as when I first got over here. I just came back from walking around outside. Boy, it made me feel good to take in some sunshine and cool breeze. The weather reminds me of back home on a nice summer day. And to top it all off it's 9:30 p.m. Friday night at home. And how nice it would be to be back there driving the Chevelle around with windows down and listening to those quiet pipes, right, Dad? (ha ha)
   One nice thing about being in the field, you never know what day it is, so a man never thinks about those things. But one sure thing, I'll have all that again someday!
   I got your package yesterday, the one with all the cans and meats in. Thanks a lot, Mom. Like I say, it's not worth the hassle and the cost. I'll have to admit that those apricots really hit the spot this morning after leaving them in the hospital's refrigerator. From now on though, if you think you've got to send something, send chocolate chip cookies. They are still No. #1. And send some mixed nuts, Butterfinger bars and some of those chocolate wafer deals I always liked. Don't worry about me getting thirsty from the nuts because they never give us our packages unless we're back at a fire base camp.

So don't send me any more cans of meats or beans. Now don't think I'm giving you hell, because I'm not! It's my fault because I've never told you what to send. Well, enough of that.

Hey, Mom, do you have any of those facial wash and dry things? They come in a little packet. If they don't cost too much, drop one or two in each letter you send. Now don't go and send me 10,000 at once, like that Kool-aid. (ha ha) Because one or two a day I can keep my face half-way clean. I've went as high as 20 days without getting a chance to even wash my face. So then I can read your letters with a clean face. But like I say, they might be expensive.

Well, I can't think of much more. I shouldn't be here much longer. And if you're worrying, you're stupid! Because I'm fine!

With love, Stan

Mom and Dad's new Mercury.

Stan sharing some of Mom Ross's homemade
chocolate chip cookies with Jayson Dale. The Folgers
coffee can served well in transporting goodies half-way
around the world.

*When I talked to Jayson "J" Dale, Stan's good friend, he remembered
sharing care packages with each other. It was something all GIs looked
forward to. By sharing their homemade bundles, it became much more
than just food, it was almost like a religious ritual, like "breaking bread"
with a brother!*

*Good 'ole Mom kept the goodies coming, and chocolate chip cookies
were Stan's favorite. When I bake chocolate cookies I always think of my
brother.*

*The face wipes were a fairly new convenience in those days. We have
wet wipes for every part of our bodies these days.*

*Stan knew that Mom would always send more than was needed. That
habit is one she still maintains.*

Ches Schneider writes, "One advantage of being the platoon 5-Mike
was that I could share in the packages of cookies and goodies that the
guys received from home. Since I gave out the stuff, I knew whose
relative had sent what. In skilled hands, one or two shakes of a package

would give away the contents. On the other hand, since I opened my packages last, I was the object of everyone else's attention. While I didn't mind sharing other's goodies, I jealously guarded the cookies sent to me by my mother." *Ches went on to recall his sharing experience,* "I peeled off the brown wrapping paper, my eyes bulged. There, before me, was a box of Brach's chocolate-covered cherries! My mouth fell open in amazement. After eating all the junk the Army called food, that box of real-world food was unbelievable. It was a wonderful treat that only a mother would think to send. Instantly, I tried to conceal my treasure from the other members of 4-6. No luck."

July 27, 1969

Dear Mom and Dad,

Well, I'm afraid my stay is about over. My temperature is normal and they're not going to let me stay when there's nothing wrong. But it has been enjoyable. I suppose I'll be out in the field tomorrow. You'll be getting up to a nice Sunday morning in a little while. It's starting to get low in the sky over here.

Boy, I'm sure glad I got to see all that moon stuff! When I'm in the field, we never know anything. This is the first week that I've known what day it was everyday. You wouldn't believe how shut off a man feels out in the field. That's why I like a radio. I hope you've got it on the way.

Well, how's everything at home? I'll bet the weather is beautiful! Boy, it takes a lot to not let thinking of home blow a guy's mind. I had a 2nd LT. tell me if I wanted to, I could probably go to Germany after I'm done here. I told him, "They could stick it all. All I want to do is step foot on the land I've been fighting for and get back to my family." I can't figure out why people always want to go to some country. There's enough for me in the U.S.

One nice thing, since I've been in the hospital, I've been able to write to everyone and to you each day. Like I say, I'll probably go to the field tomorrow, so it may be a week before you hear from me again.

How's the corn looking Dad? I'll bet it's really nice. Well, I've got 105 days out of 365 gone. That's a chunk! Time is going I guess.

Tell Dad, I remember when he started plowing for the corn. I said then, "I'll be glad when he's picking it."

Is Warren on vacation now? I was going to write him, but I didn't know if he was home or not. Tell Bill thanks for writing. In too good shape. (ha ha)

With love, Stan

Stan enjoyed field work. He helped Dad whenever he got the chance. Like so many farm families, our lives were governed by the seasons. Events were marked by planting and harvesting. For Stan, the harvest of 1969 would never come.

July 28, 1969
Dear Mom and Dad,

Well, I don't know what happened, but they're letting me stay another day. I thought for sure I would leave today. So I guess that means another nice day and sleeping between white sheets again tonight. (ha ha)

Well, I don't have much to say since I last wrote. You've got to admit, I've been pretty good to write since I've been in here.

I guess our company came in yesterday. A buddy of mine came to see me. I guess the NVA are at it again, so I'd better oil the rifle up a little more, I guess.

Boy, it will be nice to go back to shooting rabbits (ha ha) and not have to worry about them shooting back.

I heard from Bob the other day. I guess he's just got four-and-a-half months left. I wish he was home; then all I'd have left would be three and a half.

So you're canning quite a bit, Mom! Garden stuff will sure taste good next April. Every now and then we run into some pretty good farms over here. I've seen bean fields and corn fields, just as good as back home, but not very many. Up north here, this land is red and real good stuff. If the dumb bastards would quit fighting, and raise something! We've run into deserted villages with real good houses and furnished. It's a shame the way the NVA run good people off.

I'd sure like to get some pictures up north here. All the ones you've got are of the rice paddies. I think I'll buy me a nice still picture camera and send my movie camera back home. People just as well take advantage of these low prices while he's over here. It's about the only damn benefit a man gets.

Well, since I've been in the hospital I've written everyone I could think of…so maybe everyone's happy. (ha ha)

Well, bye for now, Stan

Mom, proud of her garden. She, Eileen, and little
Phillip wave for the camera and for Stan. As in
pictures from pioneer days, important family
possessions were on display in the background, Stan's
car and the camper.

The produce that Mom put up that summer would be a bitter reminder of her lost son. She had never worked so feverishly, canned so much, or kept as busy.

Farm wives and mothers have a need to provide for their families, to prepare for the unexpected, like squirrels gathering nuts for the winter. Those traits helped my mother endure and go on, to be there for the rest of us when the terrible news came.

She would later feel the pain and loss in those private places where mothers go to grieve—doing dishes, wandering around in the grassy yard that once kept her son corralled in boyhood play, in her bed at night when the darkness and quiet brought images of her boy's face and smile.

Mom was not one to spend her time going to Stan's grave. She always felt, and still does, that he isn't there. He's in a better place.

July 29, 1969
Dear Mom and Dad,

Well, another day in Vietnam. Like I figured, they have my ass right out in the field the minute I got out of the hospital. It's sure a switch from white sheets to a foxhole, and that's what I'm in right now.

Boy, there was a nice full moon out last night. It really makes a guy stop and think just how in the hell could anyone have went that far.

Well, is it getting any dryer at home? I met a kid from Iowa while I was in the hospital. He was from Ames. I showed him a clipping you sent me out of the paper. It's always nice to meet someone from back home.

Well, how's that big Park Lane coming? Did you get the dent fixed yet? Boy, I could have just seen Dad. (ha ha)

Are you doing quite a bit of camping this summer? Boy, it sure sounds like fun. Are you still fishing quite a bit, Dad? I still can't imagine you fishing! Hey, Mom, did they have a county fair this year? I figured you'd be mentioning it. Are you going to go to the State Fair?

Well, I can't think of much more. I guess we'll be humping up and over a mountain tomorrow. So it's about dark anyway, I think I'll turn in. I'll write next chance I get.

With love, Stan

One of the guys from Iowa, James Faber, became a
good friend to Stan and was a member of his squad.

Robert Gouge writes, "By the time that darkness fell, the jungle-pounding grunts had already finished digging their foxholes, rigging their 'hootches,' radioed in their positions, pre-plotted artillery fire, set up and armed the claymore mines, cleaned and re-cleaned their weapons, eaten a C-rat supper and curled up in their poncho liners for another long night of little or no sleep…that is if they were not selected to be on ambush, LP or perimeter watch."

The County Fair was something we looked forward to every summer in July. My peers will relate that in the 60s, there wasn't a constant need for entertainment that we have in the 21st century. We did have television. The whole family gathered around to watch "I Love Lucy" or "The Andy Griffith Show." There weren't video games, arcades or the obsession to satisfy a child's need for instant gratification. Movies were an occasional treat and church played a central part in providing social interaction.

We belonged to our local 4H club and participated at the fair by showing livestock, produce, and baked items. In those days the girls and boys were in separate divisions, so I had to join the girls' club if I wanted to show my Hereford calf.

Stan and I saved our money. He saved his from hay bailing and I from babysitting. The fair was an event, especially for farm kids. It was a time to get together with friends and take in the worldly sites of the carnival. Every girl wanted her boyfriend to win a stuffed animal for her, and the guys were more than willing to prove how manly they were by trying their hand at every game on the midway. The more stuffed animals a girl carried around, the more studly her date.

I got my first kiss at the fair, a special moment in the darkened Fun House, where on a sultry July night, I lost some of my innocence. It wasn't the best kiss I ever experienced, but it was the one I will always remember.

It was always fun to get our pictures taken in those small booths where we made crazy faces and captured those special moments of our youth.

Stan, age sixteen, picture taken in one of the popular
photo booths at our county fair.

Karen with her Hereford 4H calf.

July 31, 1969

Dear Mom and Dad,

Well, another day. What's the matter? It's been two days and no mail. It's OK. I don't care if you miss once in a while. I realize for you to write everyday it's quite a hassle.

Well, not much has happened since yesterday. We mostly sat around today. It wasn't too bad. I guess we've got a big operation coming up in a few days. So the President (Nixon) dropped in today. Boy, they really kept it quiet! We didn't even know about it until he left. But I knew we'd never see him out here in the jungles.

I guess we go in tomorrow long enough to get paid and a change of clothes. The guys have been out for 14 days. I was in the hospital for ten of them so I've had a little break. I sure wish I could have kept a fever longer. (ha ha) That hospital life was great!

Boy, it would be nice to go back to B&B (Long Bien) for a while and shop and really have the safe feeling again. I've just been there twice since I've been in country.

Our CO gave the whole company a talking to today. He said, "There are too many people trying to get jobs in the rear." He said, "That shit's stopping!" He said, "We're Infantrymen. We're over here for one purpose (we're trained killers) and there's no sense putting you

213

in the rear, because out on the line is where you belong, and that's where I'm keeping you!" He said for no one to even think of going in, until 30 days before he's supposed to go home.

I just thought to myself after he quit talking, what damn luck. A man doesn't have anything to look forward to. Seven more straight months of field work will blow my mind! I don't know how I'm going to take it! After hearing that kind of shit, a man sure doesn't have much to hang on to. I almost laughed out loud when he said the part about us being trained killers. (ha ha) All I've ever done is protect myself.

Well, anyway, I guess I know what the score is. I even asked our top sergeant if I could try to change to the 1st Infantry Division, or to the 1st Cavalry, but he said, "There's no way in hell, once a man's assigned (that's it)."

Well, I guess that's all I know for now. It's about C-ration time. (ha ha)

Straight from the foxhole, Stan

A job in the rear was dearly coveted by those on the front lines of the war. The grunts both wished for and loathed the rear. Feelings of hostility toward those that had safer jobs in the base camps caused friction between the men and growing unrest in the field.

Base camps were shelled from time to time and men were killed and injured, but the psychological strain and risk of death was much less.

In Edelman's <u>Dear America</u>, Chapter 4, "Base Camp at the Rear", he includes letters written by GIs feed up with the unequal treatment of the Infantry. One such letter written to then President, Richard Nixon, by the members of Delta Company 3/21, 196th Light Infantry Brigade of the Americal Division reads, "Our first major complaint is that we are spending more than we feel is our fair share of time in the field. From the time we entered Advanced Infantry Training, we realized that we, as Infantrymen, were destined to have it harder than most. We have accepted our responsibilities and have fulfilled our duties to the best of our ability. We feel that after spending a reasonable amount of time in the field, we should be given the opportunity to work in the rear or secure area for the remainder of our tour. This is standard procedure in most units here in Vietnam.

In order to clarify the matter, I think it is necessary to explain to you that basically there are two different wars here in Vietnam. While we are out in the field living like animals, putting our lives on the line 24 hours a day, seven days a week, the guy in the rear's biggest problem is that he can receive only one television station. There is no comparison between the two. The combat Infantryman would rather take permanent KP or burn human waste on a fire support base than spend another night in the field. The man in the rear doesn't know what it's like to burn a leech off his body with a cigarette; to go unbathed for months at a time; to sleep without an air mattress, let alone in a fox hole; to walk all day on feet raw from immersion foot; or to wake up to the sound of incoming mortar rounds and the cry of your buddy screaming 'Medic!' In short, he does not realize the tremendous emotional and physical strain that the men in the field are forced to endure." *Nixon never responded to this letter.*

The importance of the grunt as opposed to the men in the rear was a bitter pill that Ches Schneider would reflect on in his book, <u>From Classrooms To Claymores</u>, as he relates an incident regarding the Bob Hope tour that was scheduled to appear at a camp near his company, "I've seen every one of his Christmas specials on TV, and now he has come personally to Nam to entertain me! 'Not even, Professor!' Killjoy Karate grinned. 'He has come to entertain the brass and REMFs, not us.' Everyone groaned about the REMF's being the ones who least deserved to see the show. Jimmy our black machine gunner, concluded, 'Let the REMFs run security, and let the grunts see the show. We're the only ones doing anything in this damn place anyway."

Reflections
By
Tim "Obie" Oberst
199th Light Inf. Brigade, 4th Platoon, Charlie Co.

Karen, I'm so glad I finally got to talk to Stan's family. Stan has always remained a part of my life. We promised that we would get in touch with each others families if something happened to one of us, but as time went on, that didn't happen. I remember one time when we were at a water tank, he said, "I don't think I'm going to make it!" I got angry with him and told him not to think like that.

Sometimes I have flashbacks. I can't control it, they just happen. You and your family have really helped give me peace. It was hard for me to take Stan's pictures out of my album. It was like saying goodbye, something I can never do! We were in some scary battles together. He used to call me crazy, but I think it was the other way around.

I feel a great sense of relief now. Stan and I were good friends. His death took a great toll on my life. After talking to you guys, I feel my promise to Stan has been completed. I have buried a lot of things from that time. The battles and ambushes we were on are now surfacing, and that's OK. Thanks to you, your mom, and Phillip. Thanks so much for your kindness.

God bless, Tim

Hunter Killer Team that Tim was part of, LZ
(Landing Zone) in the jungle N.E. of Saigon,
September, 1969. Charlie Co., 2nd BN, 3rd INF., 199th
Light Infantry Brigade, (Cold Guard.) (Left to right,
front) Robert Too-Late, Tim "Obie" Oberst, Jayson
"J" Dale, (Back) Louis "Snake" Ruth, Tom Phillips,
Nelson "Baltimore" Berryman.

I first learned of Tim through David Clines and Jayson Dale. Like so many of Stan's, buddies, one contact led to another. I called and wrote e-mails to say that I was Stan Ross's sister. To say Tim was surprised and stunned would be putting it mildly. I think he felt a ghost had reached out from the past.

It was hard for him to speak for a while; I could tell it was emotional for him to recall my brother. I explained why I had contacted him and he was more than happy to recall the memories he had of Stan and his time in Vietnam. Tim fought alongside Stan and Jayson Dale on Butterfly Hill, in July of 1969.

Tim would eventually visit with my parents by phone, helping him to fulfill his promise to Stan. It's been healing for my mother and father and for me to put another name with those youthful faces from Stan's photos.

Tim said, "There hasn't been a day since Vietnam that I haven't thought of or spoke of your brother." *His wife Becky confirmed that when I talked to her and she said,* "I have heard Tim talk about Stanley Ross all these years. It's wonderful to finally talk to a member of his family. It's been very healing for my husband."

Tim is married and has two sons. His eldest son, Tim Jr., is in the Marines and has served in Iraq. Ryan, his youngest, graduated from high school in 2005, and is thinking of joining the Army. Tim and his wife, Becky, live near Cleveland, Ohio, where Tim has worked for General Motors for thirty years.

When I read Stan's letters I was curious as to what kind of person made up the VC and NVA units. Were they thugs with no sense of morality? Were they forced into service? What was the character of this elusive enemy that my brother hunted and feared?

<u>*Robert Gouge*</u> *quotes Retired Colonel David H. Hackworth who described the enemy forces he encountered in 1969,* "The Viet Cong were one of the most formidable Infantry opponents the U.S. Army ever encountered. The vast majority were locals, women as well as men... Most of the VC had cut their first teeth on war. Their older brothers, fathers, uncles, grandfathers, and great-grandfathers had fought the French, the Japanese, the French again, Saigon's troops and now the Americans. A thousand years before these battles, they'd fought the Chinese, Cambodians, Thais, and anyone else who tried to grab their

rich lands and make them slaves. Like Spartan warriors in ancient times, the VC bred fighters. Small kids started out helping their big brothers and sisters—the VC on-the-job war training program. Young boys and girls grew up spying on their enemy, carrying supplies, working in gardens to grow food, setting out booby traps, caring for the wounded and burying the dead. By the time they were teenagers, big enough to shoulder and aim a rifle, they were trained in the basic skills of guerrilla warfare. At that point they joined whatever village guerrilla unit protected their home turf and assisted any Main Force units in their area of operations. When these seasoned outfits needed replacements, the youngsters volunteered from their village units."

Gouge goes on to say, "Some joined because of personal vendettas against the corrupt, 'Puppet' regime of the Saigon government led by Thieu, Ky and others. Some joined because war against the Americans was seen as a continuation of the historic and religious Vietnamese struggle against foreign invaders. Others were forced to join the Viet Cong at gunpoint while others, although not in large numbers, joined the ranks because of Communist doctrine and ideology."

August 5, 1969
Dear Mom and Dad,
Well, another day in Vietnam. I'm sure glad things are drying up back home. I wish things would dry up here. It seems like it rains all the time. Things do seem like they are calming down lately. It's sure nice to have a little peace and quiet for a change. The weather hasn't been too hot lately either.

Hey, Mom, about all the talk about your club or whatever you're starting. I'd rather you not carry it too far. I just want peace and quiet. I'm nothing special. There are a lot of guys over here doing and going through the same kind of shit. I know you mean well, but please don't carry it too far! I don't give a damn how people feel. I've got folks back home to make my homecoming. I don't need anyone else. Don't worry. If anyone says anything, I'll hit them right in the mouth. You know all the chicken shits are around there, Mom. They're probably just saying that Rose Ross thinks her son's the only one over there. I don't want a crowd around when I get home, just peace and quiet, that's all I ask. Well, enough of that.

Well, not much news. I wish I was back in the hospital. I'm starting my fifth month pretty soon. Wow, time is going!

I wrote to Steve and Bob both while I was in the hospital, so I should be hearing from them. Well, bye for now. A whole bunch of love to the best family in the wonderful USA.

Stan

Support group started by Mom. Jerry Hankins (middle left), Bill Lane (center left) both Vietnam veterans.

Stan refers to himself as nothing special. In Donald E. Stephen's book, Bait: Vietnam 1971, Chapter 3, he speaks of his fellow soldiers and the pride he had for them, "My mind shifted to our mission and what Infantry really meant in the course of the war. A giddy feeling of pride came over me. On the ground, step for step, soldier for soldier, we were as good as any unit in the world. The whole damned war was centered around the good old American grunt." *Stan and his men were very special. They were the backbone of the war effort in Vietnam.*

Mom started a local support group that summer for parents of servicemen in Vietnam. It was a success and she helped many worried mothers and fathers put their energy in the group rather than focusing on their sons and their well being.

Guys from our community that returned from Vietnam were welcomed with open arms. That love is remembered and continues today.

When I was visited Stan's grave Memorial Day weekend of 2005, I spotted a familiar face, Jerry Hankins, a friend from high school and a veteran of Vietnam. Jerry's father was our mail man, who also had the unpleasant task of delivering the Army's correspondence after Stan's death. Mr. Hankins was a member of our church and a life long friend to my parents.

I hadn't seen Jerry for many years. He hugged me and my mother. We reminisced about Stan. His eyes were moist as he greeted Mom and held her for a long embrace. Stan's gravestone and military marker were decorated by not only our family but by many of his friends and acquaintances. It was comforting to know that Stan was still remembered. Somehow I knew he was probably laughing and saying, "Come on guys, lighten up. I'll see you all again someday!"

Captain James McGinnis.

Captain McGinnis addressing the men.

Reflections
By
Captain James McGinnis

One of the techniques I utilized throughout my Army career was to employ the best people I could find and use them in key positions of responsibility and leadership. At the time, I assumed command of C Company 2/3 199ᵗʰ, I began to search for the kind of men I wanted to build this unit upon and Stanley Ross was one of those.

I wanted men who were trustworthy, dependable and honest. It was my intention to identify several quality people that I might use at company headquarters for important things like taking care of signal operating instructions (SOI, classified secret), radio communication with other units, and management of logistics (beans and bullets). We were an outstanding organization that depended upon outstanding men to uphold the high standards we established.

Stanley Ross was intelligent, enthusiastic and dedicated to excellence. It was my intention to promote him to the highest level of my authority and utilize his abundance of skill and desire to make Company C an even better outfit. I owe my success to men like Stanley and am honored to have known some of the greatest young men America has ever produced.

Sincerely,

James McGinnis

All the men I have interviewed have had nothing but praise for James McGinnis.

As I have spoken with him several times by phone he has been gracious and supportive of my work. He still has a love and concern for his men even today that is genuine and true and even a little fatherly. His soft spoken southern manner and accent draws you in and I can see why his men trusted and loved him as a leader and role model.

Lt. Michael Lanning reflects on his first impression of Captain McGinnis as he takes command of Charlie Company in June of 1969, "My opinion of the new CO's being Number 1 was not just based on his patronization of me. McGinnis was taking charge. His calmness and willingness to listen quickly gained our confidence." *Lanning goes on to say,* "We called him the 'old man.' This seemed particularly appropriate as McGinnis was at least ten years older than the rest of us. Number 1 was a term that GIs and Vietnamese alike used for expression of praise. Number 10 was just the opposite. Everything was either 1 or 10—there were no degrees."

August 13, 1969

Dear Mom and Dad,

I sure hope you're not worried since I haven't written for quite a while, but believe me, I couldn't help it! The past 14 days has been something. (I've been scared to death!) (Beat out of a medal and flattered!) (ha ha) Like I say, it's been something.

First, we started on a sweep. It didn't seem too bad until we heard there might be some VC up ahead. 1st Platoon was walking first, 2nd, 3rd, and 4th in that order. I'm in the third, so that day I was about 75 meters from the front. Well, anyway, our luck, we heard voices up ahead. But at least it's better to hear them before they hear us. Well since 1st platoon was up there, we figured they could handle whatever was up there. They figured they heard about ten NVA. Well, 1st snuck up on them and opened up, (boy, did the shit hit the fan), but it turned out that there were about 30 NVA against about a nine-man front line. Anyway we could hear 1st Platoon calling for help, so me and my best friend and my sergeant took off. We ran about 75 meters through a fire fight to get up to the front to help those nine men out. The NVA were even shooting RPGs and that's bad shit!

Well, to make it short, the nine men got air commendation medals for valor, and they didn't give us nothing for running clear up there and helping. The more I thought about it, the madder I got. It's not the medal, because I don't want any of their damn medals, but not even a thank you! And we were the only three that went down out of the 3rd platoon. Everyone else chickened out. I'll admit it, I'll never do anything that crazy again, but when you hear guys calling for help it's hard not to help. Well, enough of all that.

Now get this, the other day the captain talked to me about being a squad leader. I told him I thought a person had to be a sergeant to be a squad leader. He said, "I think you're the man who can handle it, so I'll take care of the promotion if you want the job." Boy, I don't know what to do. To make sergeant by October or November would be great, and that means about $175.00 more dollars a month, but a person's got to look at the responsibility behind it—to be responsible for 15 men's lives. And another thing, after six months in the field a person's chance for a job in the rear is good if there's an opening. But being a sergeant squad leader most of the time spends all but about 20-30 days in the field. I don't know if I could keep my right mind out there that long, and the responsibility! Because in a fire fight, and to call out orders is a matter of life and death! So I've got to do some serious thinking about it.

My sergeant told me if I done a good job I'd make staff sergeant before my tour is up. There are some people in the Army that don't make staff sergeant (E6) for five years or more. They sure as hell don't give it to you. A guy earns it! But still and all, rank's no good to a dead man. Please write and tell me what you think I should do. My squad leader doesn't leave until Nov. so I wouldn't take over till then. There's a lot to learn—

how to call in artillery, read a map. It's no easy job. Well, enough for that, but please write and give me your opinion, Dad.

Well, enough on Army life. About a car, next time you got a chance ask the Martin kid when and what he wants for his Chevelle. I'd sorta like to have that. But I'm going to get me a '74 cycle too! I figure I'll pay cash for the cycle, maybe owe a little on the car.

Did you receive the money order I sent home last month, $200.00? Please tell me each time you receive a money order.

Hey, Mom, don't sweat the mail. I'll get it all. I'm eating cookies right now. They're great! I received the radio five days after you sent it. It's really nice. I play it a lot.

Hey, Mom, I'm sending my movie camera home. Would you please send my Polaroid, just the camera not the flash. Maybe you can find a Tupperware to put it in. If not, send it anyway. A lot of people ask for pictures of me, and the guys around here would like to have some taken, so please send it! I think it would be pretty nice. Send a couple packs of color film with, it please! Now, buy it out of my money, and like I say, if you need money for anything, Dad, feel free to use mine.

Well, I can't think of much more to write. Tell Eileen I've had to kill, but I don't want to even think about it! I've had nightmares over it at times. Enemy or not, they're still human beings that don't know anything more than what someone has told them. But that's part of this damn shameful war.

So it's pretty nice weather back home? I can imagine. Boy, I'd give anything to be there. You just don't realize how wonderful you have it. I can't imagine going to sleep without fear of not being there in the morning.

It gets so dark in the jungle at night. One sound scares the shit out of a man. (ha ha) We had a guy crack up last week. He started screaming in the night. Boy, did that shake me up!

Well, I guess I'll close for now. We get two days back this time. So I'll probably write tomorrow, too!

With love, Stan

Stan talks about purchasing a Chevelle from the "Martin kid". Merritt Martin owned a yellow, '68 SS Chevelle that Stan dearly coveted. As a twist of fate, one year to the day after Stan's death, my brother-in-law, Randy Ensminger pulled into my parent's driveway for his first date with my sister, Eileen, driving that same yellow Chevelle. Of course, my parents recognized it right away as the car Stan had wanted. Randy had no idea that the car he had purchased was the one that Stan wanted once he returned. My sister was concerned when she saw the look on my dad's face. She thought, "Well, there's the first strike against my date!"

Things turned out all right for Randy and my sister. That car was the beginning of a long and happy relationship. They have been married for 30 years and the Chevelle is still remembered with fondness. Stan would have wanted it that way.

The Third's leaders (left to right), Lt. Arrol Stewart, Sgt. SFC, Johnny Rogers, and Sgt. Greg Breeckner.

Third squad, 3rd Platoon, (left to right, front) William Perrie, Stan, Donald Mazzi, Dave Cherneski; (back) Greg Breeckner, Tom Phillips, Tommy Smith, John Vandsen, Terry Wanner, Tom Reed, Bill Stoner.

In the previous letter Stan is referring to the August 7th fire fight that he and his platoon were involved in. Lieutenant Michael Lanning and his men were pinned down and were separated from the rest of their platoon. Stan, our other squad member, and his squad leader, SGT Greg Breeckner, helped to lead them out of a very dangerous situation by getting back to the rest of their platoon. Lanning's journal account of August 7th in his book, The Only War We Had: A Platoon Leader's Journal of Vietnam reads, "Our predicament was far from over. We had withdrawn at a right angle to the original route of march and I was unsure of the Company's location. If they heard us moving through the jungle now, they might shoot first and ask questions later.

It had been nearly an hour since our last radio contact. The artillery had stopped with our loss of commo. When and where it would start again, I didn't know. I instructed the men to stay hidden. Surely McGinnis would have patrols out looking for us now that the firing had stopped.

A long ten minutes later, we heard movement in the jungle. The only sound from our hide-away was deep breathing and clicks of M-16s being taken off safety.

Through the matted vegetation a figure slowly emerged. I felt like shouting. Instead, as calmly as possible, I said, 'Sergeant Breeckner, it's us. Please don't shoot.'

Breeckner hit the dirt as he brought his M-16 around in my direction. I slowly stood up from my hiding place. A grin broke over Breeckner's face as he said, 'Hello, One-six. How are you doing?'

I wanted to hug him. Instead, I answered, 'Fuck you give me some ammo.'

SGT Breeckner was a squad leader in the third platoon. Nearing ten months in the field, he was as good as they came. He and his squad had volunteered to look for us..."

In Lanning's second book, Vietnam 1969-1970: A Commander's Journal, he mentions my brother by name and says, "Ross had been one of the men who found me and my recon team back on 7 August. I never had the chance to tell him thanks." *When I read those words in Lee Lanning's book, I was stunned and proud that he mentioned my* brother and gave him and his men credit for risking their lives for their fellow brothers in arms. Captain McGinnis is the officer that Stan referred to as asking him to become a squad leader.

When I talked to Lee Lanning in person about that day, he recalled the August 7ᵗʰ fire fight, and had nothing but praise for the courage that my brother and others in his squad displayed in helping Lanning and his men out of a very dangerous situation. As Stan said, they did not receive medals for their rescue, which they should have.

The captain Stan refers to is Captain James McGinnis. McGinnis was very gracious when I contacted him. As he said in his comments, he had high hopes for Stan in a leadership role.

Reading the part of this letter that referred to my sister Eileen's question, I knew it was something he wished he didn't have to reveal to her. It is, however, a question that a teenager would be curious about. She was 15 at the time, and very much aware of what the country was going through and what people were saying about the military and GIs who were portrayed as cold-blooded killers of women and children. She remembered a brother that once teased her, chased her with bugs, and gave her an occasional punch on the arm—a warm big-hearted brother—not someone that would callously take a life.

Stan holding baby Eileen, spring of 1954.

August 14, 1969

Dear Mom and Dad,

Well, another day off. Tomorrow we go back to the field. So I'd better write while I can. I sent my movie camera home yesterday. I didn't insure it because they said I didn't have it packed good enough. I sent it anyway. Tell me if it gets there all right. The film that's in it is almost used up. Mom, if you take movies, remember these few things about it and then you can take perfect movies every time!

1. The footage dial on the front, leave it on that dot by 25 feet, but if you take something far away put it on INF. And for close up, it's better to estimate footage and set the dial. Otherwise, leave it on the dot.

2. It's all right to use the zoom on any footage setting, but remember don't move the camera too fast from side to side.

3. A person can't really go by that film indicator, which tells when you're out of film. But when it says on the indicator that you're about out, listen closely to the sound of the camera. When there's still film in it, it will sound smooth, as if the gears aren't running, and when you open the camera and take the film out, if it doesn't say (EXPOSED) on the film, it isn't run out yet.

Well, I hope I've explained it pretty good. Please save what I've written, because there's no need in taking movies if you don't do it right! (ha ha) I think I'll have a lot of fun with that Polaroid.

Hey, Mom, I bought a camera off a guy just going home. It's a $40.00 camera and I got it for $15.00. It's real small, about half the size of a pack of cigarettes. It's really neat! I'm sending a roll of film home in this letter. Get them developed as quick as you can. I'm real anxious to know what kind of pictures it takes. He used it for slides. Make sure you tell them you want regular sized pictures.

I'm glad you're having nice weather. It's been hotter than hell here! But that's nothing new. (ha ha) Yes, that was too bad about Margaret McClure. I really got a kick out of you giving Homer my boots. You know I wouldn't get mad. (ha ha)

With love, Stan

Stan on leave, visiting Homer, who's holding up his
famous "Old Crow."

Stan's interest in taking pictures gave him something to keep his mind off of the war.

I'm always amazed at the number of photos he was able to take with his Instamatic and Polaroid cameras.

Margaret McClure was the teenage daughter of close friends of our family. She was tragically killed in an automobile accident. As kids we would often visited the McClure's home and played with their children. It's always a treat to see some of them when I'm at home. I have many fond memories of their parents (Mildred and Carlos) who were warm and hardworking farm people like my family.

Homer Kephart was my dad's first cousin on his father's side. Homer was a confirmed bachelor who hired out to many of the farming families in our community when field work or other jobs were needed. Depending on which family he was working for, that was where he made his home. He never owned a car, but drove a small Ford tractor, which he lovingly referred to as the "Thunderbird!" He drove it in all kinds of weather.

Homer was a unique and colorful character. His booming voice would announce his arrival before his six-foot-four frame would fill the door.

Homer's education consisted only of a few years of grammar school. He wasn't book smart but knew a great deal about life and could tell some interesting tales that kept young listeners glued to his every word. He was an accomplished bee-keeper and kept his hives at our farm. It was great fun to help him harvest the honey. He had a way with the bees and was rarely stung. My mother always had a well-stocked cupboard of honey.

Homer's wardrobe consisted of overalls, denim jackets and caps. He kept his money in a bulging billfold in one of the front pockets in his bibs. Folgers coffee cans served as his bank, where he kept his life's earnings.

He did enjoy Stan's boots that Mom gave him. Homer always referred to Stan as "The Little Man!"—a title that Phillip would inherit. Homer enjoyed a nip of whiskey now and then; he and Stan enjoyed a friendly drink of "Old Crow," as he called it, before he left for Vietnam. Homer died in 1982. He was 83.

August 23, 1969
Dear Mom and Dad,

Well, we're back in for one day and night. I guess we were out for a week or more. I don't really know. I have a hard time finding out the date to put on the letters. (ha ha)

Our last mission went pretty good. We saw two VC but couldn't get close enough to kill them. I sure hate it when we spot VC. Because when you spot them the Captain will make us stay in that area and walk it for a week, trying to scare up the gooks. I'll bet I've walked 5,000 miles, and through the jungle, it's hell! A person cuts with one hand and holds the old rifle in the other.

I guess we're headed for some fire support camp out in the jungle somewhere. I hope we get to stay there a while. Maybe I can catch up on some writing then. Like I've said 100 times, "Please understand why I can't write as often as I should."

Boy, that State Fair subject sounds like a dream. I'm glad to hear you're all having a good time camping and etc. Don't ever feel that I'm getting pissed because you write me about all the fun. Just remember one thing, just thank the good Lord for the opportunity to enjoy all pleasures and sights of the wonderful U.S.A.!

To me, it's just like a dream to even think about such a place. One thing sure, freedom is just a word until someone takes it away.

I look forward to coming in for a rest once in one or two or maybe three weeks at a time in the field. I've slept 14 hours at a time when we've finally come back in for rest and new ammo. Because out in the field a person might be awake all night scared to death, but that's all part of the game. OH, mail call. Wait a minute while I stop and pray for a letter. (ha ha) But old Mom came through again. They always yell here's one from Mama Ross! (ha ha) They still can't believe it, how you write everyday. I tell them that they just don't know what kind of good people are in Iowa! You're a winner, Mom, all the way, and you do better than I ever dreamed, Dad! (ha ha)

So Harold found you at the fair? He wrote to me. Do you ever think he'll grow up? (ha ha) But I like him, a person can't help liking him, and he thinks the sun rises and sets on Dad. He even writes about you in his letters, "Old Uncle Russ."

I'll bet the State Fair was really nice, wasn't it? And when you mentioned driving up there, wow, I remember when I drove across Texas that time while you guys slept. Man, it just seems like all that was a dream.

You said that that Denny Anderson came home. I'll bet he's really living it up! He deserves all the fun he can have for spending a year in this dirty rat, mosquito, red ants, leeches, messed up place, let alone being in the Infantry.

Mom, you spoke about being lonesome at times for me. Don't let it get you down. Believe me, I get so damned lonesome at times when I'm in the field sleeping in a wet foxhole, it's beyond words! But all we can do is take it. Little Phillip, I really miss! I almost forget what you all look like at times. I don't know of anything worse than being torn away from your family.

Have you sent my Polaroid yet or received my movie camera?

Well, I can't think of much more to write. I'm still alive, so that means I'm doing good! (ha ha)

With love, Stan

Stan in the field, maybe feeling lonesome.

Huey supply bird. Photo by Jim Faber.

Stan's comment about being lonely was hard for me to read. He looked forward to R&R, as so many GIs did. Edelman's, <u>Dear America</u> describes these same feelings as one soldier, 1LT Robert Michael Murray, writes to his wife, "Sometimes you have to pretend you're not really lonely or else you'd find yourself going out of your mind. But when the day is done, and you're lying alone with your thoughts, then there's no more fooling and that's when it really hurts…"

Getting mail from Stan was like taking a breath. It made the next minute, hour, and day more bearable. In the forward of <u>Dear America</u>, 1LT William Broyles JR. of Company B, 1st Bat, 26th Regiment, First Marine Div. writes, "With the possible exception of his rifle, nothing was more important to an American in Vietnam than his mail…"

Broyles goes on to say, "Everyone knew who was getting mail and who wasn't, who was having trouble at home, whose girlfriend was trying to let him down gently. It was a special time, private but also communal."

Stan would comment in his letter that he felt sorry for the guys that didn't get much mail. He probably would have shared his if he thought it would make them feel better.

I was amazed after typing Stan's letters, how he managed to write so many in such difficult conditions. Soldiers wrote on whatever they had around at the time, even used C-ration cartons.

Ches Schneider recalls the importance of mail during his year in Vietnam and how it was the lifeline between family and friends at home. He writes, "My letters to Karen, (his wife) and my parents were my lifeline to sanity. They could also serve as a chronicle of my adventures should I ever want to write a book about my experiences in Nam…The anticipation of reading mail from loved ones and friends was often more enjoyable than the actual reading of the correspondence itself. It was always nice to know that someone at home cared about you enough to take time to write."

Harold Grant was our cousin on my dad's side of the family. My Aunt Ruth, Dad's oldest sister, was his grandmother. Harold, and his sister Lucy, was closer in age to us than our other cousins. We spent many sleepovers at their house in Wayland, Iowa, and also at our grandparent's farm that lay along the river bottom banked by the Skunk River.

Stan and I enjoyed visiting them because they lived in town and didn't have chores to do, like milking and gathering eggs. Their bedrooms were heated and they had air-conditioning. There were neat places to ride their bikes, they always had the latest toys and games, and I envied their seemingly carefree life. Evelyn, their mother, and Aunt Ruth were wonderful cooks. Evelyn owned a hobby shop where I could have spent my entire life if it had been possible. She let me make and paint plaster figurines, which was a popular hobby during those days. I think that's when I first realized I wanted to be involved with art in some way. Harold and Lucy still live in Wayland.

August 23, 1969
Dear Mom and Dad,

Hey, news flash! I just got my sergeant orders. That's right. I jumped from PFC to sergeant. Now, Mom, you've got a little something to brag on me about. I'm even sorta proud of myself. There are not very many who make sergeant in four-and-a-half months in country. Boy, are we celebrating tonight! All the guys are patting me on the back. This is one time, Mom, you can put it in the paper. From here on out, I'm addressed as Sergeant Stanley D. Ross. (ha ha)

Well, I'd better quit. I've never bragged on myself like this before in my life. (ha ha) One guy said to me and I had to laugh, "There's just no stopping a hard fighting farm boy!"

But getting down to seriousness, I don't suppose I should have accepted it. Because within a month, after they get done teaching me all the tricks, I'll be a squad leader. That means I'll have about 15 riflemen under me. God, help me do a good job! Boy, am I confused, all this at once!

Well, I guess I'll close for now. I guess they're taking me to the NCO club tonight. (ha ha) Tomorrow, back to the war games, but tonight I'm really celebrating. (ha ha)

Remember, I'm addressed
SGT. Stanley D Ross (ha ha)
But I love you all just the same.
Nothing could ever change that!

The Vietnam War was fought by Iowa farm boys like Stan and other ordinary guys from unknown towns who did extraordinary things. They humped and grunted their way through Vietnam, none braver or better.

Tom Schiefer, a friend, and member of Stan's squad, arrived in Vietnam in August of 1969. He recalled his first impressions and days with Stan, "I have a soft spot in my heart for Stan because I was probably a little different than a lot of the guys who ended up in our company. I was the church treasurer back home, the only boy in the choir, the boy who played the piano in Sunday school. I think you probably get the picture. I wasn't a sissy as I was one of the best football players in the area, and basketball too. I just wasn't one of the 'good ole boys' most were. Stan, I think, saw that, and he immediately took me under his wing. He turned me into what I think was a pretty good soldier, and I have always been proud of how I conducted myself in Vietnam. I have always known that the one person who showed me the way was Stan. You probably wish your brother had not gone to Vietnam, and I understand. I just think that a lot of us went for a reason. I tried to talk to, and befriend, every new guy that I met. I have always felt that my time there was not a waste. It's a complicated life we all lead, and for some shorter than what seems fair. But it isn't how long you get, but what you do with the time."

Tom Schiefer in front of Old Guard/Charlie Co.
headquarters. Photo by Tom Schiefer.

Gouge describes who was chosen for leadership positions, "The platoon was in turn composed of three rifle squads that contained 10 men each. The squads were led by 'squad leaders,' who were either staff sergeants or 'Buck' sergeants that were, hopefully, experienced combat veterans. (It was also not uncommon to see some squads led by E-4's, otherwise known as a Specialist 4th Class)."

Platoons were reduced to smaller-sized squads and men were promoted often before they had the appropriate training for such a job. Stan had shown that he had what it took to be a successful leader—one the men could trust and follow. Stephen writes in his book, <u>Bait</u>, "There was another example of poor strategy. Our platoons were down to squad-sized elements, yet we were to act as platoons."

ROSS PROMOTED
Mr. and Mrs. Russell Ross, RFD 3, Mt. Pleasant received word recently that their son, Stanley, has been promoted from PFC to Sergeant. He has been in Vietnam 4½ months and his address is as follows:
Sgt. Stanley D. Ross
479-64-6162
Co. C., 2nd Bait., 3rd Inft.
199th Infantry Brigade
APO San Francisco, Calif.
96279.

Stan's promotion appeared in the *Mt. Pleasant News.*

August 26, 1969

Dear Mom and Dad,

Well, they brought out some paper and stuff today, and I guess we're about as far as they're going to make us go, so I thought I'd write.

Thanks for your advice on taking sergeant, but as you already know, I'm sergeant already. (ha ha)

When I first wrote you, I didn't figure they'd even think of promoting me until Nov. Dec. but this is something I don't even have to mess with SP4. But one thing sure, a man deserves it! Anyone who beats the jungles, it's beyond explaining.

It's really been hot the last few days, over 100 degrees, and humping in that kind of heat is hell!

Have you received the movie camera yet? Tell me if it gets there in good shape, especially for not having it insured.

Well, I've got bamboo poisoning on my hands now. It beats hell the way a guy gets diseases over here. There's a million and one things he can catch. I'll probably have to go to the aid station and get it fixed, but that's all right. Everyday out of the field is one less spent there.

Well, I guess that's about all for now, not much news that anyone wants to hear. (ha ha)

Love you all, from old Sarg. (ha ha)

Dad was against Stan taking on the added stress of a sergeant, because he knew the extra responsibility also meant that he would be taking additional risks. My parents didn't want a hero. They wanted their son to come home in one piece. They were proud of his promotion, but our older and wiser father knew the possible consequences, and he also knew that Stan would take the job in spite of what he said.

Lieutenant Norm Sassner's recollection of how Stan became sergeant, "I do recall how and why Stan got promoted to squad leader. We were at FB Crystal after a number of days on patrol and we had a number of rotations and people needing replacing. The Captain called me over to his bunker and told me to pick a squad leader and let him know in 15 minutes. I went back to our posting, called the platoon sergeant and said, 'give me three names to pick from for squad leader. I will do the same and then we will select.' We both wrote out names and Stan was chosen. My list had Stan's name three times, plus I had the last word. Stan was a good man, someone that was respected and looked up to. He was by far the best selection. I would do it again."

Soldiers in Vietnam were not only trying to stay alive by living through the next ambush or firefight, but from a number of other physical conditions as well. They endured everything from bamboo poisoning and leeches to insect bites and immersion foot, just to name a few. Southeast Asia's climate provided a petri dish of diseases and pestilence.

As it turned out Stan's formal sergeant ranking wouldn't come through before his death. He was classified as a Sp4.

Lanning describes bamboo poisoning in <u>The Only War We Had</u>, "Bamboo poisoning was the result of pricks from the sharp thorns. Puss-filled sores the size of pencil erasers and about four inches apart covered one of my legs…as they healed, they left small black holes."

Comments
By
Top Sgt. Melvin Ploeger

I was First Sergeant for seven years of my military career. Two of the years were spent in Vietnam. The first year in 1966, up north in the jungles, and the last down south with the 199th L.I.B. C Co. 2nd Battalion 3rd Infantry. That, of course, was the unit that both I and Stan were members.

I took my job very seriously and, of course, had very little time for joking and smiling. My interests were to get the job done and bring as many of the boys home as possible.

I am very happy to think that you are working hard to bring a closure to you and your parents about a very sad part of your lives. Memories will always carry on, but we must accept those honorable memories, as Stan was one fine soldier. There is no doubt in my mind that had he lived he would have left Vietnam a sergeant.

Please accept that it is very hard for me to discuss many of the sad days of my life in combat and would rather not mention specifics that cause sadness.

I did try very hard to get the troops hot chow as often as possible. That always made them smile.

Sincerely,
Melvin E. Ploeger 1st SG U.S. Army Retired

First Sergeant Melvin "Top" Ploeger. (Lower right)
Top and Captain McGinnis. Photo from Old Guard
Yearbook, 1969.

Michael Lanning described SGT. Ploeger in <u>The Only War We Had</u>,
"First Sergeant Melvin Ploeger was running the Company headquarters
at Black Horse. Soldiers and other officers alike called him Top. The
other first sergeants occasionally referred to him as Red…Top did his
best to be mean as hell. He was usually successful. No one had the
nerve to ask his age, but we figured he was over thirty-five, making him
the oldest man in the company.

Top had nearly twenty years in the Army. As First Sergeant, he was
responsible for the company's administration and logistics. Although
no one would admit it, we all liked the bastard."

August 28, 1969

Dear Mom and Dad,

Well, I'm finding more time on my hands than I usually do, so I thought I'd write to the folks back home.

Not really much has happened since last time I wrote. We haven't made contact for at least two weeks now. I hope it's another six months before we make contact again. That just isn't my bag. (ha ha)

Hey, Dad, if you ever want a transistor portable television, I can get one over here, (real nice) for $100.00. It would save a man quite a bit on money.

Well, how are all the crops doing? I've seen a few corn fields over here, they're not too good!

Well, almost another month gone. Pretty soon I'll be on number six. Wow. But it still seems like a long time till April, but it will come.

How's everything down at the plant, Dad? Driving a cement truck would sure seem like fun right now. But I guess everything gets old.

Well, I guess I won't have to worry about starving the way you're canning everything up, Mom. (ha ha)

Well, I guess we've got a jungle sweep this afternoon. I guess they spotted some gooks out there. So like always we'll have to go try to scare something up. I guess that's about all for now. I'll write next time I get a chance.

With love, Stan

Dad drove a cement truck to subsidize the family income. He worked at the Ready Mix plant in town that was owned by the Coder family. Dad enjoyed the work, and made many life-long friends while being there. The company was flexible in giving him time off when he had field work to do. Our little brother, Phillip, looked forward to the times when Dad, having a job close by, would stop at the house and pick him up. It was a real treat to ride in the big cab with his dad.

When we go for a ride these days, Dad likes to point out a bridge, school, or basement that he helped pour when he worked for the company.

The plant is still in operation in the same place, but has different owners.

I recall our mother proudly displaying her canned goods on the kitchen counter. She put up everything from corn, lima beans, green beans, tomatoes, peas, pickles, sauerkraut, cherries, peaches, pears, strawberries, you name it—she canned or froze it. We rarely had "store bought" produce, meat, or milk. The family farm provided for most of our needs when it came to food. Going out to eat was a real treat. A cheeseburger and chocolate malt from Van's diner was really special.

August 31, 1969
Dear Mom and Dad,

Well, another day in Vietnam, not much new. It's been real hot lately. I'm glad that I'm sorta used to it.

Well, we've been getting a lot of new guys lately. Two are from Iowa, around Cedar Rapids, I guess. They said it was sure nice in Iowa when they left. I talked to them an hour about back in good old Iowa.

Damn, I get homesick at times. It's a hell of a feeling not being able to do anything about it. A person could just scream at times. But that's war!

Well, they're still trying to break me in for the squad leader job. There's a lot to learn, but it's sure nice to be sorta at the "Boss" end. (ha ha)

Well, I guess the next mission is just nine men. They're taking us by chopper to this hill in the jungle, and for four days we're just sitting there waiting to see if we can ambush some gooks. It will be a break, from humping, but it's sorta hairy. Nine men all alone in the jungle. Wow!

It's amazing the schemes they come up with to get gooks. I get so damn tired of doing everything, just to kill someone. This Army is crazy! It's hell. A guy is brought up, taught not to kill, and then comes over here and that's all a person's around. What a world! (ha ha)

Just the other day they blew a claymore mine on three VC. They picked them up in plastic bags, laughing, bragging just like a bunch of vultures. Enemy or not, it made me sick! Well, enough of that.

Well, like I say, I guess there's not much new.

That one instance I mentioned is news, but who likes to hear it. See what I mean! It's harder than hell to write a letter, because if anything ever happens out here, it's someone getting killed or hurt.

Well, bye for now, and like you say, Mom, thank God for each new day, and believe me, I do thank him!

With love, SGT Stan (ha ha)

Helicopters coming in.

Aerial of Cam Tam village (jungle to the right). Photo by Jayson Dale.

Going through Stan's personal effects, we found his notebooks that had codes and signals he used as a squad leader. It looked like a bunch of letters and numbers to me, but to Stan it was a very guarded and important piece of equipment.

Stan's comments in this letter reminded me of a letter in Edelman's Dear America, *1LT Robert Salem's letter to his parents on October of 1969,* "There are so many things here that I've seen that make me proud to be an American, proud to be a soldier. Yet there are times too when I just wonder why things are done the way they are in the war, in the Army. I find myself a witness—and, yes, even, at times, an accomplice—to things I never would have dreamed (of). I suppose that innocence at best is not permanent, but the end of it is inevitably accompanied by some pain…"

1LT Broyles states in Dear America, "The emotions of war often swing wildly from comradeship and exhilaration to shame and guilt." *He quotes Sp4 George Olson's reflections of war in the forward of* Dear America, "The frightening thing about it all is that it is so very easy to kill in war. There's no remorse, no theatrical 'washing of the hands' to get rid of nonexistent blood, not even any regrets. When it happens, you are more afraid (than) you've ever been in your life…You kill because that little SOB is doing his best to kill you and you desperately want to live, to go home, to get drunk or walk down the street on a date again."

August 31, 1969
Dear Mom and Dad,

Well, guess what? I got pulled out of the field for about three days. That bamboo infection I told you I had, well, it got worse. So I guess they think they need to take a little better care of it. But I didn't get to go to BMB. I'm just sitting here at a fire support base.

That mission I mentioned, the nine men, well, they took off this morning. I'm sorta glad I missed it. It's pretty hairy.

Hey, Mom, that last letter you wrote about the motorcycle races and the names you mentioned—Parkers, Richards, Harold, what did you all do? Please explain what the hell went on. (ha ha)

Well, enough for that. I haven't received my camera yet. I suppose it will be here in a few days. Did you ever receive the movie camera? Tell Bill thanks for the package. I'll write him the first chance I get. We all sat around last night and ate it. Man, what a treat! A person sure appreciates things.

It sounds like everyone has got cycles now. I'm sure going to have one! That's the only thing that keeps me from going crazy, just thinking of coming home! It just seems like a dream that I ever lived in such a wonderful place!

Hey, Mom, you remember that plumber (Halson) family, the ones we sold that Red Rambler to? I ran into their boy over here. I guess he just got here. Man, what a surprise. We were back for clean clothes, and I went over to the beer stand to get a beer, and there he was. Man, he made me feel short. He'll be over here until next August, and April is coming, slow but sure. But he's not in the Infantry, so he's got it knocked. Well, bye for now.

With love, Sgt. Stan

GIs in Vietnam not only had to worry about being killed by the VC and NVA, but by a host of pests and diseases. Tim O'Brien speaks of this in his book, The Things They Carried, *"They carried diseases, among them malaria and dysentery. They carried lice and ringworm and leeches and paddy algae and various rots and molds. They carried the land itself—Vietnam, the place, the soil—a powdery orange-red dust that covered their boots and fatigues and faces." When I read Stan's letters, the paper was stained with the red dust and mud of Vietnam.*

The families (Parkers and Richards) that Stan mentions in regard to the motorcycle races were close family friends of our parents. Stan was friends with Bob Richards. They were in the same graduating class in high school. Bob joined the Marines after high school and went to Vietnam. Randy Parker was younger than my brother. He and his family lived about a mile from our home. Our families got together to camp and water ski. Stan loved those kinds of activities. How he hated missing out on such fun!

Even a world away, Stan ran into guys that he knew personally or had acquaintances with from home. He was very gregarious. He never met a stranger and could start a conversation with anyone. This characteristic would be recalled by all the men who knew and loved him.

September 1, 1969

Dear Mom and Dad,

Well, another day. I received my camera yesterday. I really had fun with it.

I'm still healing my bamboo poisoning up. But tomorrow back to the field. Man, a person can sure get spoiled in even two days. I think I'm getting by with something, by eating a hot meal.

I'm sending you a picture. Look close for the stripes! That's my home to the right of the picture (the bunker). (ha ha) Don't laugh. It's like a Holiday Inn. Sure beats the foxhole. It's not the best picture, but look what the poor camera had to work with. (ha ha)

I sure hope they get my pay records through for sergeant. But I suppose it'll be a couple of months. They had hardly started on my Sp4 orders.

Well, I'm doing pretty good at writing. Like I say, when a man's not in the field, he's got time, but out there no deal! Well, I guess I'll close.

Whole bunch of love to the best family ever,

Stan

Stan proudly wearing his "Buck" sergeant stripes.

September 8, 1969

Dear Mom and Dad,

Well, we finally stopped for a one-day break. But I guess there's going to be some kind of cease fire. Big deal! Nothing can stop this fighting. We haven't been having too much trouble. Anyway, our company hasn't. I guess we've just been lucky for a change. Our sister company got hit the other day. We got air mobiled to help them, but we didn't get in on too much fighting. No one got hurt in our company. But Bravo Company lost six men, 22 wounded, and four missing in action.

That's what's really bad. I'd rather get killed than to get drug off by the VC, and to be a captive. But that's just part of this stinking shameful war.

Well, I guess I'm a squad leader now. (ha ha) It's not easy, but it's pretty nice for a change to be one on the other end of the stick. As long as I do my job I don't hear no shit from no one. The worst thing is to keep the men alert and on their toes. Because the first wrong move you make, that's when Charlie will get you! Like four out of six that got it from Bravo Co.

The VC had set a 50-pound claymore mine on a path, and when the GIs got close enough, well, that's all it wrote!

Sometimes I wonder how a person will adapt back to civilian life after being like a scared fox for a year. I just hope my nerves last.

You probably laughed at that letter Sam Criger wrote his mom, but believe me, that's just about the way a person would be. I notice myself jumping at little sounds, and the crack of a rifle puts me going wild, and low crawling.

Well, enough on that. Boy, that makes me feel good that school has started. In two more days I start my sixth month.

Wow, damn, I'm homesick! I could cry at times. I swear if I ever get out of here I'll never go further than Trenton. (ha ha)

So Warren and Bill aren't getting along. Well, I guess they never did get along too good. It's a shame. That's funny, me and Warren could have more fun together than I could with any other kids. He writes me pretty often. I really get a kick out of him.

How soon will you be picking corn, Dad? I'd pick it by hand if I were out of here. (ha ha)

Speaking of going fishing, we ran onto a stream the other day and set up an ambush beside it. We threw some grenades in the stream to kill the fish. We fried about 20 in a steel pot. That's the only way to fish! (ha ha)

Well, not too much going on or to write about.

Tell Charlotte Smith I wish her all the happiness in the world. I'll bet they really had a nice wedding.

The new grandstand looked nice. I won't know Mt. Pleasant when I get home. Well, I guess I'll close for now.

We go in for stand-down the 12th. Remember when I mentioned the last one a few months ago? I hope this one is as nice. BMB will sure look nice after all this time in the field. But it will last two or three days.

With love, Stan

Stan wearing his ODs at LZ Blackhorse.

Adjusting to civilian life for returning vets was not easy. Jim Faber, a member of Stan's squad, recalled an incident that reminded him of that fact. He had not been home very long when he and his wife went out for an evening of fun at one of the campus clubs in Iowa City; his wife was attending the University of Iowa. While they were having drinks, someone in the establishment overheard that he (Jim) was a GI back from Vietnam. The guy spit on him. Jim said he didn't react, but thought to himself, "Buddy, I just spent 10 months in the Vietnam jungle, if you only knew what I could do to you!" *After that incident Jim tried to put Vietnam out of his mind.*

When my daughter and I boarded a flight from Savannah to Atlanta in the spring of 2006, a young GI in desert fatigues walked past our seat toward the back of the plane. I noticed him because of his uniform, of course, and that sad look on his face, that homesick look. Anyway a woman from first class walked back and offered him her seat in first class. He thanked her and headed for the front of the plane. The captain got on the intercom and asked him to stand and gave his name and told us that this young soldier had just finished a two-week furlough and was returning to Iraq. The captain praised him and thanked him for his service and reminded all of us how much these service men were sacrificing. Everyone on the plane erupted in cheers and applause. I had to think of what Jim Faber and many other GIs from Vietnam had experienced when they came home. It certainly wasn't to cheers or applause, but rather shame and disgust. How different our attitudes are today. Let's hope we never repeat such regrettable behavior again.

Trenton was a small town three miles north of our home. In its heyday the population was around 200 to 250, most of which were canine, thus the nickname Dogville seemed to stick. My dad recalled that in its more prosperous era, it boasted two blacksmiths, two doctors, barbers, a school, dance hall that also served as the Legion Hall, hotel, library, and the Royal Oak wagon factory. I especially remember with fondness the General Store where Mom would sell her eggs and cream and we would get to buy something sweet. Dad would use the blacksmith to repair farm equipment and I still remember the smell of burning coal that heated the iron needed to fix whatever was broken.

When Stan and I were growing up, it was a place to get gas, a quick snack, or to pass through on your way to a bigger town. It boasted two churches and a school that my sister Eileen attended. The General Store is gone now, along with most of the other businesses. It still has the gas station, churches, and a grain elevator.

Just like Stan, other vets talked about fishing in Vietnam with unorthodox methods. Donald Stephen writes, "One of the men said there were fish in the creek. 'Well, we've searched the area,' I said. 'Now let's destroy.' We found a deep hole and dropped a grenade in the water. Our mission was complete. We set up camp and cleaned the fish."

Stan loved to fish and he had plenty of places to do that at home. We lived close to the Skunk River that flowed into the Mississippi only 20 miles from our home. Little episodes, like the one in the above letter, helped to connect him, I'm sure, to a life he once knew.

I had the chance to interview friends of Stan's who made it back from Vietnam, gave numerous accounts of how the simplest things reminded them of the war and their experiences. Some memories were replayed in nightly dreams. For others, it was just the sight of a butterfly, reminding them of Butterfly Hill, or a rainy day.

Charlotte Smith, one of my best friends, always asked about Stan. I was her maid of honor at her wedding. We had been friends since childhood, attending the same church and spending many weekends at each other's homes. We always said we'd marry cowboys and have a horse ranch someday. Well, she moved to Texas with her husband, Jim, and we both had horses and lived on small acreages. Charlotte was a wonderful mother, wife and friend. She died in April of 1999, losing her battle with brain cancer.

My family and I have often wondered how Stan would have fit in once he returned home. Would the war have made him bitter, hard, intolerant? I'd like to think not. The way things turned out, he will always be that fun-loving, hard-living brother and son, with that great smile and big heart—forever young.

September 10, 1969
Dear Mom and Dad,

Well, not much news. I guess we go in for stand-down the 12th. I'm really looking forward to it. There's sure a lot of time between good times over here.

I guess I go on R&R the 30th of October. Tell Warren I'm going to Manila and look up some of his daughters. (ha ha) There's wine and women there, so I guess I'll check it out. I should have quite a bit of fun.

It's from the 30th of October to the 4th of November, then the 12th I'll start my eighth month. I thought it would be a good time to take one.

I'd thought about going to Hawaii and see you all. But it's so damn expensive and I don't want to say goodbye again. That's the hardest thing I ever had to do in my life was when I left last April.

Well, I guess we get air-mobiled out to some trouble spot tomorrow. But we still go in the 12ᵗʰ. Wow!

With love, Stan

Stan, home on leave, April, 1969, before going to Vietnam.

The 30ᵗʰ of October would never come for Stan. It seems the cruelest fate of all that he would never dance again, hold a girl in his arms and love again, or sleep without the fear of death stalking him.

Warren Lane was Bill's father (Stan's good friend). He was a neighbor and a hard - living, coarse character. My brother and other young guys liked to hang out at his place, because he always had a generous supply of homemade wine and other spirits. Our parents were friends, but my dad didn't approve of some of Warren's influences. Never the less, he was a good friend to my brother, sent care packages, and wrote to him during his time in Vietnam.

Reflections
By
David Garshaw

Karen, thanks for contacting me. Back in 1969 I wish I had had the chance to extend condolences for your loss. I can well imagine the pain is still there. It is for me in my own way.

Thinking about these things prompts me to dig out my old letters to my wife. I have not looked at them since the days I wrote them. Other than what they may help me remember, here are my recollections...

From Stan's first day in the field, when I asked him go out with a squad on a night ambush (which was the custom to initiate the newly arrived) to the last time I saw him, I knew him to be a friend. He wanted to do his best at whatever he was asked to do. Stan was always positive no matter what we faced. I knew I could depend on him. For some reason, his smile is what I remember so much. The last time I saw him, he was standing on the other side of the counter at the supply room at BMB, where I was delegated after my knees deteriorated to the point where I could no longer serve in the field. Smiling and laughing, he was getting his gear ready to go back out into the field. I'm sure we talked about how many days each of us had before we could go home.

I know Stan's death hit me like a ton of bricks and I have felt the loss all these years. Whenever I think of him or have an occasion to mention him, it's as the flower of America's youth.

David Garshaw.

September 14, 1969
Dear Mom and Dad,

Dad, I don't believe it! (ha ha) I read that letter five times to convince myself that you'd bought me a cycle. Man, I'm so excited! Hell, no, I didn't care! I'm just glad you had enough sense to take advantage of a good deal, because I was definitely going to have one. I can't even imagine riding it. It's just like a dream. Please send me pictures of it from every angle. (ha ha)

But I know I'll be worrying constantly about it. Please, please take care of it for me! Tell Eileen to spit polish it (ha ha) and don't let anyone ride it. Because you know how people are. When they get out of sight with it, they will try it out, and it should be drove real slow until the engine is broke in better, and you'd better take the battery out before winter comes along. Maybe you should call Fred Combs and ask him how the best way to store it would be. But like I say, please take care of it.

Well, thanks again, Dad. I wish you could drive it. But it's pretty big, isn't it? (ha ha)

Well, as you know, we're in on stand-down now, we're really having fun. They have a steak fry tonight with all the beer we can drink, and then they have a striptease show. Wow, but I won't look this time either, Mom! (ha ha) It's been two-and-a-half months since I'd seen BMB, and that means Brigade Main Base. It's the home of the 199th. But back to the jungle the 16th man, I hate to think of it!

Well, seven more months to go. Still seems like a lifetime. Tell Eileen if there's one spot of rust or dirt on the '74 when I get home, I'll never speak to her again! (ha ha)

Well, I guess that's all for now. Please write and send pictures of all details.

Excited as hell! Stan

The Harley that Dad bought for Stan.

Stan guarding the beer truck at stand-down.
Photo by Jim Faber.

Stand-down was a welcomed break, especially the guys in the field.
For a few days they could forget about the war, get clean cloths, shave, eat
real food, and enjoy some of the amenities that life in the rear offered. Stan
knew that he'd get a response from Mom when he added the information

about the strippers. I'm sure she gave him a lecture in her next letter. Dad, on the other hand, understood the mind and interests of a nineteen-year old.

Michael Lanning describes BMB in his first book, <u>The Only War We Had</u>, "The camp known in GI language as BMB, for Brigade Main Base, was composed of a multitude of wooden buildings approximately 20 by 80 feet. The floors were concrete and the top two feet between the walls and the tin roofs were covered only with screens. With fans, they were reasonably bearable. Sandbags stacked about half way up the walls protected peace of mind if not the body.

The camp also contained a PX (post exchange), a laundry, a souvenir shop, clubs for the different ranks, and all the usual administrative and support agencies required for a six-thousand man brigade."

Robert Gouge describes stand-down in his book, <u>These Are My Credentials</u>, "After spending days, weeks or months in the field on combat operations or at remote firebases, the Infantry, normally two companies or a battalion at a time, would come into BMB for a 3- to 5-day stand-down. While here, the 'boonie rats' caught up on some much-needed rest and relaxation, re-supply and conducted maintenance on individual weapons and equipment…veterans described it as 'an encampment of armed warriors.' The grunts would come in for a five-day respite from the blood and the mud, the boredom and the terror… they looked like whipped dogs."

Stan was crazy about cars and motorcycles. When Dad purchased the Harley for Stan, I doubt he let himself think about the "what ifs" or how hard it would be to look at the shiny machine Stan looked forward to riding, if he didn't make it home.

In an interview with the Mt. Pleasant Newspaper dated November 11, 2005, my Dad recalled his feeling about the Harley he purchased for Stan, "I'll never forget that motorcycle, but worse, I'll never forget that I never saw him ride it."

After Stan's death, the cycle would sit in the grain bin for weeks before Dad had the heart to sell it. An old saying came to mind when I read this letter, "If you wanna hear God laugh, tell Him your plans."

September 14, 1969

Dear Mom and Dad,

Well, another day of rest. Boy, that steak fry and stripper was all right! (ha ha) My head hurts a little this morning, I wonder why? But tomorrow back to the field. I bought a couple of things. I hope you like them.

Well, I've been in the Army a year and two days. Seems like a lifetime.

Are you taking good care of my cycle? You'd better! (ha ha) Hey, Dad, tell me how much I owe you on the cycle yet. I should have it paid off in one or two months. I don't plan on spending too much on R&R.

Well, like I say, write and send pictures of the '74, and don't let anyone ride it. I don't want it hurt.

Well, I guess not much news. Things haven't been too bad lately, "contact wise". So I can't complain.

It's really something, the way these guys have it back here; they have they're own rooms, television, even air-conditioning in some of them. Man, all the comforts of home, all the beer they want, EM clubs, snack bars, and movies. Like I say, it's too different to believe. No wonder people extend to get out of the field. The one and only good thing about the field is that time goes faster out there.

Well, not much new to write. Bye for now.

With love, Stan

Stand-down, Captain McGinnis (waving), Michael Lanning (center), LT. Divoky. Photo by Jim Faber.

257

Elden Rasmussen and Stan at BMB, Long Binh
getting ready to return to the field after stand-down.
Photo by Jayson Dale.

Edelman writes in Dear America*, Chapter 4,* "In Vietnam, not everybody humped. Most GIs, in fact, worked in rear areas as support personnel. They were a significant part of the American presence in Southeast Asia. In the bloated military bureaucracy, some did jobs that were as wasteful as they were frivolous. Others performed necessary and vital tasks, as doctors and nurses, postal clerks and paymasters, intelligence analysts and graves-registration personnel."

Donald Stephen's opinion of the guys in the field was that, "On the ground, step for step, soldier for soldier, we were as good as any unit in the world. The whole damn war was centered around the good old American Grunt."

September 18, 1969
Dear Mom and Dad,
Well, it isn't very often that I get a chance to write a letter when I'm out in the field. But we're not moving too far today so I thought I'd jump somebody for a paper and pencil. (ha ha)

We are on a seven-mile sweep of jungle. Bravo Company made contact in there twice, so I guess there must be some VC in here. So CO. C is moving through to see if they missed anything. I sure hope we don't make contact. About half of the jungle, a person's got to cut through. It's no fun, but as least I'm not point!

I've got my own radio now. He walks right behind me. My call sign is 33. I've been squad leader now for two weeks.

It's not been too hot here lately. But it's been raining every night. Man, it would be nice to not have to get soaked every night. But that's war!

I haven't gotten the pictures of the cycle yet. Boy, I've been on cloud nine ever since you told me! Please don't let anyone ride it. You know how it is.

What kind of oil did you put in it (Harley Davidson oil)? How did you get it home? Where are you going to store it?

Well, I guess that's enough questions at once. (ha ha) I won't know how to act just pushing an electric starter. I can't wait! Well, I'll close for now.

Doing as good as possible,
Stan

Stan on patrol with his squad, RTO (radio telephone
operator) Terry Wanner in the lead, Stan behind him,
northwest of Cam Tam.

September 20, 1969

Dear Mom and Dad,

Well, another day in Vietnam. Not much news, we're still on a sweep of the jungle. Still no contact yet. Maybe we'll luck out for once. (ha ha) You wouldn't believe how it's raining. I've been wet for three days. I've got a cold. Man, sure not too comfortable. The worst is sleeping in the damn rain. But I guess it's a hardship tour. (ha ha)

Well, how's my baby '74? Sure hope you're taking care of it. Well, at least in a few weeks I won't be missing much, because it will be cold. Well, I guess time is going, but it sure could go a lot faster to suit me. (ha ha) Excuse the dust on the paper. It just started raining again.

They say the last month of the monsoon is unbelievable. It sure is! It's been raining about 16 hours a day.

Well, we really had fun on stand-down. What a band. It was really good! They wouldn't allow us in some of the clubs. They figured we were too animalish like. (ha ha) They didn't want any fights. They had one fight at the EM club, just like on TV. They were throwing chairs and beer cans. Kinda nice to let off a little steam on the BMB Warriors. (ha ha ha)

Well, I suppose we'll be starting off in a little while. It's been one week not out here. The clothes seem to be getting a little dirty. (ha ha) I sure wish R&R would come. I could stand a couple out days out of here!

I got a letter from Paul. I guess they had quite a bit of fun. Well, in about six months it will be the kid's turn. (ha ha)

How's little brother? I sure miss him. There's nothing worse than being torn away from the ones you love. You said it seemed like a dream, I was ever home. Just think what it's like giving up everything and sleeping in the mud! Damn, I get so mad and disgusted some times.

I've had this jungle bamboo rash for a month now. I've even got it under my arm pits! When I sweat, man it burns! They just tell me it will go away. The doctor told me I should try to shower more often, I almost hit him. I asked him if he'd ever been in the field. He said, "No, why?" I told him showers are few and far between. Well, that's life. I'll quit "bitching." Who wants to hear it! (ha ha)

Well, I guess I'll close for now. Like I say, take care of my baby '74.

Bye for now, Sgt. Stan

Stan in the jungle, C-rations for breakfast, ponchos drying in the background.

GIs during stand-down, get a chance to let off some steam and dance with "donut dollies." (Red Cross volunteers)

All the veterans I spoke with recalled the terrible living conditions that they, the Infantry, had to put up with. The elements, pests, lack of proper nutrition and hygiene, took its toll on their bodies and their minds. Stan was not a pampered boy or man. He was used to hard work and discipline, but Vietnam challenged everything he'd experienced in his short twenty years. This was worse than bucking bales in a hot, steamy, Iowa alfalfa field. Mom wouldn't be waiting at the house with a smile, fresh-cold lemonade, and sandwich. All he could do was take it, like the rest of the guys.

Michael Lanning recalls living conditions in the field, in his book, <u>The Only War We Had: a Platoon Leader's Journal of Vietnam,</u> "The terrain and living conditions were taking their toll. Colds, infections, fungus, and malaria continued to lessen our morale as well as our numbers." *Lanning goes on to write,* "Personal hygiene was difficult in Vietnam. When time permitted, we secured both sides of a stream or water-filled bomb crater and took turns bathing. Occasionally a soldier would strip his shirt off and wash it in the punctual afternoon showers."

September 23, 1969

Dear Mom and Dad,

Well, another day in Vietnam. Dad, I probably won't know you when I get home. You've went to fishing and riding motorcycles. (ha ha) Tell me why in the hell you wouldn't do things like that when I was there to enjoy it too! (ha ha) Dad I'm real proud of you. I never figured you'd ever ride the '74. You're finally enjoying one of the biggest pleasures in the world. One thing sure, you don't have to take a back seat to no one on that baby. It's not that hard to ride either is it? Somebody just as well get some good out of it. All I say is just you ride it, don't let anyone else ride it. I just hope you'll let me have it when I get home. (ha ha) I'd hate to buy another one. (ha ha) Well, have all the fun on it you can, Dad. It really makes me feel good to know you're enjoying it!

That's just too bad about Harold. If he can't afford one nice cycle, it's nobody's fault but his own. I'd give my right arm to be home riding around on the nice '74. But it's coming.

Well, as far as for over here, things aren't any better or worse than they have been. We've been riding and working off tracks the last couple of days. They've got it pretty good too! Anything beats walking.

Hey, Mom, if you can, send me some food seasonings. These C-rations are a lot better if a guy can dope them up. Send some hot sauce/pepper, garlic salt, Barbeque salts, anything that works. (ha ha) And if you see any of those cans of pudding (ready-to-eat). A guy got some in the mail, it was real good. Get chocolate if you can.

Well, enough on that. I got my pictures that I took with my little camera. They're not too good. I think I'll sell it. I don't suppose those pictures you had developed turned out any better, did they?

Hey, about those cycle pictures, I never have got them. That's my damn luck. I've really been looking forward to them. But they probably got lost in the mail.

Well, bye for now, Stan

Dad holding a beer, sitting on the Harley that he
purchased for Stan.

Squad loaded up, and heading out for the field.
(Front, right) Jim Faber, Greg Breeckner.

Robert Gouge describes the Army's culinary delights, "The cuisine for the Infantry consisted mainly of C-rations, which were small meals packaged in a cardboard box that contained anything from Beans and Franks, Spaghetti and Meatballs, to Chicken and Tuna, and also Ham and Lima Beans which were affectingly called Ham and motherfu----s. There were twelve different meals in all and each package contained an accessory pack that contained toilet paper, a spoon, cocoa mix, coffee and cream, a P-38 can opener and small pack of four cigarettes, which were usually Winstons, Pall Malls, Marlboros or Salems. Each soldier would carry between three to five days worth of meals, depending on the length of the mission and the likelihood of being re-supplied in the field."

Dear Karen   Sept. 26

Well I had almost figured you
were mad at me. But I guess
I can't talk. I'm not the best
at keeping up letter writting
either. HA HA I guess you are
pretty busy and alot of changes
are made. Well theres been a
few things changed at this
end to. I'm a squad leader now
I've got 15 men under me. Thats
why they made me sargeant. It's
got its disadvantages, but at
least I'm usually the boss. I don't
catch much hell from anyone.
unless I mess up. We got
made contact the other day. We
got 4 VC, but other wise things
have been pretty quiet lately.

I hope I never see contact again.
It really puts a guy praying. HA.
HA. But otherwise thats about all
the news. We're still in this
messed up jungle. Its impossible
to get rid of the VC.
They'll be fighting these gooks for
10 more years. We had standown
2 weeks ago. We really had
fun. It was the second time
I'd been to the rear since I've
been here. Those guys have got
it made back here. "But that luck". HA.
HA. I'm real happy for you, going
back to school and all. Like you
say it will be worth it
someday. I've thought about
Colledge a few times. But I've
got to get out of this hell
hole first. My 1st lieutenant
said his been to York, Neb.

3.

quite a few times. I guess he lives about 20 miles from there. He's a pretty good guy. We get along real good. "Hey" did you know dad bought me a 1967, Electra slide motor cycle. It just had 836 miles on it. It's really beautiful. I can't wait to get home. Well I guess lil close for now. Like I say not much new around this place. Well I'll have plenty of women and women the 30th of next month HA HA. I should have fun HA. HA. Well write me again sometime and good luck in school.

Stan.

Men attending wounded, ready for "dust off," a GI reaches up to grab a hook that lifts the injured up to the medivac chopper. Photo by Jim Faber.

(Left to right) Captain McGinnis and 1st Lieutenant
Ronald Divoky.

September 30, 1969
Dear Mom and Dad,

Well, I don't know what to write. It's all about the same old shit! Not much new happening. We are working in some elephant grass now. It's a bitch! I've been sorta worried about scaring up an elephant. That would be the shits. (ha ha) We're always finding big piles of shit. But there's not many around here.

We haven't been in contact for almost three weeks. Wow, thank God for that! Boy, things are really different around here from when I first got here. There are just three guys left in the field that have more time in the country than I do. A lot of guys have gotten jobs in the rear, but I suppose I'll rot out here. (ha ha)

I've been having a little trouble out here with one of the guys in my squad. All he wants to do is stay drunk. I can't blame him much. But a guy just can't do some things out here. A guy can't keep his cool when he's drunk! I told him, I'd take him off by myself and he could forget I'm a sergeant and try to make me see things his way. That pretty well set him straight. Just like a lot of guys, all mouth! We have trouble with pot smokers too! I told my men if I ever catch them smoking it, I'll put them in jail. But actually I've got a pretty good bunch of men.

Well, how's the '74 running, Dad? Will it go 120 MPH, or haven't you tried it yet? (ha ha) Well, not much longer and I start my seventh month. Wow, 30 days till R&R. That should be quite a bit of fun. Well, like I say, not much new. Don't worry. Things are as good as can be.

With love, Stan

Stan's concern about drug use was justified. His life, as well as his men's, depended on everyone being alert and aware. Anything less would lead to disaster!

When I talked to other vets about the drug problems we heard so much about in Vietnam, their response was that it was more of a problem in the rear than in the field.

However, there were exceptions, as Donald Stephen writes from experience, in his book, Bait, "For three months prior to OCS (Officer Candidate School), I'd been assigned to a holdover platoon in Fort Gordon, Georgia. While I was there, I saw many kinds of methods used, from sucking shoe dye poured over a sock, to every pill imaginable, so I know what grass smelled like.

"I never smoked before, nor taken any other kind of drug, so I didn't try my cigarette that day. I sat and watched captains and majors light up. They enjoyed every bit of the grass. Not all officers partook, and several did as I, and refused even to light up. Still I thought, 'These are the people who are going to lead men into combat.'"

Stephen goes on to write later in his book, "I had heard the rumors about drugs in Vietnam, but I had never taken any, including marijuana, so I didn't know the effects. I had been in the bush forever, and I couldn't imagine using drugs when everyone's lives depended on alertness and quick reaction." *He goes on to say,* "When we were on two-day stand-downs, some of the men smoked a little, and some got a little drunk, myself included. But it was a different story in the bush."

Ches Schneider recalls drug use of various sorts during his tour, "I noticed that once we hit the rear area, our close-knit platoon broke up into factions. The Blacks all formed soul-brother groups, and the heavy boozers started to buddy up. A few potheads emerged, and they sought out REMF dopers and soon they were zonked. I can truly say that until that time, I hadn't seen any of our guys do any dope in the field or on a fire support base."

October 6, 1969
Dear Mom and Dad,

Well, how's things at home? Please excuse me for not writing sooner. I guess you were right, Mom. We hadn't had contact for about three weeks, but they just keep building up. It's been hell the last few days. We ran into a company-sized NVA force. They put us on tanks because we couldn't handle them by foot. We were in contact for two days (off and on).

Believe me, I've written three letters and tore them up. I just don't want to worry you no more than you are. They pulled me out of the field for two days for outstanding leadership of my squad. I was flown to Xuan Loc for dinner with the General of the 199th Infantry BDE. It was a real honor, almost too much for a farm boy! (ha ha)

I'll tell you one thing, Mom and Dad, I had an experience man to man with the enemy that you wouldn't believe, so I won't even tell you until I get home. Because I know you must worry.

But anyway, when they told me I was going before the General for outstanding leadership, I told them I was going to speak for my men. I'm more than proud to serve with men that will stick by a person under extreme hostile fire. I talked with him for more than 45 minutes.

Well, I'm closing for now because you're going to hear all about it anyway. Please don't say nothing to anyone. I'm really looking forward to R&R. I'll call you the first thing!

Love and miss you all so much! Stan

Brigadier General of the 199th,
Warren K. Bennett.

The medal that Stan received and the recognition from the General was a result of his confrontation with an enemy soldier that was hidden behind jungle vegetation, waiting in ambush. Jayson Dale, Stan's friend, described what happened; "Stan saw movement near some brush. He moved a bush with his foot, rather than his rifle, uncovering the enemy. Stan was lucky to get the first shot off, saving himself and his squad." *Stan told Jayson, had he used his rifle to move the bush instead of his boot, he wouldn't have had time to get his gun in position. That was quick thinking. Stan received the Bronze Star for his action.*

Stan was awarded his first Bronze Star for killing the enemy at close range on October 5, 1969. He received his second after his death on October 20, 1969.

A letter from Mom, expressing the concern she held for her son, as well as the pride she felt for him being recognized and honored by his superiors.

October 13, 1969

My Dearest Son, Stan,

Sweetheart, your letter's beside me. Yes, it's been the longest we've waited for a letter.

Oh, Sweetheart my burden wasn't in vain. Two weeks ago on Monday I had such a burden for you, Stan. I spent time on my knees before God—all I could do was pour my heart out to the Lord. Watch over my Stan. No other words would come out. Yes, we're proud of you. But we hate it that you're under such hardship (nerves).

I've committed you into God's hands; He knows and holds the reins. All we can do seemingly is to sit tight, like on a time bomb. That's how we feel here at home. Faith is our only refuge, honey. Stan, I'll try to write more.

I just can just imagine how thrilling it is to be treated royally for a change. You deserve every ounce of it, honey.

I bet you're counting the days to R&R. I've got new to tell you in a new letter, hometown news, some good and some bad.

Take care and thank God for every day sweetheart! I do for you, and every one of the men. Please keep your cool, sweetheart. Don't try to go it alone. You've got great men.

Love, Mamma

(A letter to Mom and Dad from Stan's friend, Steve Klaus.)

October 6, 1969

Dear Rose and Russ and all,

Hi, I got your letter. Seems I never hear from Stan. I don't know if the mail don't get there or it is just harder to send letters in country.

They sent me into Cen Chi. Been working with some LRRP's last three days. I've got to get my weapon cleaned. I met a guy from the 199th 2/3 Alpha Co. He says he's going to look Stan up for me. I wish Stan would try to get to go to sniper school. I'd be able to see him a couple days.

It sounds like you had some good luck hunting. No, I never knew about the '74 Harley. I expect Stan will put on a few miles.

I was really glad to hear Bob gets to come home in November. Twelve months is long enough for anybody to stay in this _____ country.

How does Bill like college? I hear Stan sent home pictures. I've seen the type. They are really good pictures. I've a notion to get one.

Am glad to hear the weather is nice. I know winter is right around the corner. I hear R. Scarff joined the N. Guard, and friend R. Waterhouse is about to go into the Army. I wish he could wait to go in January, and then he could be my replacement. (ha ha)

Well, best close now. Hope all are fine. I'm OK.

Steve

Steve Klaus, Stan's friend and sniper in the 25th Inf.

October 8, 1969

Dear Mom and Dad,

Not too much time to write. Things haven't been the best lately. But I'm still alive, so I guess that's all that counts.

The General of the 199th INF. BDE gave me a three-day leave to Vung Tau, but like a fool I turned it down. The squad is hurting for men, so I figured I'd better stay and do my job. The VC have been hitting pretty regular lately, but we've got some good men out here. Believe me it's been like killing rabbits. (It's hell.) Well, enough on that. All I can do is just worry you more.

Hey, Dad, please find out for me if there's any way I can get an (AK 47) NVA rifle home. I've got a nice one. You wouldn't believe the fight we had! I took it from a dead gook. I'd sure like to get it home. So maybe I can get it home through the VFW, or American Legion, as a war trophy. I know it's going to be hard to get it home, but please see what you can do. One thing sure, it's got quite a story behind it. Well, got to go. (Not long until R&R.) (ha ha) Be looking forward to a letter about it.

Love, Stan

Stan and Willie Thorpe in the rubber plantation.

I don't know, but I'm guessing that the AK47 Stan was talking about was the gun he took from the Vietnamese soldier he mortally wounded. Taking war trophies was always a sensitive issue.

Stan's own destiny would come in a similar confrontation, when he would be ambushed by the enemy. There would be no letter home this time, describing what happened.

One of the last pictures Stan sent home reflects a haunting gaze into the camera of a weary soldier, tired of the killing, exhausted from the living conditions, and lack of nutrition. It is the one photograph that always makes me weep.

I remember the nationwide Vietnam moratorium. I was attending Bethel College. I could hear the bell those three days, at home, in class, walking through campus. I thought of Stan. It was a constant reminder of despair and heartache a world away. I wanted the ringing to stop; it was like a metronome counting off the tragedies of war.

Mom's following letter to Stan, regarding the moratorium, and the rifle he asked about, reflects the worry and stress she and my dad were feeling after hearing about his hand to hand combat with the enemy. It frightened her to think about what Stan had done and what could have happened. Sadly, her fears and dread would become a reality in a few short days.

October, 15 1969
My Dear Stan,

Today is moratorium day in Mt. Pleasant. We've had special meetings in the town square for our four sons who have given their all (life), in Vietnam. If their moms were there, I didn't know them. We had a large group, all sons in Vietnam and overseas were remembered in the service of their country. I was proud to be among the numbers, not proud of the nasty war—but you, son— please don't press yourself, sweetheart. I even took your letter right in to Daddy about the rifle. Thought maybe he could see someone after work about it.

It's almost 5:30 p.m. and mail leaves the post office soon. I'll write you more information tomorrow. Oh, please take care sweetheart, when you're face to face with the enemy, Stan. Oh God, help my son! Please don't do that again! We don't want a medal, we've told you that. Please!

Love, Mamma

Stan with that look of despair and exhaustion, after
being in the field for an extended period of time.

Stan's Final Letter Home

This letter, the last that Mom and Dad received from my brother, was the hardest for me to read and record. He was killed on October 20, 1969. My parents received this letter on October 22, 1969. They had already heard the news that he had been killed.

I had sent a care package (cookies, hand lotion, gum, candy, etc,) a couple of weeks before his death. My package never reached him, and it was sent back to me days after he was killed. It was heartbreaking to open it and look over everything I had so carefully packed a few weeks prior. The cookies were a little crumbled, but everything was there. It broke my heart as I lifted each item, and thought of Stan and the fact that this box had been to Vietnam and back.

It reminded me of the letters in the last chapter of Edelman's <u>Dear America</u>, letters that would be treasured as one of the last correspondence of a son, husband, father, nephew, or daughter. Letters that held such pain, yet promise that, just maybe, they would make it home to those they loved.

This was the first time I had read many of the letters that Stan had written home to my parents. It was heart wrenching as I took in each of his words and listened to his voice describe his life in the field. The homesickness, fatigue, loneliness, and disillusionment that he felt each day must have been a terrible weight!

It was painful to read the letters after all the years that had passed since Stan's death. He wrote as he spoke in that "country boy" slang. The battles he fought were not only in the field, but in his heart as well. He fought the enemy, but he also respected him, and said so many times. There was no delight or satisfaction in killing for Stan. He did what he had to do for his country, his men, and his survival. He would often comment that he "was still alive!"

He loved his family more than life itself. He praised our mother for her unwavering support through the letters of encouragement she wrote almost daily. She kept Stan informed of the latest gossip, news from the community, and family happenings. I'm sure he poured over each letter until the ink was barely readable or because he had to destroy them for security reasons.

Stan wrote often, in camp, foxholes, the jungle, and in rice paddies, leaving trails of his muddy finger prints along the margins. I would trace over those prints like a blind woman reading brail, hoping my fingers would some how connect with his spirit.

I mourned that he would never be a husband, father, or grandfather, that he missed family gatherings, Christmas celebrations, the 4th of July, and high school reunions. I wish he could have known his nieces and nephews and that we could have laughed about the silly things we did as kids.

He wanted so much to come home again and see the "Little Man" (Phillip) and be, as he said in one of his letters, "back in the picture again!" He did come home again, but not the way he or we wanted.

Stan left us with fond memories of his brief 20 years. He was a risk taker, dare devil, and a fun loving guy. He was a macho guy on the outside, but inside his chest beat a tender heart.

Stan was a good brother, friend, and son. He was a normal guy who dreamed, loved, planned, and cared too much. He was passionate about life and never did anything halfway. Maybe if he would have taken that three-day leave that he mentions in this last letter, he would have made it back, but he didn't want to leave his men, and as my Dad said many times, "You can drive yourself crazy wondering, what if!"

Perhaps that's why he paid the ultimate price and sacrifice...he took the chance and gave his all.

October 17, 1969
Dear Mom and Dad,
Well, how's everything at home. Sorry I haven't written for a while, but we've been on the move. Things have calmed down a little, maybe the VC have moved away. (ha ha) I hope!

They have built a fire support base right in the middle of where we were making heavy contact. Boy, it was a nightmare. But it's all over. I just hope we don't run into them again.

When I talked to the General, he said he thought it was a supply route for NVA supplies, so we're just working clover leaves out of the fire support base. I told them I'd like to take my men on a three-day search and ambush mission. I don't want to hang around here while they're building this place up. And my men feel the same way.

Don't worry about those little problems I wrote you about. I've got a good bunch of men. Matter of fact, you wouldn't believe it but I took the platoon out the other day (28 men). I've even had the 1st Lieutenant ask me for an answer. (ha ha) I don't catch hell from no one anymore. Like I told you when I was home, your shit until you prove yourself and your ability. Please don't get the idea I'm bragging, because I'm not! That's just the way it is. I think I've had a conversation with every captain and on up clear to the General, and I've told them all just what I think of this F_ _KED up war! I told the General they should do more for the morale of the Infantryman, and before I flew back to the unit they had already set a schedule for a USO show, so maybe I done a little good. But it's terrible the way they treat the Infantry. We can't even get any beer anymore. But one thing sure, no matter what happens, I'm not breaking down now. I'm over half way through this shit, and I've go too much to look forward to, RIGHT! Just 13 days till I can talk to you. Wow, won't that be something!

What did you ever find out about getting the AK 47 home? I sure hope there's a way. Did you get my Bronze Star? Boy, I never figured I'd ever earn that! I'll get the certificate that proves it and the story for the paper in a couple of weeks.

Well, I suppose you're all happy about the Mets getting the series, huh, Dad! Yes, I've got the cycle pictures. What a beauty! I look at them every day. Well, bye for now,

Love, Stan

October 20, 1969

In late January and early February of 2006, I spoke with men who were with Stan on that fateful day. For all it was a difficult memory to revisit. Stan was not the only comrade they had seen mortally wounded, but for these men, speaking with a relative about what happened made the facts of that day more sensitive. I felt a bond with these men, a connection even though we had never met. We were from the same generation. I understood the decades they had been through, the innocent, carefree 50s and the raw, turbulent 60s.

As I listened to each one, I don't know what it was, exactly, that I wanted to know. I read the official, type-written, government statements my parents received 36 years ago. But somehow I had to hear it for myself. Did he speak after it happened? Where was the wound exactly? Did he cry out? Did he moan? Was there someone to console him? Were there any last words? Did he suffer?

Memories of that day came back in fragments to them; one thing triggered another, and so on. They would pause and say, "Oh, yea, I remember now," and then go on. It all seemed so surreal. Stan was smiling, smoking his pipe on the trail one moment, the next, he was on the ground motionless, his pipe lying beside him. There were no enemies captured to avenge their friend, no ceremony to mark his passing, just the automatic reaction that every GI acted on during a fight, survival of the group and self-preservation.

The following are their accounts to me…

Tom Schiefer right with buddy Jim Faber, Cam Tam.

Reflections
By
Tom Schiefer
199ᵗʰ, Charlie Co.
October 20, 1969

Let me start off by stating my feelings as they probably affect my point of view of this day that left its mark on about a dozen young men for the 36 years since then.

I had been in Vietnam for about two months at this point and most of the time had been more of a battle with the elements and longing for those we all missed back in what we called the "world." Funny how we GIs developed our own language with words like, Gook, World, Freedom Bird, FNG and Short timer. I think about those words once in a while, and they bring back a kind of serendipitous feeling that I don't think I'll ever understand.

That morning started off like most, with one notable exception, we were going back in for a two-day stand-down after being in the field on an ass kicker of a mission that had lasted about three weeks. I think few people understand 21 days without a hot meal or a shower, but all of us were long over due and feeling a sense of excitement.

I remember 3rd squad went on point that day as we left our overnight NPD (night perimeter defense) and we moved back east. We had about 10 miles to go before meeting up with the rest of the 2nd and 3rd and an artillery group, where we would build a small base camp that night. That meant hot meals and at least a change of clothes.

Tad was walking point and Ben Jackson was second. This was our new formation as a couple weeks earlier I had taken over the M60 and John had moved back in the squad. Stan Ross was walking 3rd with Faber behind him and then me and Calahan. Bobby was my AG, so I'm pretty sure of this but some of it is hard to recall as we were probably short about three people from a normal squad. I think following Bob and Blasik was the lieutenant. It's funny, but I have no recollection of who was in formation after that, but I'm sure Doc and a few others were very involved that day, but things got out of hand and some of it isn't clear and has never been for me.

We had just started north off a tank trail about two miles from our overnight and I heard a couple snaps in the air. That is a sound you hear when you are on the other end of automatic weapons. Once I hit the dirt, I tried to take a real quick assessment of the situation and the first thing that came to mind was, we were in four-foot-high grass that made seeing ahead or even seeing the other guys hard. Bobby plopped down in the grass beside me and said something like, "Oh, shit!" I looked to my left and saw Faber trying to do the same thing I was, which was to get high enough to see what the hell was going on without catching a bullet. At this point I heard an M16 empty and a couple AK's incoming just sputtering at us. About five seconds later, Faber called to me that Stan and Ben had both been hit. I got up and moved over about 10 feet where I saw Stan who had been shot once in the chest and had a look on his face I will never forget. About then the lieutenant yelled at me to move up and open fire on the tree line about 100 feet in front of me and to the right. Bob and I ran up and went through about 300 rounds just trying to get things under control which seemed to work, because I never heard any return fire after that moment. At this point, you're probably talking about two minutes since the first shot (things happen very fast in combat and then it's over).

My next memory of that day is crawling back a ways to ask how everyone was and seeing Benny Jackson. I knew he was not going to make it. Stan had a sucking chest wound and Doc had put a dressing on it like we had been taught to do and I thought Stan, being a big tough guy, was going to make it. But he looked so pale and scared that he probably went into shock. I remember the guys loading him on the Medivac which seemed to get there in just a few minutes. I was thinking they could get him turned around.

Well, after the chopper left we hung around for a while and I remember the guys on the chopper calling us and saying Stan didn't make it. That was one of the toughest days of my life. Ben Jackson and I went to Vietnam together, all the way from Oakland through the induction center, he was the only guy I knew, and there he was dead. Just as devastating a loss was Stan Ross, one of the guys who, when I got to the platoon, made me feel welcome, talked and joked and seemed just like one of my friends back in the world. It was a damn sad day. That's probably why 36 years later I remember it so well.

I remember that we never really talked about it even back then. I think it was a very personal thing that just dug up too many feelings that we didn't want to deal with. I know we sure missed those guys and we were all changed forever.

Tom Schiefer lives near Bucyrus, Ohio where he has been employed with General Electric for 39 years, as an engineer. He went to school on the GI Bill. Tom also owned a computer business, building computers for clients and businesses. Tom is married and has five children. He and his family like to spend their summers on Lake Erie boating.

Jim Faber.

James Faber's Recollections
October 20, 1969

I spoke with Jim Faber on February 26, 2006. Jim arrived in Vietnam in early July of 1969. He had gotten married to his wife, Lou Ann, four weeks before he shipped out, as he thought he probably wouldn't make it back. Jim spent ten months in the jungle, some of which was in Stan's squad. Jim had tried to put Vietnam out of his mind all these years, until I contacted him. The memories were too painful to talk or think about.

He remembered my brother and the day he was killed. He recounted Stan's final moments to me. After Stan was wounded he told Jim that he had that "million dollar wound" soldiers often referred to, the wound that would get him home without dying. Stan had a "sucking chest wound." Jim knew it was crucial that they Stan get air-lifted out as soon as possible. Twenty to thirty minutes was as much time as they could spare. It took the Medivac helicopter about 45 minutes to land because of the fire fight they were engaged in. Stan was awake and said he would beat Jim home to Iowa and all the girls before he would.

Jim and his wife Lou Ann are Iowa natives, and Lou Ann knew many of Stan's friends while attending the university. Jim and Lou Ann have two grown sons. Jim is a successful business man who works for Thermo Electron Corporation. His job takes him to many foreign countries, but he has never returned to Vietnam.

Jim provided several pictures that appear in this book. He, like Stan, took many pictures while in Vietnam. I'm thankful for their documentation of a difficult time in their lives and in the history of our nation.

Reflections
by
Ronald Divoky
April 22, 2006

As I reflect on Stan I recall the good times we had. He was a great guy and we had a lot in common. We both came from a farm background and it was not uncommon, when possible, for us to sit around and talk about farming and raising hogs and livestock. He would tell me about farming in Iowa and I would tell him about farming in Nebraska. At those times it was more like being at home and talking to a friend and neighbor over the fence instead of where we really were.

Third platoon was an exceptional group of guys and I am proud to have served with all of them. I look forward to seeing everyone in July. Unless something major comes up, we are planning on being at the reunion.

Ronald Divoky, was the lieutenant with Stan's platoon on October, 20 1969. He remembers that day as many of the men do who were with my brother. He has fond memories of Stan and said, "He was a good soldier." Ron said that after Stan and Jackson were hit, he instructed his men to concentrate on the tree line where the shots had come from. His medic took over the care of the wounded.

Ron's daughter was born while he was in Vietnam. A son came later while he was stationed at Fort Riley, Kansas. Ron made captain after he extended his tour for one more year. He was discharged from the Army in January of 1972.

Since then he has worked in the telephone industry as an accountant and in other positions. Ron lives in Lincoln, Nebraska, with his wife.

Recollection of a Squad Member
Anonymous
February 1, 2006

"I was a member of Stan's squad, walking on a path that day in October, when he was mortally wounded. We were on patrol in high elephant grass, going down a winding trail. I was behind Stan, Jackson, and Kawahira, the point man. When Stan was hit along with Jackson, we all hit the dirt. We opened up a fire-line with automatic weapons, toward the enemy. I crawled forward and located Stan. He was lying on his side, his pipe on the ground beside him. He looked like he was asleep. At first I thought he was going to be all right. Jackson was badly wounded. He died on the helicopter on the way to the hospital; Stan went into shock, I guess, and never regained consciousness. There was so much weapons fire that the brass shavings—the shrapnel from the firing—was hitting my neck. I pulled up my collar because my neck felt like it was on fire.

"I always remember Stan saying that there was nowhere else he'd rather live than Mt. Pleasant, Iowa. He loved it there. Stan said that the day he left for Vietnam, his little brother, Phillip, cried and asked him not to leave. He always talked about his family and going home again."

This brave soldier and friend of my brother asked not to be named. Our visit by phone was difficult for him. We dredged up memories that he has tried to forget since 1970. I thanked him for sharing his memory of that day, when Stan's body fell and his spirit lifted from this earth.

Tadaaki (Tad) Kawahra.

Reflections
By
Tadaaki Kawahira
Point man 3rd Platoon, Charlie Co.
February 1, 2006

Tadaaki (Tad) Kawahira, point man in Stan's squad the day he was killed, was very gracious when I spoke to him by phone on February 1, 2006. "I was twenty years old when I went to Vietnam," he said. "We were all very young." He remembered Stan with fondness, "I remember Stan as a big guy, handsome. I used to tease him that he should go to Hollywood when he got out of the Army. He would laugh. I remember him as being a very caring person, always looking out for his men. He was smart and meticulous with the details of his job.

"He was behind me when I heard the shots. I hit the dirt and turned and saw him go down. Everything happened so fast. I remember him lying there, not moving. We lost two good men that day. You can be proud of your brother. He was a good soldier and friend."

Mr. Kawahira is a Japanese American, who bravely served with the 199th in Vietnam. He lives in Los Angeles, California where he owns and operates a landscaping business.

Terry Wanner.

Terry Wanner
RTO for Stan's squad and 3rd Platoon
October 20, 1969

March 3, 2006

Dear Karen,

I am writing to you to try to tell you what happened the day Stan was shot. I have to tell you, that most of that year I spent in Vietnam, I have blocked out in my mind, but there are four or five incidents I remember pretty well and the day that Stan was shot is #1. I will try to tell you as best I can, after almost 37 years.

As I can remember, we were out on a platoon-size mission. I can't remember how long we were out there, but I do remember our rations were gone and we had not been re-supplied. I recall digging in the ground the night before Stan was shot, hoping to find some rations that GIs before us might have left behind. I found an old can of C-rations, peanut butter, and it tasted so good, not having anything to eat in quite awhile. Usually I would throw peanut butter away, that's probably why I found it. Some GI before me probably threw it away.

The next morning we left from our night defensive perimeter and I believe we were heading back to our Fire Base at Cam-Tam. We came into a semi-circle area on a trail, which reminded me of a logging trail. It was probably used by water buffalo drawn carts, which was common to the Vietnamese.

I was the RTO (radio man) for the platoon commander, Lieutenant Divoky. Stan was behind me and Private Jackson was in front of me. We were walking in a staggered formation down a path, in high elephant grass. Five minutes before shots rang out, we heard what we thought were chickens. This put us on edge a bit knowing that chickens didn't belong there. Stan then turned and looked at me, as if to say, "Here we go again." He had his pipe in his mouth and grinned. I'll always remember that look.

It was probably a half an hour after that, we turned off that trail and headed up a secondary trail. We started through some really high elephant grass—taller than us. We always called it elephant grass because it was so high.

We started heading through the grass toward an old rubber plantation when two shots rang out. The sniper fired from a tree line ahead of us. The first shot hit Jackson, and the second hit Stan. Stan was walking behind me. That's why I remember that day so well, because of Stan being behind me. I was walking with my radio; its 10-inch antenna was sticking up in the air. I feel that the sniper, who shot Stan, may have sighted on my antenna, and missed me and hit Stan. The enemy got the drop on us. Stan and Jackson fell on either side of me. The last time I saw Stan he was lying in the elephant grass. I didn't see or hear him after that because we were all taking cover. I couldn't believe I didn't get hit since they usually aimed at the radio antenna first. We called in an air strike right after. A Cobra helicopter came in and worked the area. A search was made after the fire fight, but we didn't find the sniper. Stan and Jackson were dusted off in a Medivac.

I drew a map on the next page to try and show you where we were that day.

I'm glad to hear you're writing a book, and hope you'll stay in touch.

Best Wishes,
Terry Wanner

Terry Wanner was very gracious when I asked him to share his memories with me. I know it wasn't easy for him. He recalled that day in a three-page letter with vivid detail. Terry even included this map of the trail and the squad's positions marked on it.

Terry lives with his wife in West Virginia.

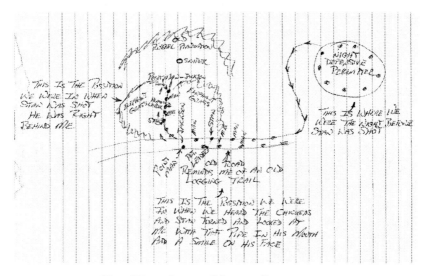

Terry Wanner's map of the squad's position on
October 20, 1969.

"We all thought Stan would make it, which makes it all the harder for us to accept. Things can't be changed, but for us, if there was any way to change it we sure would have. He was a damn good guy and we sure missed him after all that. I was reminded by Jim Faber that one time, while in the rear, Stan, Jim and I procured a mess of steaks form the mess hall." (Ha ha) Tom Schiefer, 3rd Platoon, Charlie Company .

Words of Comfort

Letters from platoon members, squad leaders and friends, came to my parents after Stan was killed. These men were dedicated to each other through blood, sweat, and a bond like no other. They had been through the hell that was war everyday, and had witnessed the horror and grief that claimed their friend.

I was moved as I read each letter and card, how these men, with all they had going on around them, took the time to reach out to my grieving parents, giving their sympathy, condolences and recollections of my brother, their friend.

The following letters are to my parents from Steve Klaus, while he was in country, as well as a letter from his mother, telling him of Stan's death. Steve was a boyhood friend and joined the Army shortly after Stan. He became a sniper in Co. C, 2nd Battalion, 27th Infantry, 25th Infantry Div, and was decorated for his bravery during his tour of Vietnam.

Steve and his wife, Diane, still live in Iowa and named their son Benjamin "Stanley" Klaus. I know how proud that would have made Stan. I want to express my deepest thanks to Steve for sharing his memories and letters of my brother over Memorial Weekend, 2005. I think Stan would have gotten a few chuckles himself!

October 23, 1969

Dear Steve,

Some letters are hard to write. This is one. I've had the Red Cross send you a telegram so that by now you know that Stanley is gone.

Marjorie called me first. I then called Flora Richards. Flora is indeed a wonderful person. She got Raymond and they went to Ross's. I believe Russell's sister and aunt also went right away. Then about 2 p.m. she stopped here and we decided to have the Red Cross let you and Bob know right away. So I called and evidently she called when we got over to Ross's about 7 p.m.

Rose said that Flora had got in touch with them too! I've found that bad news don't ever get any better. I know a little of how you must feel. Rose is going on shock and Russell too, but Rose is better able to cope with it than Russell. The little sister, Eileen, went to sleep, so Rose covered her up. Sleep is nature's healer in time of such trouble.

Here it's work as usual, we put some round bales up in the mow and then moved the elevator, had just a little trouble getting it out of the north end of the barn. It was not lined up right, but got that straightened out. I remember last year you parked it by that tree in the south lot. How did you get it to stay up in the air? We rested it on a fence post, but will probably use it for the corn. He got a load up late day before yesterday. Well then, about 11:00 a.m. we got up some little steers and the Vet came. We now have some little delicacies for the deep freeze. Also weaned a few calves. Sounds like the anvil chorus here. "Home Sweet Home."

Well, in the afternoon we put woven wire around most of the lot fence starting by the faucet and part way up the big gate. Well, then, Bill came briefly and had coffee with us, and now the man called to say we are combining beans today. So I'll be busy hauling beans.

Well, Steve, I better stop now and get breakfast. We are renewing our vigor on the prayers for your safe return, and of course I always ask the Lord to make room for a brand new angel in Heaven.

All our love,
Take care, Mom

Soldiers enjoyed hearing about the mundane chores back in the world. They would have given anything to be home combining beans or mending fences rather than securing concertina wire.

November 25, 1969
Dear Mr. and Mrs. Ross,

I am Sgt. Greg Breeckner. I was your son's squad leader for most of the time he was here. I would have written sooner, but I really don't know what to say. Everyone wants to write, but when they try, they can't find anything to say.

We'll all miss your son very much. He had many friends over here. He always had everyone laughing and making things a little more pleasant.

Stan and I used to spend many nights on ambush talking about motorcycles, and he used to show off the pictures of his new cycle.

I offered to make Stan sergeant, and he really wanted it, so I used to sit with him every night and teach him all I knew. It wasn't long before he took over the squad and I moved on to take over a special squad.

Well, now I am going to be coming home in 18 days. My year is finished. My next station is Ft. Hood, Texas. I would like to stop by and see you folks on my way down there, OK?

Well, I must go. I hope this letter is of some comfort to you. By the way, I am Italian.

Greg

A Sympathy Card from Stan's Platoon

The following three letters are from Stan's close friend, Jayson Dale. Jayson and Stan were together until the end of August of 1969, when they were assigned to different units. I located Jayson in the spring of 2005. He has been a wonderful source in filling in some of the everyday life that he and Stan experienced while serving together. The letters he sent to my parents were a great comfort to them. They would later visit Jayson in Washington State, when he returned home. He was very gracious in answering some of their painful questions.

December 9, 1969
Dear Mr. & Mrs. Ross,

Have to scribble a short note as it is starting to get dark. Sorry I'm so late in writing.

We don't really need anything except your prayers, which I know are with us.

Stan never did change. He was always sensitive and cared very much for his friends, as you know. I guess one of the reasons Stan and I became so close was that we came into the company and platoon at the same time. We grew to understand each other and were about like brothers. The coincidence is that my younger brother's birthday is May 13, 1948. I'm 22.

I can remember when he bought your Bible, June 4. I bought one for my parents that day and since then I have gotten one for my grandmother.

Do not worry, Stan was a Christian! I guess the good Lord just decided he wanted him. He told me that he could make you very happy, Mrs. Ross, by being one, and he was. He carried a pocket-sized Bible with him in the field.

I can still remember when it happened. I was stunned! He was supposed to go to Manila in ten days. After it happened, they offered it to me. I couldn't take it. I hope you understand why. I just came back from Singapore and had a very good time.

Things are getting pretty rough here and as Stan always said, "We may not like it, but it's our job, and we're proud to be American!"

It's getting real dark so I'll have to close. Will try to write tomorrow. May the Good Lord bless and take care of you.

Yours, Jayson

P.S. Will try to answer all your questions.

January 2, 1969

Dear Mr. & Mrs. Ross

Thank you so much for your letters. It picks a guy up. All the guys said to say thank you for the Christmas cards. Also, it's nice to know that there are people like you back in the world, that care what happens to us. All we ever hear about over here is about the protests and moratoriums.

Well, I lucked out and got a job in the rear. Detail NCO at Blackhorse. Sure hated to leave all the guys, became quite attached. But things are just getting too hot. Tet is about to start and the NVA and VC are trying to mass, so they can hit the bases.

We went to BMB Dec. 28, for stand-down, first one in 62 days. Had cleaned the lockers out, found Stan's Polaroid camera! Someone had put it in an old duffle bag. You should be getting it within a couple of weeks. Also, I found his blue rope. Will send it as soon as I get a chance.

Did you ever receive his movie camera? I'm pretty sure he sent it home on our stand-down, Sept.15. I do know that he sold his Minolta camera to Sgt. Faber, as he told me.

Let me know if there's anything else I can do. I know you asked about something else, but I lost your letter.

Well, I have 102 days left over here. It's still a long time.

Better close, so take care and God bless you all,
Jayson

February 3, 1969
Dear Mr. & Mrs. Ross
Sorry I've taken so long in writing, but I ran into a slight problem, my appendix! The 23rd I went to the 93rd Evac Hospital and had it taken out, then came up here to Cam Ranh Bay for convalescence. Guess I'll still be here for about six more days. It's nice here, but I wish I was out of here. Time goes too slow.

Greg Breeckner went home December 12. I think he's in Fort Hood, Texas now.

Tet will officially start in three days. Hope they don't have anything planned for us. It could be bad, but I doubt it. From all the P.O.W.s and documents we've been able to get, they are having trouble getting enough supplies. They have plenty of weapons and ammo, but not food. But imagine they'll try something.

This place is supposed to be secure, but I don't feel too safe. The guards only get to carry two magazines of ammo and that wouldn't hold off a fly. At Blackhorse it's the same thing. The reason for it is racial disturbances. Yes, we have that over here, too!

I'm becoming a little prejudiced, even though I have five good friends in the company that are Negroes, and I'd do anything for those guys. We had one Negro who said he wouldn't fight with us. Hard to believe, isn't it. Then he got a job in the rear as a K.P. Guess he was messing up so they were going to send him to a firebase as a K.P. He refused to go. Five sergeants wrote up statements, one of them was colored. It was a clear cut case. The Colonel dropped the charges and said he could go no further than BMB. Just what the guy wanted. What it amounts to is the Army is afraid of them, and will do anything to keep them from hollering prejudice. Yet Obie lost his job because they quit the platoon. He went back to the field. I know what would have happened to him if he would have refused. He goes home the same day as I do. Keep this under your hat as I could get into trouble for telling you. I've seen that happen a couple of times.

About those pullouts, they're a big joke! They say they're bringing the whole 1st division home, (Ha) only guys with 11 months in country. (2,000 men) They're supposed to have 18,000 men, but only have 15,000. So 3,000 will go home that aren't even here. A total of 5,000, but actually only 2,000 will be going. The rest, 13,000 will be redeployed into other units. You remember after the 9th Div went home, only 400 went! What's bad is it gets the guys' hopes up over here and then they end up staying, big letdown! But they don't tell you that at home, or do they?

Only way to end this war is by a complete pullout. Otherwise, we'll be here five to ten more years. The ARVN's CS Vietnam soldiers don't do anything—just sit in their base camps. Most they go out for is three days, while we're out 10 to 20. That's around where we're at. I wouldn't fight either if I had some idiot doing it for me. (Ha) That's what bugs us the most. It should be going the other way around, and I'm speaking for all the guys in my platoon. Better close as it's time for chow.

God bless you all, Jayson

Jayson's letter reflects many of the concerns and frustrations that GIs were feeling in Vietnam. Men were in the field too long, and racial tensions were getting worse, mirroring what was happening in the States. News reports weren't always accurate and misled the public as to the true picture of the war.

Saying Goodbye

Stan was killed on October 20, 1969—a heavy year of casualties in Vietnam. It took several days for the Army to ship his remains home to us. The distance and red tape added to the long wait we had; those days would be torture for us. We knew he was gone from this earth, but wouldn't really believe it until we saw it for ourselves. It sounds crude, but we were relieved to know that there was a body. So many parents, wives, and loved ones got nothing back, nothing to give them closure.

The summer of 2005, the last MIA from Wichita, Kansas was returned to his family. Their situation was far worse, not knowing if their soldier was alive or dead, or in some horrible POW camp.

When Stan's body was returned to us, as a family we viewed his remains at the mortuary in Wayland, Iowa—a small town northwest of our home. The couple that owned and operated it were old friends of the family. They had taken care of many of our relatives.

Stan's coffin was sealed in glass. It's strange what your mind reflects on in such times. It reminded me of Snow White, when she was in the glass coffin in the woods, and the animals and dwarfs circled around her, mourning. I'm not sure what the purpose of the glass seal was; I know it took several days for Stan's body to be sent home from Vietnam. Perhaps it was to make sure there was no contamination from the body or for preservation.

I watched my stooped parents approach the casket, holding on to each other as children do when they are afraid of the dark. Their wails of grief sent shock waves through my body. It was a scene that a child rarely witnesses. Parents are supposed to be strong and resilient, holding you. It was one of the most helpless feelings I ever experienced. There was nothing I could say, no gesture that would comfort. I simply stood and watched as they looked at the child they had made together, the son they had pinned their future on. My mother rubbed her hands across the top of the casket, wanting to touch her eldest son, but her tears puddled on top of the glass, as she stroked the transparent seal, up and then down, trying to touch her son.

When I approached his casket, I was afraid to look inside, my heart beat fast and I felt light headed. It was like a movie in slow motion. Finally, I peered in. It resembled Stan, but it felt like I was viewing a mannequin in a department store. I looked for evidence of his wounds, something that would tell me he had been injured, but there was nothing but the stiff uniform he so proudly wore a few months before.

That chilly October, when we laid him to rest, the corn stood proudly, as if saluting my brother's return. The gray skies and piercing winds added to our grief and sorrow that week. I felt chilled most of the time, unable to warm myself. My teeth would chatter for no apparent reason other than my grief. I would never look at that month or corn harvest the same again.

For months after his funeral I would try to conjure up his face and imagine his voice. I would talk to him while driving in my car, away from everyone. I didn't believe in ghosts, but I felt his spirit, and it helped to tell him how sorry I was, and how much I missed and loved him. I turned my pain inward, locked away where it would stay until I let the grief out, thirty-five years later.

Lt. Arrol Stewart.

Arrol and his wife, Jan, Stewart, 2005.

On August 29, 2005 my brother, Phill, and I visited Arrol Stewart who was Stan's platoon leader in August of 1969. 1st Lt. Arrol Stewart was asked to identify Stan's remains. He did, at the Long Binh hospital.

Phill and I knew the circumstances of Stan's death—that he was killed by a sniper while on patrol near a rubber tree plantation, and went into shock, never regaining consciousness. We knew all that, but we needed to hear it from someone who was there, who saw Stan last. It sounds morbid, but we wanted to hear it first hand. Did he suffer? Did he die instantly? Those were our questions. Arrol answered some of our questions with guarded compassion.

Arrol related much of his tour experiences to us. He remembered Stan as a good soldier, who was a leader, and always had a smile and kind word. We looked at old pictures that I shared from my brother's collection and ones that he had. I asked him what it was like to be in a fire fight not knowing what the next minute would bring. He said he didn't think about anything but keeping his men safe and keeping his head down. He didn't feel fear as we think of it. His response was that, "I was too busy trying to do the job that had to be done." His second day in Vietnam was the fire fight of August 7, 1969. He had been trained as an officer at Fort Benning, Georgia. His ability to read maps and lead his men was something that saved his platoon casualties.

Jayson Dale, Stan's friend from Charlie Company recalled Lt. Stewart as, "A good man, and damn fine officer; he put our welfare and safety above all else."

Arrol now lives in Albion, Illinois with his wife, Jan. He owns and operates an antique store that once was the town's grocery. It was established in 1875 by his great-grandfather.

My brother's death changed my parents forever. It changed how they related to each other and to their children. It tested their trust and faith in God. It jaded their view of our government and its leaders. It changed the look in their eyes. Behind their gaze seemed a sadness that could never be healed. It changed holidays for many years. The joy and anticipation was gone.

Having a grown son of my own, I can't imagine how terrible it would be to lose him. He is my flesh, a part of me that I knew before I saw his face. I have seen the effects of loss and sorrow, how it sucks the life out of the soul. It made me, at times, too protective of my children. I would worry and fret for their safety, in unreasonable ways. They say "Time heals all wounds." I know, for a fact, it does not. It just makes them less tender. The years have passed; our family has experienced weddings, births, graduations, and now great grandchildren. My parents have mellowed; they sense their mortality. They know that by leaving this earth, they will once again be united with their son.

When I sit with them now, they reminisce, laugh and try to recall their history. They remember the things that made them proud as parents and some of the less shining moments. They know more than I thought they did. It seems we didn't fool them.

They like to point out the family traits and resemblances in their grandchildren—who looks like whom. In the end, the conversation almost always comes back to Stan. My parents will stop, shake their heads and go on with the story. Still far from forgotten, these memories live on. Stanley's childhood dislike for school, his passion for hunting, his knack for getting into harmless trouble, and his obvious love for his family are just some of the things discussed when our family gets together. As my brother Phill remarked, *"We treasure our memories. There is not a single time when I visit my parents that we don't talk about and remember Stan. It keeps him alive and with us."*

My parents described what happened that day and how they felt, *"No sooner did I hear the knock at the door. When I opened the door, there was a gentleman in full uniform standing at attention, and even then I couldn't comprehend what was happening. I told him to come in, and when he did, he just said, 'I'm sorry Mrs. Ross,' and then he told me."* My dad saw the car pull in our drive from the barn, where he had just finished milking, *"I knew exactly what was going on, and I ran up to the house and threw open the back door with the bucket still in my hands. I have never been madder in my life; I just threw the bucket as hard as I could. I was so mad even though at that point I had not heard the words, 'Stan's been killed,' but you have to lay it on someone, and that poor man just happened to be there."*

Mom and Dad do not re-read Stan's letters. They don't watch the 8-mm movies. It's too painful. They are pleased that I have honored him in this way and that he will not be forgotten. There are enough memories to sustain them.

Many asked my mother about her faith after Stan was killed; her response was this, "Some may say, 'Where was your God when your son was killed in Vietnam?' Our answer is 'The same place He was when His only son was killed.'"

Dad and Mom Ross, 2005.

Purple Heart
By
Karen Ross Epp

It came in a nice box
That Purple Heart
Mother's hand
Moved over it
A trade for the real thing
That beats no longer
In your young chest
Hand to hand
Bayonet to flesh
Bullet to breast
From where from whom
It had no face
Death that claimed you
Perched in a rubber tree
We only knew
Your heart we sent
Traded for purple
Cold
Metal
Packaged returned
Cookies crumbled
Never received
Never opened
No way to touch you
Through sealed
Clean-clear glass
Mother's tears
Splash
Father's fists
Clenched
October sky gray
Ground so cold
Receives your casket
So young so sweet
Handsome you lay
You gave them your heart
They gave you a medal
Years gone by
Still the pain is sharp
Your face so clear
You were my brother
Our Mother's dear

Preston Pena
4th Division
September 1969-September 1970
E-mail responding to poem

I just finished reading your poem (a touching tribute to your brother and to all those who made the ultimate sacrifice). As I have browsed the Virtual Wall, one sentiment in particular rings so true, "To live on in the hearts and minds of those left behind, is to never have died." And so it is with your brother. Still, you must be left wondering, "What might have been had he been able to live out his life?" He died a hero and a patriot in the service of his country (and forever that will be his legacy).

I am among the fortunate to have survived my tour of duty. I was born in the same year as Stanley and served in Vietnam (with the 4th Division) from September 1969 through September 1970. I will never forget those of my comrades-in-arms who lost their lives in that far away land (in what is fast becoming a forgotten time in our history). May all their families and friends be sustained by their loving memories.

Best regards,
Preston Pena

Local Young Man Killed In Vietnam

The parents of Sgt. Stanley Dennis Ross, 20, were notified early Wednesday morning that he had been killed in action in Vietnam. He was the fifth fatality in the Vietnam war from Henry county.

He was in the "Blackhorse operation", according to members of the family and announcements were made this week the operation was involved in some contact with the enemy.

* * *

He was killed on Monday of this week, according to the message received by Sgt. Robert Martinez, army adviser for the Army Reserve unit here, of Mt. Pleasant who went to the home of the parents, Mr. and Mrs. Russell Ross, about six miles northwest of Mt. Pleasant to inform them. Sgt. Martinez's information was that Sgt. Ross was killed "during a sweep". A telegram is to follow later giving more information.

* * *

Sgt. Ross entered the service in September, 1968, and went to Vietnam in April, 1969. He was a mem-

Sgt. Stanley D. Ross

ber of Company C, Second Battalion, Third Infantry Division. His parents had watched the television program at 2:15 Wednesday morning telling of the nine killed in skirmishes around Saigon this week and suspected that Stanley was fighting in that area. A few minutes later they saw Sgt. Martinez approaching their house.

* * *

Sgt. Ross was graduated from Mt. Pleasant high school in 1968. He had served as a bus driver while in school.

Besides his parents, the immediate surviving relatives include: two sisters, Karen, a student at Bethel College, Newton, Kan., and Eileen, a student at Mt. Pleasant high school and a brother, Phillip, four years old.

The other four from Henry county who died in Vietnam were Michael O'Connor, Maraelle Ford, Charles Miller and Woodrow Warth.

9 Americans Killed And 31 Wounded

SAIGON (UPI) — U. S. headquarters today reported 216 Viet Cong and North Vietnamese killed in the latest rounds of battle — 34 of them when U. S. troops and armor turned the tables on two highlands ambushes.

Military spokesmen said a total of nine Americans died and 31 were wounded in the scores of skirmishes and Communist shelling attacks that dotted the command's war map Tuesday and this morning.

Five flights of B52 bombers followed up the fighting with two raids within a half mile of the border Demilitarized Zone, one in the Central Highlands near the ambush sites and two north of Saigon.

The battle lull that began six weeks ago was still considered in effect, with Sen. Mike Mansfield, D-Mont., saying in Washington that U. S. forces already were observing a virtual unilateral ceasefire.

Mt. Pleasant News notice and related article about the war.

Bearers bring the casket of Sgt. Stanley Dennis Ross from First Baptist church where services were held. He was the fifth Henry county man killed in Vietnam.

Military Service Held For Sgt. Stanley D. Ross

First Baptist church was filled to capacity Tuesday afternoon for military funeral services for Sgt. Stanley Dennis Ross, 20, Mt. Pleasant, route 3, who was killed in South Vietnam on October 20.

The Rev. Peter Siemens, pastor of the church, officiated. Mrs. Rog-er Martin and Mrs. Dale Schillerstrom sang selections. Mrs. Peter Siemens was organist.

Bearers were Warren Lane, William Lane, Harold Grant, Leonard Ridinger, Robert L. Smith and Donald Scarff. Military rites were conducted at the graveside in For-est Home cemetery by an honor guard and firing squad from Fort Leonard Wood, Mo.

The flag from the casket was presented to Sgt. Ross's mother, Mrs. Russell Ross, by a sergeant from Fort Riley, Kan., who came here to be with the family during the services.

Services were held at our church, First Baptist, where
Stan was a member.

Karen Ross Epp

BY DIRECTION OF THE PRESIDENT
THE BRONZE STAR MEDAL
(SECOND OAK LEAF CLUSTER)
IS PRESENTED POSTHUMOUSLY TO
SERGEANT STANLEY D. ROSS

For distinguishing himself by outstanding meritorious ser
in connection with ground operations against a hostile fo
in the Republic of Vietnam during the period

May 1969 to October 1969

Through his untiring efforts and professional ability, he
consistently obtained outstanding results. He was quick
to grasp the implications of new problems with which he
was faced as a result of the ever changing situations in-
herent in a counterinsurgency operation and to find ways
and means to solve those problems. The energetic appli-
cation of his extensive knowledge has materially contributed to the efforts of the United States Mission to the
Republic of Vietnam to assist that country in ridding itself of the commmunist threat to its freedom. His initia-
tive, zeal, sound judgment and devotion to duty have been
in the highest tradition of the United States Army and reflects great credit on himself, his unit and the military
service.

Bronze Star Medal with V Device: Was awarded for acts of
valor on 5 October 1969.

The 1st Oak Leaf Cluster is the second award of the Bronz
Star Medal for acts of valor on 20 October 1969. The 2nd
Oak Leaf Cluster is the third award of the Bronze Star
Medal for meritorious service from May 1969 - October 196

Purple Heart: Awarded for wounds received in combat.

National Defense Service Medal: Awarded to all members
of the Armed Forces of the United States.

Vietnam Service Medal: Awarded to all members of the
Armed Forces of the United States serving in the Republic
of Vietnam.

Vietnam Campaign Ribbon: Awarded for participating in th
Vietnam Campaign.

Expert and Sharpshooter Badge: Degree of proficiency wit
each weapon

DEPARTMENT OF THE ARMY
Headquarters 199th Infantry Brigade (Sep) (Lt)
APO San Francisco 96279

The following AWARD is announced posthumously

ROSS, STANLEY D. 479646162, SERGEANT
UNITED STATES ARMY, COMPANY C 2D BATTALION, 3RD INFANTRY
199th INFANTRY BRIGADE (SEPARATE) (LIGHT)
Awarded: Bronze Star Medal with "V" Device
Theater: Republic of Vietnam
Date action: 5 October 1969
Reason: Sergeant Ross distinguished himself by exceptional heroism in connection
with ground operations against an armed hostile force in the Republic of
Vietnam on 5 October 1969 while assigned to Company C, 2d Battalion, 3d
Infantry, 199th Infantry Brigade. On that date, Sergeant Ross was par-
ticipating in a search and destroy mission when his unit made contact
with an enemy force of unknown size. After the initial contact, Sergeant
Ross came upon an armed enemy soldier concealed in thick underbrush. Wit
out regard for his personal safety, he assumed an exposed position in an
attempt to capture the enemy. At point blank range, the enemy chose to
fight and Sergeant Ross returned fire, mortally wounding the enemy soldie
His alert and aggressive actions contributed significantly to the success
ful completion of the mission and earned him the respect and admiration o
all with whom he served. Sergeant Ross' valorous actions and devotion to
duty were in keeping with the highest traditions of the military service
and reflect great credit upon himself, the 199th Infantry Brigade and the
United States Army.
Authority: By direction of the President, under the provisions of Executive Order
11046, dated 24 August 1962.

FOR THE COMMANDER: JAMES L. MEIDL
                                            Major, AGC
                                            Adjutant General

Awarded: Bronze Star Medal with "V" Device (First Oak Leaf Cluster)
Theater: Republic of Vietnam
Date action: 20 October 1969
Reason: Sergeant Ross distinguished himself by exceptional heroism in connection
with ground operations against an armed hostile force in the Republic of
Vietnam on 20 October 1969 while assigned to Company C, 2d Battalion,
3d Infantry, 199th Infantry Brigade. On that date, Sergeant Ross was
serving as squad leader as his unit moved through tall grass toward a
rubber plantation. As the pointman entered a small trail he spotted an
enemy soldier who engaged the unit at close range. With complete dis-
regard for his personal safety Sergeant Ross maneuvered his squad into
a protected defensive position. While in his exposed position he was
fatally wounded by enemy fire. His valorous actions and unrelenting
devotion to duty at the cost of his own life were in keeping with the
highest traditions of the military service and reflected great credit
upon himself, the 199th Infantry Brigade and the United States Army.
Authority: By direction of the President, under the provisions of Executive Order
11046, dated 24 August 1962.

FOR THE COMMANDER: JAMES L. MEIDL
                                            Major, AGC
                                            Adjutant General

In June of 1970, the Mt. Pleasant School District held a memorial service on the front steps of the Mt. Pleasant high school. Board members and past administrators accepted a Bronze plaque as a memorial to Stan. The plaque honors Stan and his service. It was displayed inside the main entrance of the high school, the same high school Stan attended.

Pictured below at the dedication are (left to right) Principal Richard Van Tuyl, Past Principal George Stanley, Superintendent Robert Formenack, and Rev. Chester Potts from Open Bible Church. The plaque was moved to the new high school in 1999, where it now hangs in the library.

Funds for the plaque were donated by family, friends, and the community.

Plaque dedication at Mt. Pleasant High School.

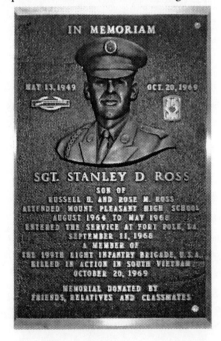

IN MEMORIAM

MAY 13, 1949   OCT. 20, 1969

SGT. STANLEY D. ROSS
SON OF
RUSSELL R. AND ROSE M. ROSS
ATTENDED MOUNT PLEASANT HIGH SCHOOL
AUGUST 1964 TO MAY 1968
ENTERED THE SERVICE AT FORT POLK, LA.
SEPTEMBER 11, 1968
A MEMBER OF
THE 199TH LIGHT INFANTRY BRIGADE, U.S.A.
KILLED IN ACTION IN SOUTH VIETNAM
OCTOBER 20, 1969

MEMORIAL DONATED BY
FRIENDS, RELATIVES AND CLASSMATES

Bronze plaque that now hangs in the new high school.

In 1975, Newsweek contacted my parents about doing an interview with them regarding their feelings on the war, what they had sacrificed, and the value of it all. Their interview was part of an article that reflected other stories of the same vein. This is part of that interview, edited for the final publication. My Dad was not happy with it, because he felt they had left out important things he wanted to say.

Dad had always been a solid Republican, and voted a straight party ticket every election throughout his life. In the last election, my Dad voted for John Kerry. It's not that he has changed his view on military service, but he sees the ominous similarity of the war my brother fought in Vietnam. He sees the folly that is spewed from our nation's leaders as they talk about "staying the course."

He cries more easily now and feels the grief all over again, knowing how the parents of this generation feel as their sons and daughters are brought back from Iraq in their flag-draped coffins. It breaks his heart all over again.

It was my pleasure to hear from Mr. Jeff Lowenthal, the photographer that took the picture for Newsweek in 1975. He is an accomplished photographer, with many awards and accomplishments behind his work. He said he often thought about my parents and brother over the years, and wondered how they were. His permission to use his photo once again is very much appreciated.

Jeff Lowenthal

The Rosses: 'Terrible sorry'

Newsweek

In the dusk of a late summer evening six years ago, Russell Ross took his boy Stanley, 20, to the Burlington railroad station near little Mount Pleasant, Iowa, and put him on a train to join the Army. In the moments before he climbed aboard, Stanley talked about going, and about how maybe he wouldn't owe his country as much when he got back. Then he was gone, and Russell Ross stood for a long time watching the train lights twinkle away into the darkness and feeling "just real proud for Stanley . . . standing up for what he believed" at a time when kids his age in distant cities were picketing and rioting for peace. His heart full, he decided on the spot to do something nice for his boy, and settled on buying him a new motorcycle. He began laying away cash, saved up for a Harley-Davidson and wheeled it into a shed on the family's 160-acre farm to await Stanley's return.

Last week, a spring blizzard blanketed Mount Pleasant, and in Forest Home Cemetery, an icy wind knocked a plastic Easter wreath off the grave marked STANLEY ROSS. They had sent Stanley home from the war in a government-issue casket, too soon after the night he had left; the Harley had stood long after in the shed until Russell Ross mustered the heart to sell it. And now he reads the dispatches in the Mount Pleasant News with a daily deepening sense of frustration and loss. "All it seems to come to," he says wanly, "is a waste of lives. All we've done is create a lot of homeless people and orphans. I feel terrible sorry for them people over there. But I feel terrible sorry for Stanley, too." He pauses for a moment, remembering their good-bys in the darkness at the Burlington station. "I guess he doesn't owe anybody *anything* now," Ross says. "I guess he done more than anyone had a right to expect."

—PETER GOLDMAN with TONY FULLER in Chicago and bureau reports

Newsweek picture and article, April 14, 1975.

In the late 80s I went to Washington D.C. as a delegate to the NEA (National Education Association) Convention. While I was there I visited the Wall. I was not prepared for the emotion that it evoked in me. After all, it was just another monument in a city where statues and monuments appear every few hundred feet. But as I gazed at the long stretch of black marble, a feeling of sorrow, pride, and astonishment fell upon me. I knew that I had lost a brother, and I knew that several thousand soldiers had lost their lives as well, but to see the names etched in stone going on row after row, the enormity of loss, stunned me. There were so many names, so many fathers, husbands, and sons embedded in stone. It was beautiful and yet ominous at the same time.

I saw veterans weeping—rubbing their fingers over the name of a friend or family member. I saw mothers and wives placing artifacts along the wall where their loved ones name was etched. There were pictures, drawings, stuffed animals and flowers. There were letters, ribbons, and much more— objects that provided a connection to the souls on that wall.

The Wall is one of the finest examples of tribute to a fallen generation that I have ever seen. In its simplicity it says much more than a verse or platitude could proclaim. "It is the names that say it all!"

I made a rubbing that day, as many were doing. My children watched me with curiosity and concern. They never knew their uncle, except through my recollections of him. With each stoke I thought of Stan and wondered if anyone had come to see his name as I had. I have learned since, that many of his friends have made the trip, and reverently touched the stone that bears their friend's name.

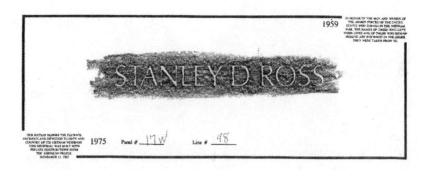

The rubbing I did of Stan's name on the
Vietnam Memorial.

The Vietnam Memorial.

JOSEPH V CAMERLENGO · JAMES CO
D G CURTIS · DENNIS C HALL · THOM
DS · MARTIN W ESSARY Jr · PATRICK M
E KEITH · DENNIS W KIPP · RICHARD D
POLING · STANLEY D ROSS · MICHAEL
VIGIL · JOE N WATSON · MICKEY R AL
CLAYTON · GLENN R COOK · JOHN E
THOMAS V FELDHAUS · FLOYD E GOL
NNEDY Jr · TIMOTHY F LARMON · KE
PAYNE · MARTIN Y NAMER · JOHN D

Stan's name on the wall.

Author's Final Thoughts

This has been a labor of love, and at the same time, a painful process for me. I found myself waking up in the middle of the night thinking about what I had read in Stan's letters. I thought about what his friends had told me. I visualized him sleeping in the rain, sweating in the jungle, cutting through elephant grass while holding on to his rifle, and trying to stay one step ahead of death.

In the past, I had refused to let my mind go to that dark place where the images of my brother's violent death festered and waited for closure. I neatly tucked those mental pictures away in the dark corners of my consciousness.

Still, Stan was always a constant force in my life, even after his death. When difficult, overwhelming situations arose, I always thought of Stan. My strength and determination became stronger realizing that if he could endure the battlefields of South Vietnam, I could handle teenagers, stress at work and even breast cancer.

Reading his letters brought back bittersweet memories, as I'm sure they will for those who read this memorial to him. His words are sometimes crude, harsh, loving and funny. It is the writing of a nineteen-year-old boy who became a man in a matter of months—growing from an inexperienced private to a squad leader who unselfishly gave his life for his men and his country. He never tried to add stripes to his uniform or become a hero; he simply wanted to get the job done and come home to those he loved.

As I read and copied his letters it became clear to me how much we take for granted. His decision to serve his country was not one he took lightly. He echoed the phrase so many of us heard in the 60s, "War is hell!" Young men, just out of high school, were the ones who paid the highest price for freedom. The Vietnam War was fought by nineteen-year old, blue-collar foot soldiers…grunts.

Stan was proud to be a grunt, humping in the Infantry. He took on the unspeakable tasks of war while the rest of us watched a sanitized version on the nightly news from the comfort of our living rooms. They suffered unimaginably. We went on with our lives, raised our families, and pursued our careers.

My gratitude to my brother and those brave service men and women can never be expressed in words. Stan and those like him still live on in our hearts. His courage should inspire all of us to do a better job of living.

Going home in 2005—Memorial Weekend and again over the 4th of July—gave me time to reflect as I looked around the home were we both grew up and out in the fields where we played and where Stan hunted.

I slept in the same room I had occupied in my youth, just across the hall from Stan's old room. The memories brought tears to my eyes many times during my stay. I conjured up the misty images of our younger selves doing what kids do…what siblings do. I could almost hear the laughter, the footsteps running up and down the stairs, chasing one another around, trying to scare each other, calling back and forth across the hall, or straining to listen to the muffled voices of our parents down below, maybe overhearing what our Christmas presents might be, or what family secrets were never discussed in our presence.

In 2005, we took new family photos with my parents. We posed on the same front porch where we had spent so many summer evenings keeping cool, kicking back on the swing, or enjoying homemade ice cream. Our pictures revealed growing families, aging parents and, yes, "Little Phillip" all grown up, alongside his daughter who is now about the same age as he was when Stan left. Today, there are babies about to be born. As always, life goes on. I thought of what Stan had said in one of his letters, "I can't wait until I'm back in the picture." How we wish he were still in our family picture and not just in our hearts.

It was wonderful to see everyone together, but I felt such sadness as I thought about the one family member that was not with us. I knew, however, that in a way, he was there…smiling big, taking it all in, and wishing us well.

Finding the men who were with my brother those last months of his life and connecting the dots to his life at that time has been an experience like no other in my life. I have been blessed by the connection to them though my writing, as I have listened to and read their recollections of that treacherous year of their lives. I have heard how they have reached out to each other after 37 years. I've learned that the human body and spirit can endure terrible acts of physical and mental abuse, but it never forgets the love and devotion of a brother!

This summer, July 28-29, 2006, the men I have written about and who were part of my brother's life for those seven months in the rice paddies and jungles of Southeast Asia, will gather at our family farm in rural Iowa, the home where Stan and I grew up. The men will meet for the first time in 37 years. If nothing else comes from writing Stan's story, the wounds, memories, and, yes, the joy that will be shared that weekend, will have been worth every hour, every tear, that went into seeing this work completed.

In closing, I want to thank all those who contributed to Stan's story and supported me at every turn, even when I wasn't sure I could go on. I also want to thank the wives who waited for their husbands and sweethearts to return to them, in some cases returning as different men, than the ones they said goodbye to. Thank you for being there for them over the years when the dark cloud of Vietnam would darken their thoughts. You have been brave as well, and deserve our respect and honor. All of you helped filled in the blanks for me and gave me what I was looking for all along—a way to remember Stan and, at the same time, a way to say goodbye. With your help I have found my brother and found closure as well.

Our home has had a few face-lifts since 1969, but
looks much the same.

Mom decorating Stan's headstone,
Memorial Day, 2005.

Mom and Dad, back, Karen, Phill, and Eileen,
July, 2005.

Melvin and Dorothy Ploeger today, 2004.

Greg Breeckner and Liz on the beautiful shores of S.C.
March, 2006.

Jim and Lu Ann Faber, 2006.

(Left to right) Karen, Michael Lanning, Arrol Stewart,
Phill Ross, Oct, 2005.

James McGinnis and wife, Joan.

Wanda and Mike Kitch, May, 2005.

Appendix

CLASS OF SERVICE
This is a fast message unless its deferred character is indicated by the proper symbol.

WESTERN UNION
TELEGRAM
W. P. MARSHALL, PRESIDENT

1220 (R 11-54)

SYMBOLS
DL=Day Letter
NL=Night Letter
LT=International Letter Telegram

The filing time shown in the date line on domestic telegrams is STANDARD TIME at point of origin. Time of receipt is STANDARD TIME at point of destination

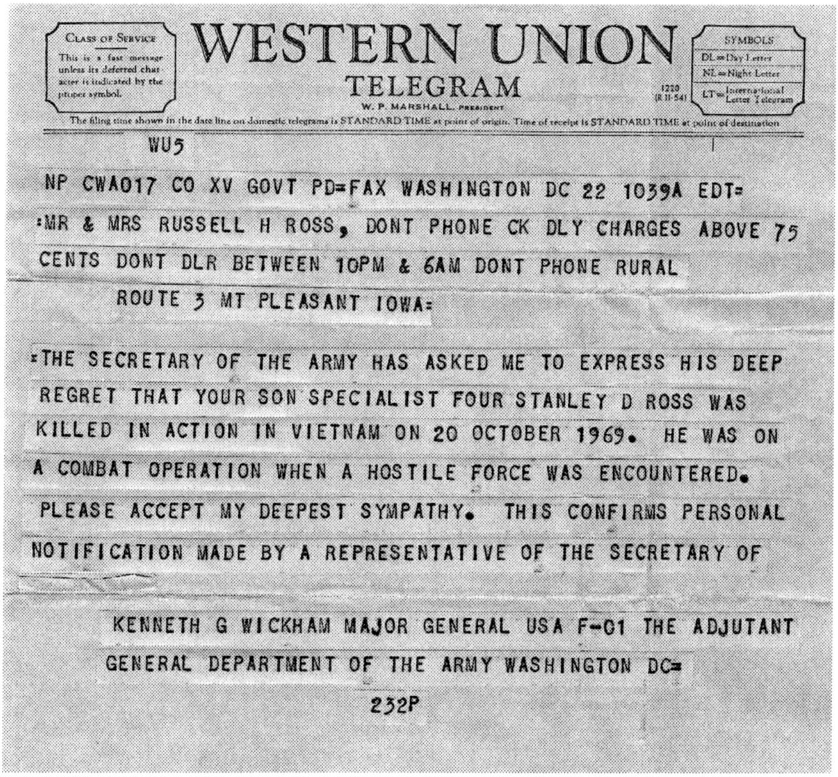

WU5

NP CWA017 CO XV GOVT PD=FAX WASHINGTON DC 22 1039A EDT=
:MR & MRS RUSSELL H ROSS, DONT PHONE CK DLY CHARGES ABOVE 75
CENTS DONT DLR BETWEEN 10PM & 6AM DONT PHONE RURAL
ROUTE 3 MT PLEASANT IOWA=

:THE SECRETARY OF THE ARMY HAS ASKED ME TO EXPRESS HIS DEEP
REGRET THAT YOUR SON SPECIALIST FOUR STANLEY D ROSS WAS
KILLED IN ACTION IN VIETNAM ON 20 OCTOBER 1969. HE WAS ON
A COMBAT OPERATION WHEN A HOSTILE FORCE WAS ENCOUNTERED.
PLEASE ACCEPT MY DEEPEST SYMPATHY. THIS CONFIRMS PERSONAL
NOTIFICATION MADE BY A REPRESENTATIVE OF THE SECRETARY OF

KENNETH G WICKHAM MAJOR GENERAL USA F-01 THE ADJUTANT
GENERAL DEPARTMENT OF THE ARMY WASHINGTON DC=

232P

Telegram informing family of Stan's death.

WU6

CT WA239 HB XV GOVT PDB=WASHINGTON DC 22 331P EDT=

RUSSELL H ROSS, DONT PHONE CHECK DLY CHGS ABOVE 75 CTS=

RURAL RTE 3 MT PLEASANT IOWA=

THIS CONCERNS YOUR SON SP4 STANLEY D ROSS. THE ARMY WILL
RETURN YOUR LOVED ONE TO A PORT IN THE UNITED STATES BY
FIRST AVAILABLE MILITARY AIRLIFT. AT THE PORT REMAINS WILL
BE PLACED IN A METAL CASKET AND DELIVERED (ACCOMPANIED BY A
MILITARY ESCORT) BY MOST EXPEDITIOUS MEANS TO ANY FUNERAL
DIRECTOR DESIGNATED BY THE NEXT OF KIN OR TO ANY NATIONAL
CEMETERY IN WHICH THERE IS AVAILABLE GRAVE SPACE. YOU WILL
BE ADVISED BY THE UNITED STATES PORT CONCERNING THE MOVEMENT
AND ARRIVAL TIME AT DESTINATION. FORMS ON WHICH TO CLAIM
AUTHORIZED INTERMENT ALLOWANCE WILL ACCOMPANY REMAINS.
THIS ALLOWANCE MAY NOT EXCEED $75 IF CONSIGNMENT IS MADE
DIRECTLY TO THE SUPERINTENDENT OF A NATIONAL CEMETERY. WHEN
CONSIGNMENT IS MADE TO A FUNERAL DIRECTOR PRIOR TO INTERMENT
IN A NATIONAL CEMETERY, THE MAXIMUM ALLOWANCE IS $250;
IF BURIAL TAKES PLACE IN A CIVILIAN CEMETERY, THE MAXIMUM
ALLOWANCE IS $500. REQUEST NEXT OF KIN ADVISE BY COLLECT
TELEGRAM ADDRESSED: DISPOSITION BRANCH, MEMORIAL DIVISION,
DEPARTMENT OF THE ARMY WUX MB, WASHINGTON D.C., NAME AND

ADDRESS OF FUNERAL DIRECTOR OR NAME OF NATIONAL CEMETERY
SELECTED. IF ADDITIONAL INFORMATIONCONCERNING RETURN OF
REMAINS IS DESIRED YOU MAY INCLUDE YOUR INQUIRY IN THE
REPLY TO THIS MESSAGE. PLEASE DO NOT GET DATE OF FUNERAL
UNTIL PORT AUTHORITIES NOTIFY YOU DATE AND SCHEDULED
TIME OF ARRIVAL DESTINATION. PLEASE FURNISH AREA CODE
AND TELEPHONE NUMBER OF FUNERAL DIRECTOR SELECTED=

DISPOSITION BRANCH MEMORIAL DIVISION DEPT OF ARMY
WUX MDB==

351P

Telegram regarding casket arrival and burial
arrangements. (2 and 3, cont.)

THE WHITE HOUSE

WASHINGTON

October 28, 1969

Dear Mr. and Mrs. Ross:

It is with great sorrow that I have learned of the death of your son, Specialist Four Stanley D. Ross.

Of all the hardships of war, the cruelest are the losses of men such as your son. The only consolation I can offer is the profound respect of the nation he died to serve, and the humble recognition of a sacrifice no man can measure and no words can describe. Those who give their own lives to make the freedom of others possible live forever in honor.

Mrs. Nixon joins me in extending our own sympathy, and in expressing the sympathy of a saddened nation. You will be in our prayers, and in our hearts.

Sincerely,

Richard Nixon

Mr. and Mrs. Russell H. Ross
Rural Route Three
Mount Pleasant, Iowa

Condolence letter from President Richard M. Nixon.

DEPARTMENT OF THE ARMY
Company C, 2d Battalion, 3d Infantry
199th Infantry Brigade (Sep) (Light)
APO San Francisco 96279

7 NOV 1969

Mr. and Mrs. Russell H. Ross
Rural Route #3
Mount Pleasant, Iowa   52641

Dear Mr. and Mrs. Ross,

I extend my most profound sympathy in the recent loss of your son, Specialist Four Stanley D. Ross, of Company C, 2d Battalion, 3d Infantry, 199th Infantry Brigade, who died of wounds received in the service of his country.

On 20 October 1969, your son's platoon was moving from their night ambush position. Stanley was the squad leader for the point squad. While nearing a grove of rubber trees, the point man for his squad observed one enemy soldier walking toward them. The point man opened fire on the enemy, at which time, an unobserved and unknown size enemy force returned fire. During the initial contact Stanley was seriously wounded by small arms fire. He was immediately administered first aid and evacuated by helicopter. Stanley never regained consciousness and died enroute to the 93d Evacuation Hospital in Long Binh.

News of your son's death came as a shock to all who knew him and his loss will be felt deeply in the company. I sincerely hope that the knowledge that Stanley was a fine man, exemplary soldier and leader will comfort you in this hour of sorrow. A memorial service was conducted in Stanley's honor near the area where he was mortally wounded.

Once again, personally and for the officers and men of this command, please accept this letter as a symbol of our sympathy.

Sincerely yours,

JAMES V. MCGINNIS
CPT, Infantry
Commanding

Enter Sept 12. 1968
death Oct 20 1969

Condolence letter Captain James McGinnis. Mom's
writing of dates.

DEPARTMENT OF THE ARMY
Headquarters, 2d Battalion, 3d Infantry
199th Infantry Brigade (Sep)(Light)
APO San Francisco 96279

7 NOV 1968

Mr. and Mrs. Russell H. Ross
Rural Route #3
Mount Pleasant, Iowa 52641

Dear Mr. and Mrs. Ross:

Your sorrow and grief at the death of your son are shared by all from this Battalion. We hope you will accept this letter as an expression of our sorrow at his death.

We knew him not only as an exemplary soldier but also as a gentleman. His kindness and concern for the men he lived and worked with made him dear to them all.

In times of grief our consolation comes not from human things but from a deep Faith in God. His words to us through His Apostle enable us to see beyond the present and find hope for the future. "If anyone lives and believes in me, he will never die."

Your son's life has been an inspiring example for us all. We pray that the common burden of sorrow that we bear will be tempered by the realization that he died valiantly for his country and is now close to God. Please accept our sorrow, our sympathy, and our prayers.

Sincerely yours,

HERBERT H. HICKS
Chaplain (CPT) USA
Battalion Chaplain

Condolence letter from Chaplain Herbert Hicks.

Hq 199th Infantry Brigade
APO San Francisco   96279

Dear Mr. and Mrs. Ross:

Our entire brigade is deeply disturbed by the death of your
son, Specialist Four Stanley D. Ross, 479646162, while fighting
with the 199th Infantry Brigade. In a close-knit unit such as
ours this news leaves me with a feeling of personal loss as well,
and it must be especially difficult for you inasmuch as your son
was serving so far from home and family.

The example which Stanley set as a soldier reflected the highest
standards of self-discipline and courage. His devotion to duty,
understanding of the job to be done, and willingness to protect
and preserve the ideals which we Americans hold dear, characterized
his service to our country.

Certainly no words of mine can diminish your deep sense of
loss, but we all hope it will be of comfort to you to know that
your grief is shared by all the men of this brigade. Our hearts
and prayers are with you at this most difficult time.

Sincerely,

WARREN K. BENNETT
Brigadier General, USA
Commanding

Mr. and Mrs. Russell H. Ross
Rural Route #3
Mount Pleasant, Iowa   52641

Condolence letter General Warren Bennett.

327

Guys from Third Platoon, (left to right) Willie Thorpe, Stan
(middle), John MCCombs, Dave Cherneski,
Greg Breeckner, Jayson Dale,
(back), Richard Sims Jr., Elden Rasmuseen, Tom Reed.

Photo by, Tad Kawahira

Bibliography

Edelman, Bernard. <u>Dear America: Letters Home From Vietnam</u>. New York: W.W. Norton & Company, Inc., 2002.

Gouge, Robert J. <u>"These Are My Credentials" The 199th Light Infantry Brigade in the Republic of Vietnam, 1966-1970</u>. Bloomington: AuthorHouse, 2004.

Lanning, Michael L. <u>The Only War We Had: A Platoon Leader's Journal Of Vietnam</u>. New York: Ivy Books, 1987.

Lanning, Michael L. <u>Vietnam 1969-1970: A Commander's Journal</u>. New York: Ivy Books, 1988.

O'Brien, Tim. <u>The Things They Carried</u>. New York: Broadway Books, 1990.

Schneider, Chess. <u>From Classrooms To Claymores: A Teacher At War In Vietnam</u>. New York: Ivy Books, 1999.

Stephen, Donald E. <u>Bait: Vietnam-1971</u>. St. Joseph: L & L Printing Service, 1986.

Goldman, Peter with Tony Fuller. "It All Seems A Waste" <u>Newsweek</u> April 14, 1975; pp. 34, 35

Lowenthal, Jeff. *Newsweek*, photographer.

Porter, Bekah. <u>Mt. Pleasant News.</u> "Ross Family Still Proud of Son's Sacrifice." Mt. Pleasant, Iowa: November 11, 2005

Map of Vietnam, <u>www.maps.com</u>. 3/25/06

Map of Iowa www.com/map/Iowa 6/8/06

Printed in the United States
202123BV00003B/1-84/A